The Caribbean Novel in English

The Caribbean Novel in English

An Introduction

M. Keith Booker
and Dubravka Juraga

HEINEMANN
Portsmouth, NH

IAN RANDLE PUBLISHERS
Kingston

JAMES CURREY
Oxford

ISBN 978 0 85255 560 6 (James Currey paper)
ISBN 978 0 325 00252 1 (Heinemann cloth)
ISBN 978 0 325 00212 5 (Heinemann paper)
ISBN 978 976 637 024 4 (Ian Randle paper)

Transferred to digital printing

First published in Jamaica 2001 by
Ian Randle Publishers
11 Cunningham Avenue
Kingston 6, Jamaica

James Currey
www.jamescurrey.com
is an imprint of Boydell & Brewer Ltd
PO Box 9, Woodbridge, Suffolk IP12 3DF, UK
and of Boydell & Brewer Inc.
668 Mt Hope Avenue, Rochester, NY 14620, USA
www.boydellandbrewer.com

Heinemann
A division of Reed Elsevier Inc.
361 Hanover Street
Portsmouth
NH 03801-3912
www.heinemann.com

Library of Congress Catalog Card Number 00-025366
A catalogue record is available from the British Library
A catalogue record is available from the National Library of Jamaica

This publication is printed on acid-free paper

Dedicated to the memory and legacy of Franz Fanon

Contents

Chapter 1

Introduction: Historical Survey of the Caribbean Novel in English

The Caribbean has long played a central role in the history of the English novel. As critics such as Ian Watt (1957) have long argued, the eighteenth-century rise of the novel as the dominant genre in English literature can be associated directly with the rise of the middle class, or bourgeoisie, as the ruling class in England (and elsewhere in Europe). Meanwhile, the rise of the bourgeoisie and their capitalist market system, supplanting the aristocracy and the Catholic Church as the dominant powers in Europe, was enabled largely through the opportunities and resources made available through colonization. The islands of the Caribbean, "discovered" by Columbus in 1492, were the first non-European lands to be conquered and subsequently colonized by Europeans. Many of these islands, especially through the production of sugar and other cash crops, remained for hundreds of years among the most profitable sites of colonial exploitation.

The islands of the Caribbean were also central to the rise of the middle class in other than purely economic ways. As C.L.R. James outlines in *The Black Jacobins* (1938), the Haitian Revolution of the 1790s, which eventually led to the establishment of Haiti as an independent nation, was an integral part of the French Revolution, which most historians regard as the single most important event in the establishment of bourgeois rule in Europe. The Caribbean colonies played an important symbolic role for the emergent European bourgeoisie, whose imaginations (and ambitions) were immeasurably stirred by the very existence of these rich colonies in such distant, exotic locales. It is thus not surprising that so many early English novels draw inspiration from the Caribbean. For example, Aphra Behn's *Oroonoko* (1688), sometimes regarded as the first English novel, takes place in Surinam, on the Caribbean coast of South America. Similarly, Daniel Defoe, in another founding work of the English novel, selects the Caribbean as the location of the exotic island on which he maroons the title character of *The Life and Strange and Surprising Adventures of Robinson Crusoe* (1719).

Defoe's novel has been widely interpreted (by Watt, among others) as a representative allegory of the capitalist system, so that its setting recognizes the Caribbean as the paradigmatic site of capitalist economic activity. Meanwhile, the Caribbean continues to hover in the margins of any number of British novels through the nineteenth century, typically as a source of wealth for the generally affluent characters who populate those novels. The Bertrams of Jane Austen's *Mansfield Park* (1814) derive their wealth from a plantation on the island of Antigua, and their genteel way of life is seriously threatened when profits from the estate begin to decline. In Charlotte Brontë's *Jane Eyre* (1847), Edward Rochester expends some of his youthful sexual energies in the West Indies, returning to England with a mad Creole wife. The Caribbean, with its legacy of notorious pirates, provided inspiration for late nineteenth-century adventure stories such as Robert Louis Stevenson's *Treasure Island* (1883). And the trend continues into the twentieth century, when novels such as Ronald Firbank's *Sorrow in Sunlight* (1924, published in the United States under the unfortunate but telling title, *Prancing Nigger*), Alec Waugh's *An Island in the Sun* (1956), and Graham Greene's *The Comedians* (1966) have continued to find the Caribbean fertile soil for the nourishment of the British literary imagination.

The Caribbean has also played an important role in the history of American literature, which is not surprising given the geographical proximity of the United States to the Caribbean and the extensive amount of cultural interchange that has occurred between Americans, especially African Americans, and the Caribbean. For example, the Caribbean naturally impacts the seagoing fiction of Herman Melville from time to time. And the Caribbean, with its extensive connections to the Harlem Renaissance of the 1920s (in which the Jamaican Claude McKay was a central participant and for whom the Jamaican Marcus Garvey was an important inspiration), was at the very forefront of the development of American modernism.[1] Meanwhile, the Haitian Revolution, in which former slaves organized an army that fought off major invasions by both the British and the French to establish an independent black republic, helped to inspire several North American slave rebellions. In addition, the Haitian demonstration of black collective power and capability has long played an important symbolic role in African American culture and in the culture of the American Left. Even so early a work as Melville's story "Benito Cereno" (1856) seems to have been based extensively on the events in Haiti, with Melville's rebellious slave leader, Babo, having much in common with Boukman, the Haitian slave leader who was the source of the title character of Guy Endore's *Babouk* (1934), perhaps the most successful American leftist novel to have been based on the rebellion in Haiti. Arna Bontemps's *Drums at Dusk* (1939) and Madison Smartt Bell's recent *All Souls Rising* (1995) are also based on the Haitian Revolution.

The Caribbean has also played an important role in a number of major works of modern American literature, from John Dos Passos's *U.S.A. Trilogy* (1930–1936) and William Faulkner's *Absalom, Absalom!* (1936) to Toni Morrison's *Tar Baby* (1981). What is different about the twentieth century, however, is that the Caribbean has developed a rich and varied literature of its own, answering American and British representations of the islands with works that allow the people of the Caribbean to speak for themselves. Given the long history of cultural and economic contact and exchange between the Caribbean, Great Britain, and the United States, it is clear that Caribbean literature, even if designed primarily for Caribbean readers, should be of great interest to American and British readers. However, it is important for American and British readers to understand that certain aspects of the historical and cultural background of the Caribbean dictate that Caribbean literature must be approached on its own terms and not merely read as if it were a subset of British or American literature.[2]

The Caribbean was the first non-European region to be colonized by Europeans; the original Native American inhabitants of the Caribbean were the first non-Europeans to suffer genocide at the hands of European expansionism; and brutal economic exploitation, in the particular form of slavery, dominated the subsequent history of the Caribbean as nowhere else, not even in the American South. As a result, many of the issues that have recently been of concern to postcolonial and multicultural scholars take an especially clear form within the context of the Caribbean. Partly because of the unique historical background of the Caribbean region and partly due to the influential work of major Caribbean intellectuals such as C.L.R. James, Frantz Fanon, Aimé Césaire, Eric Williams, and Walter Rodney, Caribbean writers have tended to be intensely aware of the social and historical issues that set their work apart from that of their European and North American predecessors and contemporaries. Indeed, Ashcroft, Griffiths, and Tiffin conclude that, because of this sophistication, the Caribbean can be considered "the crucible of the most extensive and challenging post-colonial literary theory" (1989, 145). In order fully to appreciate Caribbean literature, then, readers need to be aware of the many issues that inform such theory.

To an extent, the issues that surround Caribbean literature are similar to those that inform African and other postcolonial literatures.[3] For example, Caribbean literature takes on a particular urgency and importance because it plays a central role in the attempt to construct new cultural identities that escape the domination of the colonial past.[4] Moreover, because of the conscious understanding of the need to exorcise the ghosts of the past and find ways to draw upon that past in an attempt to build a new and better future, Caribbean writers, like other postcolonial writers, quite often engage history in their work. Caribbean literature differs significantly from African literature in that African postcolonial writers can draw upon indigenous African cultural traditions that date back thousands of years, while the indigenous cultures of the Caribbean (primarily those of the Arawak and Carib Indians) were essentially wiped out by the particularly brutal forms taken by European colonization in the early years of Caribbean conquest. But Caribbean literature also differs dramatically from the postcolonial cultures of "settler" colonies such as Australia, Canada, and the United States, where the indigenous cultures were replaced by the imported cultural traditions of European settlers. In the postcolonial Caribbean, the descendents of such settlers constitute only a small minority of the population, which tends to be dominated by the descendents of African slaves. In some areas, though (particularly Guyana and Trinidad), the descendents of East Indian indentured laborers, brought in after the abolition of slavery in the British Empire in the 1830s, also constitute a substantial portion of the population.

The postcolonial culture of the Caribbean, then, consists of a rich mixture of imported European, African, and East Indian cultural traditions. East Indian culture, itself extremely diverse, obviously remains marginal to the culture of the Caribbean, while white Europeans constitute such a small percentage of the total population that European culture is not fully hegemonic in the region, despite the long history of political and economic domination of the Caribbean by Europe. Meanwhile, African culture does not really dominate Caribbean culture, either. During the long centuries of slavery in the Caribbean, slave owners often used extreme measures to alienate their slaves from their African cultural heritage, fearing that it could provide the basis for a sense of solidarity that could encourage slave revolts. In fact, the Caribbean has a rich history of slave rebellions, of which the Haitian Revolution is the best known and most successful. But the historical experience of slavery nevertheless denies Afro-Caribbeans the kind of direct access to African culture that is available to African writers.

As a result of this complex heritage, the crucial project of constructing viable postcolonial cultural identities is particularly complex in the Caribbean. It is thus no surprise that subgenres, such as the bildungsroman, which are thematically concerned with the construction of identity, have been particularly prominent in the Caribbean novel, but this search for an identity informs Caribbean literature in more subtle ways, as well. For example, African writers work in a postcolonial context in which traditional African languages, such as Swahili, Gikuyu, Igbo, Yoruba, or Wolof, are still living languages. Virtually all Africans, in fact, speak one or more indigenous African languages, yet most postcolonial African novelists, for a variety of reasons, continue to write in former colonial languages such as French or English, a phenomenon that has caused considerable controversy in recent years.[5] In the Caribbean, however, no such indigenous languages are widely spoken. Language does, however, remain an issue because, even though English remains the dominant language in all of the former British colonies of the Caribbean, it is often spoken there in distinctive dialectical forms. Thus, while Caribbean writers may not have the choice of writing in a separate indigenous language, they do have a choice of writing either in "standard" English or in Caribbean dialects. Indeed, some of the most interesting experiments in Caribbean writing have involved efforts to make productive use of Caribbean dialects as literary languages. British and American readers need to be aware, though, that such experiments are not mere exercises in style, but have powerful social and political implications involving a potentially subversive engagement with the long history of cultural domination of the Caribbean by Britain and, more recently, the United States.

Because of this long domination, Caribbean literature shows a strong European influence. Indeed, the very fact that the novel has been the single most important form taken by Caribbean literature is itself a legacy of the area's European heritage. And the first Caribbean novels, produced at the beginning of this century, were essentially attempts to emulate the European novel. While one can trace the beginnings of Caribbean literature to a variety of educational and cultural phenomena that evolved through the nineteenth century, to some extent it is fair to say that indigenous Caribbean literature owes its birth, in the early years of the twentieth century, to the efforts of a single individual: Thomas Henry MacDermot. Publishing under the anagrammatic pen name "Tom Redcam," MacDermot, with works such as *Becka's Buckra Baby* (1903) and *One Brown Girl and —* (1909), can lay some claim to being the first indigenous English-language novelist of the Caribbean. Moreover, MacDermot, a white Creole and longtime editor of the *Jamaica Times*, was a Jamaican nationalist who sought to further a distinct Jamaican cultural identity, not only through his writing but through his sponsorship of "The All Jamaica Library," a short-lived and ill-fated publishing effort that encouraged the development of literature written by Jamaican authors for Jamaican readers.

Unfortunately, only five volumes were issued in this series, three of which consisted of the two Redcam novels, the second of which was published in two volumes. But the stage had been set for the development of the Caribbean novel, and MacDermot/Redcam was soon followed by other gifted authors, such as H. G. de Lisser, who published a number of novels from *Jane: A Story of Jamaica* (1913, reissued in 1914 as *Jane's Career*) to the posthumous *The Arawak Girl* (1958). The quality of de Lisser's writing is uneven (and tends to decline as his career proceeds and his politics fade from anticolonial Fabian socialism to downright reactionary support for the British Empire), but at least one of his novels, *Jane's Career*, deals with important issues of race and class in colonial Jamaica—and intelligently enough that the book is still worth reading.[6] It was the first Caribbean novel to feature a black protagonist and the first to be published by a British publisher. Also still read is de Lisser's *The White Witch of Rosehall* (1929), though this book is essentially a romance that already suggests the decline of de Lisser's talents.

De Lisser, like MacDermot, was a member of the small white minority in Jamaica. Meanwhile, Claude McKay's participation in the Harlem Renaissance led to the publication of three novels—*Home to Harlem* (1928), *Banjo* (1929), and *Banana Bottom* (1933)—which can to an extent be regarded as the founding texts of the black Caribbean novel. The first two of these novels are set in Harlem and Marseilles, respectively, but both feature a Caribbean intellectual (the Haitian Ray) as a central character. *Banana Bottom*, considered by many critics to be McKay's finest novel, is something of a pastoral fantasy set in Jamaica. While containing comic moments, it also includes anticolonial commentary in its treatment of life in British-ruled Jamaica at the beginning of the twentieth century, and McKay's vision of black racial pride makes the book an extremely important one in the evolution of the Caribbean novel.

McKay, however, was a rather isolated phenomenon. Moreover, he was linked at the time more to the Harlem Renaissance and other movements abroad than to Caribbean culture. Black literature in the Caribbean, and Caribbean literature as a whole (in the sense of being a distinct literary phenomenon), was essentially born in the 1930s, when economic pressures brought about by the global collapse of capitalist economies in the Great Depression triggered a variety of radical activities in the Caribbean. The most important of these was the growth of a militant trades union movement throughout the British Caribbean, but this movement was part of a larger growth in awareness that, among other things, greatly spurred the development of a Caribbean culture that began to challenge, rather than emulate, the British (and European) literary tradition.

Crucial to this phenomenon was the so-called Beacon Group in Trinidad, whose members were associated with the *Beacon* magazine, published in Port of Spain from 1931 to 1934. Three of these members, Alfred Mendes, C.L.R. James, and Ralph de Boissière, would go on to become important Caribbean novelists.[7] Mendes's two published novels, *Pitch Lake* (1934) and *Black Fauns* (1935), which show a great deal of sympathy with the poor and downtrodden of Trinidad, while often bitterly criticizing the white Portuguese middle class into which Mendes himself had been born, set the tone for the socially-conscious fiction that would dominate Caribbean literature through the remainder of the twentieth century. James's only novel, *Minty Alley*[8] (1936), is somewhat in the same vein, though of course he would ultimately be far more important as an editor, activist, historian, cultural critic, and political theorist than as a novelist. Born to a middle-class black family in Trinidad in 1901, James would in fact go on to become one of the central figures in the intellectual history of the modern Caribbean. Indeed, he was one of the world's leading intellectuals of the twentieth century.[9]

James, like so many subsequent Caribbean writers, spent a great deal of time in both Britain and the United States and was highly influential in both countries as well as throughout the Third World. In 1937, he published *World Revolution*, a study of the Communist International that established him as a major voice in modern Marxism. The book was opposed to many of the bureaucratic tendencies of Stalinism and importantly influenced by Stalin's rival Leon Trotsky; at the same time, it provided an analysis of world Marxism from a Third-World perspective distinct from the main trends in Marxist thought in Europe. *The Black Jacobins* (1938) may be his most important single work. It was reissued in a revised 1963 edition that included an appendix by James linking the revolution in Haiti to the recent revolution in Cuba as part of a historical quest for an independent Caribbean national identity. James is also the author of *Beyond a Boundary* (1963), a complex and highly original work of cultural history that was to be one of the founding texts in the burgeoning field of cultural studies. Among James's numerous other works was *American Civilization* (1993), a sweeping posthumously published Marxist study of American society and culture emphasizing the crucial role played by mass production in their development.

Born in Trinidad in 1907, de Boissière was heavily influenced by the literary circle that gathered around Mendes and James in the early 1930s and began writing in that decade. In 1937, he observed the major social upheavals that engulfed Trinidad in the wake of a bitterly fought strike by the island's oil field workers. As a result, he became involved in radical trade union activism, a commitment that would greatly inform his subsequent writing. In 1947, after a brief stay in the United States, he immigrated to Australia, where he worked in a General Motors plant in Melbourne, thus enriching his understanding of and sympathy for the urban proletariat. Among other things, this experience led him to substantially revise his first novel, already in manuscript when he came to Australia. That novel was eventually published in 1952, as *Crown Jewel*. It was followed in 1956 by a sequel, *Rum and Coca-Cola*.[10] Both of these novels, which show a strongly leftist sympathy for the working class and for the attempts of workers to organize to resist oppression by their capitalist bosses, are rooted in the labor movements of the 1930s, not only in Trinidad, but worldwide.[11] Indeed, Hazel Carby (1988) has persuasively argued that the entire Trinidadian Literary Renaissance of the 1930s needs to be understood within the context of the global leftist culture of that decade.

The ongoing development of Caribbean literature was slowed by the onset of World War II, though at least one major Caribbean novelist, Guyana's Edgar Mittelholzer, began his career as a published novelist during the war. His first novel, *Corentyne Thunder* (1941) brought a new dimension to Caribbean literature as the first novel to be set in an East Indian working-class community in the Caribbean region, though its protagonist, Geoffrey Weldon, observes this community from a mixed-race, middle-class perspective. Mittelholzer followed in 1950 with *A Morning at the Office*, a somewhat Freudian study in repression in the context of a colonial Guyana stratified by divisions based on both race and class. It is sometimes considered his finest novel, though the "Kaywana Trilogy," a sequence that comprises *Children of Kaywana* (1952), *The Harrowing of Hubertus* (1954, later republished as *Kaywana Stock*), and *Kaywana Blood* (1958), may, in its epic retelling of the history of Guyana, ultimately be his most important work.

The years after the end of World War II saw a second renaissance in Caribbean literature, this time involving numerous writers from a variety of different Caribbean locales. During the 1950s, Caribbean literature was dominated to some extent by the widespread recognition that Britain's European colonies were rapidly moving toward independence. Mittelholzer's continuing production was an important part of this second flowering, though it is probably appropriate to identify V. S. Reid's *New Day* (1949) as the founding text in this emergent movement. Important for its casting of Jamaican history as a gradual movement toward inevitable self-rule for Jamaica and for its deft use of Jamaican dialect in its narrative voice, Reid's novel inspired a number of later writers who drew upon both Caribbean history and the rhythms of Caribbean language in their work. Reid himself was born in Jamaica in 1913, reaching adulthood during the tumultuous events of the 1930s. His work grows directly out of the political climate of Jamaica in that decade, when widespread labor unrest combined with anticolonial agitation to produce social upheavals. These upheavals eventually led, in 1944, to the establishment of a new constitution, which mandated universal adult suffrage and the end of direct colonial rule of Jamaica by Great Britain, though complete independence would not be gained until 1962. *New Day* draws directly upon these events, though it may be premature in its declaration of the dawning of a new postcolonial day in Jamaica.

Reid continued his interest in the history of anticolonial resistance with the publication of *The Leopard* (1958), a historical novel set in colonial Kenya, focusing on the Mau Mau rebellion of the early 1950s. Anticipating the later work of Kenyan novelist Ngugi wa Thiong'o, Reid presents the Mau Mau movement as a legitimate and heroic response to colonial oppression, rather than an outbreak of native African savagery, as it was often portrayed in the Western press at the time. Reid returned to Jamaican history in his novel, *The Jamaicans* (1976, revised 1978), which seeks to provide access to a positive usable past for a postcolonial Jamaica undergoing considerable economic hardship and social turmoil. In addition, Reid is the author of a number of children's novels that focus on Jamaican history, including *Nanny-Town* (1983). He is also the author of *The Horses of Morning* (1985), a biography of Jamaican independence leader Norman Manley. Reid is recognized as one of the great pioneers of Caribbean literature, as can be seen in the special issue of the *Journal of West Indian Literature* devoted to his work (Baugh 1987).

Another Jamaican writer of crucial importance to appear in the 1950s was Roger Mais, who broke new ground in his depiction of the urban slums of Kingston and of their inhabitants, including the (at the time) widely feared and despised Rastafarians. Mais was born in Kingston in 1905. After completing his high school education in 1922, he worked at a variety of jobs, including work as a journalist and later as the publisher of his own magazine, *The People* (1946), the title of which indicates Mais's early socialist political consciousness. This consciousness, among other things, led him to publish a criticism of British colonialism in 1944, leading to his incarceration in a British colonial prison for six months. In the late 1940s, he wrote a number of plays, then turned to the writing of novels with the publication of *The Hills Were Joyful Together* in 1953. This novel was soon followed by *Brother Man* (1954) and *Black Lightning* (1955).

Both Reid and Mais would prove influential for a number of subsequent Jamaican writers, including John Hearne and Andrew Salkey, who both also began to publish in the 1950s. Though born in Montreal, Canada, in 1926, Hearne returned to Jamaica with his Jamaican parents at a young age. His first novel, *Voices Under the Window* (1955), emphasizes the importance of political commitment in the sometimes confusing years leading up to Jamaican independence from British colonial rule. Hearne's next four novels, all set on the fictional Caribbean island of Cayuna, continue to explore social and political issues associated with the coming of independence, though Hearne's focus gradually shifts from public politics to private, personal concerns in the movement from *Stranger at the Gate* (1956), whose protagonist, Roy McKenzie, is an idealistic communist who sacrifices his life for the cause, to *Land of the Living* (1961), which emphasizes the importance of personal emotional attachments. In 1981, after a twenty-year gap, Hearne published his sixth novel, *The Sure Salvation*, which focuses on the journey of a slave ship, but ends up being a highly pessimistic meditation on the breakdown of human relationships amid the radical alienation that marks the contemporary world.

Salkey, who would also develop a reputation as a critic and poet, began his career as a novelist in 1958 with the publication of *A Quality of Violence*, which focuses on poor Jamaican peasants in a mode somewhat reminiscent of Reid, detailing the negative impact of colonialism on the communal peasant culture of the island. Salkey's next novel, *Escape to an Autumn Pavement* (1960), explores the alienation of educated middle-class Jamaicans in the years leading up to independence, while *The Late Emancipation of Jerry Stover* (1968) examines the confusion of identity that marks life in postcolonial Jamaica. Subsequent novels, such as *The Adventures of Catullus Kelly* (1969) and *Come Home, Malcolm Heartland* (1976), focus on the experiences of Jamaican immigrants in England, where Salkey in fact spent most of his career before moving to the United States in 1976. Salkey has also written a number of novels for children and has shown an interest in the traditional folk culture of the Caribbean. He has, for example, published several collections of modern Anancy stories, featuring the spiderlike trickster figure who is a major character in many African and Caribbean folktales.

Another important novelist to emerge in the late 1950s was Guyana's Jan Carew (born in 1925), though Carew, who has traveled widely and has spent most of his career living and working in the United States, addresses themes that go beyond the Caribbean and is probably more properly regarded as a cosmopolitan writer than as a purely Caribbean one. His first two novels, *Black Midas* and *The Wild Coast* (both published in 1958), show the influence of Fanon's Marxist analyses of colonialism in their examination of the exigencies of race and class in colonial Guyana. Carew's next novel, *The Last Barbarian* (1961) is set in Harlem and explores racism in the United States, while *Moscow Is Not My Mecca* (1964), follows a black radical to the Soviet Union, where he discovers that racism is still a problem even in this seemingly egalitarian society. *Save the Last Dance for Me* (1976) extends Carew's coverage to London, continuing his exploration of the various forms of racism in diverse modern societies.

Perhaps the most important Caribbean writers to emerge in the 1950s were three young men who emigrated to England at the beginning of the decade, subsequently pursuing successful writing careers there. Two of these writers, Sam Selvon of Trinidad and George Lamming of Barbados, traveled to England from Trinidad on the same ship in 1950. The other, Trinidad's V. S. Naipaul, traveled to England the same year to attend Oxford University, from which he graduated in 1954. Born in San Fernando, Trinidad, in 1923, Selvon was the eldest of these three. He was also the first to become a published novelist. Indeed, *A Brighter Sun*, Selvon's first novel, was apparently complete in draft form when he left Trinidad. Published in 1952, this novel became one of the founding texts of the Caribbean literary renaissance of the 1950s and helped to establish trends that would be important in Caribbean literature for years to come.[12] The style of the book makes important use of Trinidadian dialect, especially in the dialogue of the characters, thus helping both to enhance the verisimilitude of the book and to challenge the hegemony of standard British English as a literary language. The content of the book contains important autobiographical elements and much of it derives from the author's personal multicultural experience as a Christian East Indian in colonial Trinidad.[13] It is essentially a bildungsroman in form, detailing the growth to adulthood and maturity of its initially immature protagonist, but it shows an intense awareness of social and political issues, framing the story of the protagonist within the context of the story of the multicultural society of colonial Trinidad.

Selvon quickly followed with other novels set in Trinidad, including *An Island Is a World* (1955) and *Turn Again Tiger* (1958), a direct sequel to *A Brighter Sun*. He also began to publish novels about the expatriate West Indian community in London, including *The Lonely Londoners* (1956) and *The Housing Lark* (1965). These latter novels, while sensitive to serious social issues (such as the racist resentment encountered by West Indian immigrants in England), show a fine comic sensibility, breaking new ground in Caribbean literature. They also continue Selvon's successful experiments with the use of Trinidadian dialectical English as a literary language. The later novels *I Hear Thunder* (1963), *The Plains of Caroni* (1970), and *Those Who Eat the Cascadura* (1972) return to Selvon's early focus on peasant life in Trinidad. Among Selvon's most important works are a pair of sequels to

*The Lonely Londoners, **Moses Ascending** (1975) and *Moses Migrating* (1983).
Selvon has also published short story collections, essays, and plays. In 1978,
he migrated to Canada, continuing his writing career there, while also teaching at Canadian universities. He died in Trinidad in 1994.[14]

George Lamming was born in 1927 in Carrington Village, near
Bridgetown, Barbados. After finishing high school in Barbados, he traveled
to Trinidad, where he taught at the College of Venezuela and developed an
increasing interest in writing. After his move to England in 1950, he began
his writing career in earnest. He has remained one of the most important
Caribbean novelists since the 1953 publication of *In the Castle of My Skin*,
his first novel. A partly autobiographical bildungsroman about a poor boy
growing up in colonial Barbados, that novel won immediate international
recognition and provided an important boost to the Caribbean novel, then
still in its infancy. Lamming went on to write several more important novels, including *The Emigrants* (1954), *Of Age and Innocence* (1958), *Season of
Adventure* (1960), *Water with Berries* (1971), and *Natives of My Person* (1972).
He also gained a substantial reputation as an intellectual and theorist of the
postcolonial condition, as represented in such nonfiction collections as *The
Pleasures of Exile* (1960) and *Conversations: Essays, Addresses, and Interviews,
1953–1990* (1992). Though continuing to regard his native Barbados as his
permanent home, Lamming has traveled widely and has taught at important universities in the Caribbean and on almost every continent.

On an international scale, V. S. Naipaul, born in Chaguanas, Trinidad,
in 1932, is probably the most widely recognized of all Caribbean novelists.[15] His writing is marked by an impeccable English prose style that has
drawn wide praise, but has been seen by some as an attempt to emulate
British culture and deny Naipaul's Caribbean/Indian heritage. Indeed,
Naipaul is a highly controversial figure, having been widely criticized for his
negative depiction of the Third World, including Trinidad and the Caribbean, as a dark land of backwardness and ignorance. After emigrating to
England to study on a Trinidad government scholarship, Naipaul would
remain a resident of England from that time on, though he has traveled
widely and is well known as a writer of travel books, in addition to being a
widely admired novelist. Much of his travel writing deals with the Third
World, as in *The Middle Passage* (1962) and *An Area of Darkness* (1964),
which include bitter criticisms of Caribbean and Indian society, respectively.

Miguel Street, a collection of interlinked stories detailing the lives of
various inhabitants of an urban yard in colonial Port of Spain, was Naipaul's
first work of fiction, though it was not published until 1959, by which time
The Mystic Masseur (1957) and *The Suffrage of Elvira* (1958), which are also
set in colonial Trinidad, had already appeared. His fourth novel, *A House for*

Mr. Biswas (1961), detailing the struggles of an unfortunate East Indian in colonial Trinidad, is often considered his masterpiece. Mr. Biswas still has a certain earthy vitality, but later Naipaul novels, including *The Mimic Men* (1967), *Guerrillas* (1975), and *A Bend in the River* (1979), tend to lose sight of such vitality in favor of an emphasis on Third-World poverty, violence, and corruption. Naipaul's 1971 novel/story collection, *In a Free State*, was awarded England's prestigious Booker Prize, making Naipaul the only Caribbean novelist to be so honored.[16] Naipaul's latest novels include *The Enigma of Arrival* (1987), a largely autobiographical work set in England, and *A Way in the World* (1994), which combines autobiography with history in a complex meditation on the impact of the past on the nature of Caribbean reality in the present.

Most of the important figures from the renaissance of the 1950s continued to write in the 1960s. A number of new novelists emerged as well, contributing to an extensive diversification of Caribbean literature, as various writers attempted to find ways to contribute to the development of viable postcolonial cultural identities in the new Caribbean nations that gained independence one after another, led by Jamaica and Trinidad and Tobago, beginning in 1962. Of the new writers to emerge at the beginning of the 1960s, the most unusual, and perhaps the most important, was Guyana's Wilson Harris. Born in New Amsterdam, Guyana, in 1921, Harris worked for several years as a surveyor in the interior of Guyana, then moved to England in 1959. He has spent most of his time since then living in England, though he has traveled widely.

Like Lamming, Harris has produced a substantial body of critical commentary, and together these two writers are indicative of the sophistication and self-consciousness that have come to be regarded as typical of Caribbean novelists in recent years. However, Harris is best known for his numerous novels, which draw upon history, myth, and a variety of other cultural texts, employing a complex combination of modernism, surrealism, symbolism, and magical realism to express a distinctive vision of the nature of Caribbean reality. Among his best-known novels are the four volumes of the "Guyana Quartet," which begins with *The Palace of the Peacock* (1960), Harris's first novel, and also includes *The Far Journey of Oudin* (1961), *The Whole Armour* (1962), and *The Secret Ladder* (1963). Harris's fifth novel, *Heartland* (1964), is also related to this sequence, though it is not generally regarded as a member of the group. Also important are *Carnival* (1985), *The Infinite Rehearsal* (1987), and *The Four Banks of the River of Space* (1990), published jointly as the *Carnival Trilogy* in 1993. While these novels and others published in the 1960s are set mostly in Guyana (or at least in a surreal version of Guyana), Harris has also written a number of novels that take place in other settings, including Scotland, England, Mexico, and India.

The charged political climate of the years immediately before and after independence can be seen in the appearance of novels such as Frank Hercules' anticolonial *Where the Hummingbird Flies* (Trinidad, 1961) and Ismith Khan's *The Jumbie Bird* (Trinidad, 1961), which explores the confused cultural identity of Trinidad as it moves toward independence. Also notable is Khan's *The Obeah Man* (1964), a powerful political novel that presents the futility of life in postcolonial Trinidad as a direct consequence of the legacy of colonialism. Namba Roy's *Black Albino* (1961) draws upon the legacy of Jamaica's fugitive communities of escaped slaves, or Maroons, in an attempt to help develop a positive historical base for new Jamaican identities, while the protagonist of Denis Williams's *Other Leopards* (Guyana, 1963) goes from Guyana to Africa in search of his cultural roots. Williams's exploration of cultural and historical links between Africa and the Caribbean is also central to the life and work of the Jamaican novelist and poet Neville Dawes, who spent extensive periods in Ghana, where he was a supporter of Kwame Nkrumah, first president of the postcolonial state there. Dawes's two novels, *The Last Enchantment* (1960) and *Interim* (1978), are interesting for their exploration of Jamaican politics before and after independence, respectively. Both novels feature protagonists who rise from peasant backgrounds to receive elite educations, then reject elitist ideology in favor of socialism and anticolonial nationalism. The latter novel is particularly biting in its warnings of the negative impact of the threat of U.S. military intervention in the Caribbean.

One of the most important Caribbean novelists to begin his publishing career in the 1960s was Trinidad's Earl Lovelace. Born in Toco, Trinidad, in 1935, Lovelace grew up in Tobago with his maternal grandparents. He returned to Trinidad to attend high school and later worked as a proofreader for the *Trinidad Guardian* in 1953–1954. He worked in forestry and agriculture from 1956 to 1966, during which time he published his first novel, *While Gods Are Falling* (1965). Lovelace then moved to the United States to further his education and hone his craft. He studied at Howard University, then later at Johns Hopkins University, where he received the M.A. in English in 1974. The novel, *The Wine of Astonishment* originated as Lovelace's creative M.A. thesis at Johns Hopkins. By the time of its eventual publication in 1982, though, he had already published two other novels: *The Schoolmaster* (1968) and *The Dragon Can't Dance* (1979). In 1977, Lovelace accepted an appointment to teach in the English Department of the University of the West Indies. In 1980, he attended the International Writing Program at the University of Iowa, supported by a Guggenheim Fellowship.

Since that time, he has taught at a number of universities in the United States and the Caribbean. Lovelace concentrated on writing journalism, stories, and plays for a number of years, but returned to the forefront of Caribbean novelists with the impressive 1996 novel, *Salt*, which won the Commonwealth Writers' Prize.

Other major figures publishing their first novels in the 1960s included Jamaica's Orlando Patterson, Trinidad's Michael Anthony, Barbados's Austin Clarke, and St. Lucia's Garth St. Omer. Patterson, a distinguished social scientist, was born in Jamaica in 1940. He attended the University of the West Indies in 1962, then received a Commonwealth Scholarship to continue his studies in England, where, in 1965, he received a Ph.D. from the London School of Economics, whose faculty he joined upon graduation. Patterson is the author of three naturalistic novels about the urban poor of Kingston that hark back to the work of Mais and that also reflect a strong influence from European existentialism. They include *The Children of Sisyphus* (1964), *An Absence of Ruins* (1967), and *Die the Long Day* (1972). However, Patterson is probably better known as a scholar. An expert on the history and sociology of slavery, he is the author of such studies as *The Sociology of Slavery* (1967) and *Slavery and Social Death* (1982). As a respected intellectual, he became a key advisor to Jamaican political leader Michael Manley in the early 1970s. Since 1973, Patterson has been on the faculty of Harvard University, where he is currently the John Cowles Professor of Sociology.

Anthony, born in 1932 in rural Trinidad, has enjoyed a long and prolific career as a novelist and historian. His first three novels, written while he worked at a variety of jobs in England between 1954 and 1968, include *The Games Were Coming* (1963), *The Year in San Fernando* (1965), and *Green Days by the River* (1967). They center on autobiographical descriptions of childhood experience in colonial Trinidad. These novels, rich in evocation of the landscape and atmosphere of rural Trinidad, also begin to map out the parameters of Trinidadian national consciousness. To some extent, these same characteristics also inform later works, written after his return to Trinidad in 1970, such as *Streets of Conflict* (1976) and *All that Glitters* (1981). However, these works begin to focus on more adult characters and more public situations, such as the student riots that are central to *Streets of Conflict*. Anthony's latest works, including the novel *In the Heat of the Day* (1996), have an even more public, historical focus, reflecting the interest that led Anthony to write a number of works of Trinidadian history.

Clarke, born in Barbados in 1934 and educated at the University of Toronto, later settled in Toronto and became a prominent figure in Canadian literature. His first novels, *Survivors of the Crossing* (1964) and *Amongst Thistles and Thorns* (1965) draw upon his own childhood experience growing up in colonial Barbados, while the later *The Prime Minister* (1977) critiques political corruption in postcolonial Barbados. But Clarke is best known for his novels about West Indian immigrants in Canada, where they experience considerable racial discrimination but somehow manage to endure, with determination and even good humor. His most important work is the so-called Toronto Trilogy, which comprises the novels *The Meeting Point* (1967), *Storm of Fortune* (1973), and *The Bigger Light* (1975). Clarke has also published several volumes of short stories.

St. Omer was born in 1931 in Castries, the capital city of St. Lucia in the Windward Islands. Originally educated at the University of the West Indies in Jamaica, he went on to receive his Master of Fine Arts degree from Columbia University (1971) and his doctorate in comparative literature from Princeton University (1975), thus joining Patterson in establishing the tendency of recent Caribbean novelists to achieve extremely high levels of education. St. Omer began his career as a fiction writer with the publication of a novella, *Syrop*, in 1964. He then produced four novels in quick succession between 1968 and 1972, including *A Room on the Hill* (1968), *Shades of Grey* (1968), *Nor Any Country* (1969), and *J–, Black Bam and the Masqueraders* (1972). Particularly critical of the damaging role played by British colonialism and the Catholic Church in the history of St. Lucia, St. Omer employs an essentially naturalistic style to express a sense of futility and pessimism that is often compared to the early works of the Irish writer James Joyce.

The 1960s also saw the initial rise to prominence of women writers in the Caribbean, though a few works, such as Phyllis Shand Allfrey's *The Orchid House* (Dominica, 1953), had been published in the 1950s. Indeed, one might consider Jean Rhys's *Voyage in the Dark* (1934) to be the first Caribbean novel in English by a woman writer. Rhys, like Allfrey, was a white Creole (descendant of European settlers) from Dominica. However, though *Voyage in the Dark* includes important segments set in the Caribbean, it and all of Rhys's early novels are set primarily in Europe and are often considered to be European novels. In 1966, however, Rhys published **Wide Sargasso Sea**, which is set primarily in Jamaica and the Windward Islands. In this novel, Rhys gives voice to Bertha Mason, the "mad" wife of Charlotte Brontë's *Jane Eyre*, thus providing a Caribbean response to this classic English novel.

Paule Marshall, born in 1929 in Brooklyn, New York, to Barbadian parents, established her ongoing sense of connection to Caribbean culture in 1969 with the publication of **The Chosen Place, the Timeless People**, which presents the history of the fictional Bourne Island, somewhere in the Caribbean. In so doing, the book addresses a number of issues that have been crucial to recent Caribbean history, including the ongoing legacy of slavery and the continuing poverty of the Caribbean in the postcolonial era. She also initiates important dialogues between North American and Caribbean culture, enacting an exchange that has long been crucial to both cultures. An extremely sophisticated writer whose work obviously draws both upon North American and Caribbean cultural traditions, Marshall is an excellent example of the important cultural exchanges that have long occurred between these two traditions, especially between African American artists and thinkers and black Caribbean artists and thinkers. Indeed, this dialogue of cultures had already been central to Marshall's work as early as her first novel, *Brown Girl, Brownstones* (1959), a partly autobiographical account of a first-generation American of Barbadian parents who must negotiate sometimes difficult and conflicting terrain in an attempt to integrate her complex cultural heritage. Marshall's later novels, including *Praisesong for the Widow* (1983) and *Daughters* (1991), also involve complex interchanges between the Caribbean and North America.[17]

Merle Hodge, born in Carapichaima, Trinidad, in 1944, can be seen as the first of a new generation of Caribbean women writers who built upon the work of forerunners such as Rhys and Marshall to initiate a new era in Caribbean women's literature in the 1970s and (especially) the 1980s. Indeed, Hodge's 1970 novel, *Crick Crack, Monkey*, in some ways marked the coming-of-age of the Caribbean women's novel. A bildungsroman based partly on Hodge's own childhood experience, this novel also, in a sense, narrates the coming-of-age of Trinidad and Tobago as an independent nation. *Crick Crack, Monkey* remains Hodge's major work of book-length fiction, though she published an additional novel, intended for an adolescent audience, *For the Life of Laetitia*, in 1993. She has published several short stories since the publication of *Crick Crack, Monkey* in 1970, but has devoted most of her time and energy to writing criticism and other nonfiction works as part of her political activism in Trinidad. She has worked especially hard in support of better education, which she sees as a key to the island's development and, in particular, to the improvement of the social and economic condition of Trinidadian women.

The 1980s saw a veritable explosion in production by a new generation of highly skilled, professional Caribbean women novelists, beginning in 1980 with Erna Brodber's *Jane and Louisa Will Soon Come Home*. Brodber, born in Jamaica in 1940 and trained as a historian and sociologist, won considerable acclaim for this first novel, which explores the condition of modern psychic fragmentation via the use of a complex and convoluted structure and a rich mixture of languages and styles. Brodber's second novel, *Myal* (1988) also gained considerable acclaim, winning the Commonwealth Writers' Prize for the Caribbean/Canadian region. As in *Jane and Louisa Will Soon Come Home*, *Myal* examines the psychic condition of a troubled female protagonist. However, both novels extend beyond mere subjectivism and explore important historical and political issues as well, especially the importance of Afro-Caribbean cultural traditions as background for a continuing sense of community in rural Jamaica. Brodber's latest novel, *Louisiana* (1994), is set in the United States.

Following somewhat in the footsteps of Brodber is Michelle Cliff, another sophisticated woman novelist from Jamaica. Cliff was born in Kingston in 1946, but moved as a child to New York City with her family. She was educated in public schools there and later at Wagner College, where she received a B.A. in European history. She subsequently studied in London, where she received a doctoral degree from the Warburg Institute of the University of London, concentrating on studies of the Italian Renaissance. Since that time, she has taught at several American universities and is now the Allan K. and Gwendolyn Miles Smith Professor of English Language and Literature at Trinity College in Hartford, Connecticut. Cliff's first book was an autobiographical prose poem entitled *Claiming an Identity They Taught Me to Despise* (1980). She then followed with her first novel, **Abeng** (1984), an important contribution to the emerging genre of the Caribbean female bildungsroman. It was followed by its sequel, *No Telephone to Heaven* (1987), then by a third novel, *Free Enterprise* (1993), a historical novel that focuses on women who participated in John Brown's rebellion at Harper's Ferry. She is also the author of *The Land of Look Behind* (1985), a collection of poems and essays, and two collections of stories: *Bodies of Water* (1990) and *The Store of a Million Items* (1998).

To American readers, the best-known Caribbean woman writer to appear in the 1980s was probably Jamaica Kincaid, born Elaine Potter Richardson in Antigua in 1949. An accomplished writer of short stories, Kincaid turned to the novel form in 1985 with the publication of *Annie John*, another example of the autobiographical bildungsroman of a Caribbean girlhood. Kincaid's next novel, *Lucy* (1990), is in some ways an extension of the first, though not a sequel. It follows its protagonist/narrator as she migrates to the United States, focusing on the theme of feminine sexuality, but in a way that addresses topics such as class, race, and colonialism. Kincaid's latest novel, *The Autobiography of My Mother* (1996), a complex meditation on race, sexuality, and the mother-daughter relationship, was a national bestseller in the United States.

Another important young novelist to emerge in the 1980s was Zee Edgell, who began her career with the publication of *Beka Lamb* in 1982. Born in Belize in 1940, Edgell can lay claim to being the first Belizean novelist, and her first book, again an autobiographical bildungsroman, is rich in its evocation of culture and history of Belize. She studied in Belize, England, and Jamaica, where she began her professional career as a reporter for the *Daily Gleaner* in Kingston. From 1966 to 1968, she edited a small newspaper in Belize, where she also taught at St. Catherine Academy. Since that time, she has traveled widely with her American husband, Al Edgell, spending time in Britain, Afghanistan, Nigeria, Bangladesh, and the United States, while writing her first novel. She spent much of the 1980s back in Belize, teaching and occupying official posts such as being director of the Department of Women's Affairs. She is currently an assistant professor of English at Kent State University in Ohio.

Edgell's second novel, *In Times Like These* (1991), is also partly autobiographical, relating the personal and political experiences of a Belizean woman who returns to her homeland after a period of study in England. Like *Beka Lamb*, it deals in a central way with the transformation of Belize from a British colony into an independent nation. It is, in fact, set at the moment of independence in 1981. Her third novel, *The Festival of San Joaquin*, was published in 1997. Here, Edgell departs from autobiography to tell the story of a mestiza woman who is accused, then cleared, of murdering her husband. The woman, Luz Marina, then attempts to rebuild her shattered life in a context that allows Edgell to depict and explore the complex and dynamic ethnic and cultural mix that is contemporary Belize.

Merle Collins joined the ranks of highly-educated and sophisticated Caribbean women novelists with the 1987 publication of *Angel*, an autobiographical bildungsroman that also explores the history of Grenada, building up to the U.S. invasion of the island in 1983. Born in Grenada in 1950, Collins grew up and went to school there, later attending college at the University of the West Indies in Mona, Jamaica. After serving as a teacher, first in St. Lucia, then in Grenada, she came to the United States to continue her studies, receiving a master's degree in Latin American studies from Georgetown University in 1981. She then returned to Grenada to serve as a research coordinator for the Ministry of Foreign Affairs in the People's Revolutionary Government of Maurice Bishop. A strong opponent of the U.S. invasion of Grenada in 1983, Collins left Grenada after that invasion toppled the People's Revolutionary Government. She went to London, where she pursued her doctoral studies, focusing on the political history of Grenada from 1950 until the revolution of 1979. She received her doctorate in government from the London School of Economics in 1990 and is now a professor of English at the University of Maryland.

Collins has published two collections of poetry: *Because the Dawn Breaks!: Poems Dedicated to the Grenadian People* (1985) and *Rotten Pomerack* (1992). She has also published numerous short stories and has coedited (with Rhonda Cobham) *Watchers and Seekers* (1987), a collection of poems, stories, and autobiographies by women writers from Europe, India, Africa, and the Caribbean. *Angel* was followed by another novel, *The Colour of Forgetting* (1995).

The 1980s also saw the emergence of Jamaican-born Joan Riley with the publication of *The Unbelonging* (1985), *Waiting in the Twilight* (1987), and *Romance* (1988), all of which focus on the experiences of Caribbean-born women in England. In 1992, Riley published the controversial *A Kindness to the Children*, about sexual and religious abuse of children and adults in a rural Jamaican village. Also productive beginning in this period was Guyana's Beryl Gilroy, who published the novel *Fragipani House* in 1986, followed by *Boy-Sandwich* (1989), *Stedman and Joanna* (1991), and *Inkle and Yarico* (1996). Guyana's Grace Nichols and Janice Shinebourne also published interesting novels in the 1980s, as did Jamaica's Marlene Nourbese Philip.

The maturation of the Caribbean novel as a phenomenon in world literature during the 1970s and 1980s can also be seen in the increasing variety of novels by male writers during those decades. One of the most unusual works to appear during this period was Michael Thelwell's *The Harder They Come* (1980), based on the 1972 Perry Henzell film of the same title. Though the film was set in the 1960s, it was based on the real story of notorious Jamaican gunman Ivanhoe "Rhygin" Martin, who became something of a popular hero in Jamaica in the late 1940s after a highly publicized shoot-out with police made him a cult figure among the poor and dispossessed of the island. Thelwell himself was born in Kingston, Jamaica, in 1939. The son of a middle-class politician, Thelwell studied at Jamaica College and later (1964) received his B.A. in English literature from Howard University in the United States. He received his M.F.A. from the University of Massachusetts, Amherst, in 1969 and then became a teacher at that school, where he is now a full professor in the W.E.B. Du Bois Department of Afro-American Studies.

In America, Thelwell became heavily involved in the civil rights movement of the 1960s, an experience that informs many of his early short stories, as well as many of the writings in his collection *Duties, Pleasures, and Conflicts* (1987). While *The Harder They Come* remains his only published novel, his short stories, polemical essays, and political activism have made him a prominent voice in African American and Caribbean culture.

Thelwell, a strong proponent of literary realism and a critic of what he sees as the pretentious artifice of modernist literature, has identified Jamaican novelists such as Reid, Mais, and Salkey, all of whom chronicle working-class Jamaican life, as his important literary predecessors.

Thelwell's career, like those of Marshall, Cliff, and Collins, suggests a blurring of boundaries between Caribbean and North American literature. Meanwhile, novelists such as Roy Heath have tended to blur the boundary between Caribbean and British literature. Heath traveled from his native Guyana to England in 1950, the same year as Selvon, Lamming, and Naipaul. However, he did not immediately become a writer, but instead spent his first decades in London studying both law and modern languages. He eventually qualified for the bar in both England and Guyana, but chose to pursue a career teaching in a London comprehensive school rather than practicing law. Heath did not publish his first novel until 1974, when *A Man Come Home* appeared. A study of violence and sexual aggression in a Guyanese family, this novel, like much of Heath's work, also comments upon the political corruption and economic underdevelopment of postcolonial Guyana. Heath has gone on to enjoy considerable critical and commercial success in Britain, publishing a variety of works. One of his best-known novels, *The Murderer* (1978), is a psychologically complex detective story that won the *Guardian* prize for fiction. Heath's most important novels may be the trilogy of works about the Guyanese Armstrong family, including *From the Heat of the Day* (1979), *One Generation* (1981), and *Genetha* (1981). These novels are dark meditations on class, race, and the futility of life in modern Guyana. Much lighter in tone are *Kwaku* (1982) and its sequel, *The Ministry of Hope* (1997), about a modern trickster figure whose seeming simplemindedness provides a comic perspective for some trenchant social observations.

Caryl Phillips, born in St. Kitts in 1958, is a young novelist who has also enjoyed particular prominence in British literary circles in recent years. Taken to England at the age of one, he has remained there ever since, though he now shares his time between England and St. Kitts. An elegant stylist noted for his well-constructed plots, Phillips began as a playwright, but gained immediate recognition as a novelist with the publication of such works as *The Final Passage* (1985) and *A State of Independence* (1986), which deal, respectively, with the disappointments sometimes faced by West Indian immigrants in England and with the difficulty of returning home to the Caribbean after living abroad for an extensive time. In *Higher Ground* (1989) and *Cambridge* (1991), Phillips begins to perfect the technique of constructing novels out of multiple, thematically-linked stories, generally focusing on issues such as racism and slavery. The same technique and subject matter are used in *Crossing the River* (1993), which was short-listed for the Booker Prize. His latest novel is *The Nature of Blood* (1997).

The recent award-winning fiction of writers such as Lovelace and Phillips has demonstrated the ongoing vitality and growing global prominence of Anglophone Caribbean fiction in the 1990s, as did the awarding of the 1992 Nobel Prize for Literature to the St. Lucian poet and dramatist, Derek Walcott. Not only are most of the important novelists from the 1960s onward still working, but new novelists have added renewed vigor and versatility to the Caribbean novel. These new novelists include Fred D'Aguiar, who was born in London in 1960, but spent most of his childhood in his family's native Guyana before returning to England to complete his education, which included African and Caribbean studies at the University of Kent in Canterbury. Already established as a poet in the 1980s, D'Aguiar burst onto the scene as a novelist in 1994 with the publication of *The Longest Memory*, which focuses on the whipping death of a slave in the American South before the Civil War, and which won the Whitbread Prize for best first novel. It was followed in 1996 by *Dear Future*, which pictures small-town life in Guyana from the point of view of Red Head, who has been a bit off since receiving a blow to the head at age nine, and in 1997 by *Feeding the Ghosts*, about the barbaric conditions aboard a British slave ship. D'Aguiar now teaches at the University of Miami.

In a somewhat similar vein, Guyana's David Dabydeen, well known in England as a scholar and poet, turned to novel writing in 1991 with the publication of *The Intended*. And Toronto's Dionne Brand (born in Trinidad in 1953), already known as a poet, essayist, and filmmaker, turned to novel writing in 1996 with the publication of *In Another Place Not Here*. Meanwhile, Jamaica's Evan Jones (born in 1927) had established himself as a scriptwriter in film and television before the publication of his first novel, *Stone Haven*, in 1993. Other Caribbean writers who have moved in new directions in the 1990s include Trinidad's Kevin Baldeosingh (born in 1965), who has produced postmodern comic satires such as *The Autobiography of Paras P.* (1996) and *Virgin's Triangle* (1997), which show the influence of writers such as Salman Rushdie, but are written in a lighter vein than Rushdie's work. Meanwhile, the Haitian-born novelist Edwidge Danticat, who emigrated to New York in 1981 at the age of twelve, has introduced a new dimension to the literary relationship between the United States and the Caribbean with the publication of acclaimed fiction in English in the 1990s, including *Krik? Krak!* (1995), a collection of stories that was nominated for a National Book Award. Danticat's two novels—*Breath, Eyes, Memory* (1994) and *The Farming of Bones* (1998)—have also received extensive praise. Other new novelists to emerge in the last decade or so include: Trinidad's Neil Bissoondath, Robert Antoni, and I. J. Boodhoo; Jamaica's Patricia Powell and Vanessa Spence; Barbados's Glenville Lovell and Kwadwo Agymah Kamau; and Grenada's Jean Buffong. Such new developments promise a diverse and healthy, if unpredictable, future for the Caribbean novel in English.[18]

The following chapters present extended discussions of individual Caribbean novels in English. The first group of these discussions includes full-length critical essays on eight different novels, written at a level that is intended to be useful to graduate students and scholars, but accessible to undergraduate students. These essays are arranged chronologically according to the publication dates of the novels being discussed, ranging from George Lamming's *In the Castle of My Skin* (1953) to Michelle Cliff's *Abeng* (1984). In this section, some preference has been given to postcolonial novels, though the novels in general have been selected to provide broad coverage of the Anglophone Caribbean novel as a literary phenomenon. The second group of essays, also arranged chronologically, are shorter discussions of an additional ten novels, selected for their historical importance and in order to broaden the coverage of the current study to include as many as possible of the various kinds of novels that have contributed to the growth of the Caribbean novel as a genre. Together, these essays should provide readers with a broad introduction to the Caribbean novel in English, and are also intended to provide an introduction to the theoretical issues involved in reading the Caribbean novel. They are supplemented by brief sections discussing the historical backgrounds of the various Caribbean countries represented in this study.

Notes

1. On the Harlem Renaissance as a crucial phenomenon in the development of American modernism, see Hutchinson 1995.

2. For a useful recent attempt to explain the distinctive features of Caribbean literature in English, see James 1999.

3. In the case of African literature, these issues are conveniently summarized by Booker (1998a, 1–28).

4. In the Caribbean, of course, this project was well underway before the actual granting of independence. However, Caribbean literature, even as early as the 1930s, is often aimed toward the development of cultural identities independent of the legacy of British rule. Thus, virtually all Caribbean literature is postcolonial in the sense defined by Declan Kiberd of literature produced from "the very moment when a native writer formulates a text committed to cultural resistance" (1995, 6).

5. The Kenyan novelist Ngugi wa Thiong'o, who now writes exclusively in Gikuyu, has been particularly vocal in his opposition to Africans writing in former colonial languages. See Ngugi 1992.

6. See Ramchand (1983, 57–62) for an excellent brief discussion of *Jane's Career*.

7. For an excellent extensive study of the Beacon Group and their work, see Sander 1988.

8. Titles indicated in boldface are discussed at length in the later chapters of this volume.

9. James's work has become even more prominent since his death in 1989, and critical appreciation of his achievement is still growing, as can be seen in the recent publication of the critical study by Nielsen (1997), biographical studies by Buhle (1988) and Worcester (1996), and collections of critical essays on James edited by Buhle (1986) and by Cudjoe and Cain (1995).

10. These two novels were later republished in significantly revised forms, in 1981 and 1984, respectively. Our discussion of *Crown Jewel* in this volume refers to the revised edition.

11. De Boissière eventually published one additional novel, *No Saddles for Kangaroos* (1964), based directly on his Australian experience.

12. On Selvon's role in the Caribbean literary renaissance, see Birbalsingh 1977.

13. For a fuller discussion of the role of autobiography in the book, see Salik 1992.

14. Selvon's work has received substantial critical attention, some of which is summarized in the compilation edited by Susheila Nasta (1988). See also the book-length study by Mark Looker (1996).

15. Naipaul was the son of Seepersad Naipaul, himself a writer of journalism and short stories. Naipaul's brother, Shiva, was also a fiction writer of some repute.

16. Naipaul has, in fact, won numerous awards, and his work has received extensive critical attention. See, for example, the book-length studies by Cudjoe (1988) and Nixon (1992) and the collection edited by Hamner (1979).

17. Marshall's work is beginning to receive more and more significant critical attention, including one recent book-length study (Denniston 1995).

18. For an additional and somewhat more detailed historical survey of Caribbean literature in English up to the beginning of the 1990s, see the first section of King 1995.

Chapter 2

George Lamming:
In the Castle of My Skin

In the Castle of My Skin (1953) is a largely autobiographical work based on Lamming's childhood and adolescence in colonial Barbados. However, like all of his work, it moves beyond the personal dimension to establish an important dialogue with the history of Barbados and the Caribbean. Although the book is essentially a bildungsroman, relating the growth and maturation of its protagonist, designated simply as G., from age nine to age eighteen, *In the Castle of My Skin*, as Lamming notes in his introduction, focuses on the "collective human substance" of the village in which G. lives, so that "community, not person, is the central character" (xxxvi). The book does not simply focus on the story of an individual childhood; rather, it focuses on the larger question of colonial identity, on the problems faced by colonial subjects attempting to attain maturity amid a colonial environment that seeks to keep them in a condition of perpetual childhood. Indeed, the book itself enacts a similar dynamic: Just as G. seeks to develop a viable personal identity amid the confining restraints of colonialism, so too does Lamming seek a viable mode of cultural expression amid a literary tradition dominated by European models. As Helen Tiffin notes, such questions are central to all of Lamming's writing, which seeks "to grapple with the central dilemma of colonialism and its post-colonial legacy—how to recreate an indigenous personality and destiny when the only literary forms and language available are those of the former colonizer" (Tiffin 1986, 253).

The private story of G.'s childhood and the public story of colonial Barbados are carefully interwoven throughout *In the Castle of My Skin*. As Sandra Pouchet Paquet points out in her foreword to the book, "G.'s individual predicament is always dissolving into the collective predicament of other village boys, and into the adult world of social and political relations of which the child has only partial awareness" (Paquet 1991, xvi). Lamming, moreover, is highly aware of these relations. He addresses in a sophisticated way a number of issues that would later become central to the field of postcolonial studies, focusing on the difficulty of establishing viable and stable individual or communal identities amid the fundamentally demeaning and alienating context of colonialism. And he does so through both content and form, detailing G.'s experience with and growing awareness of the impact of colonialism on the society around him in a mode that departs in many ways from the conventions of the Western bourgeois novel. The book derives important energies from Caribbean oral folk culture, representing the rhythms of popular life in Barbados, while eschewing the focus on plot and individual characterization typical of the Western novel. In particular, Lamming seeks, through a variety of strategies, such as alternating between first-person and third-person narrative voices, to establish a connection between public and private experience of precisely the kind that has been obliterated in the bourgeois novel (and bourgeois society) since the middle of the nineteenth century.

To the extent that G.'s personal experience is presented as a version of the experience of his entire community, G.'s story can be understood as a form of "national allegory," as described by Fredric Jameson. In an important, though highly controversial, article from 1986, Jameson suggests that all "third-world texts"—and particularly the major characters in those texts—must necessarily be read as "national allegories." For Jameson, the allegorical nature of such texts arises from the fundamental nature of Third-World societies, in which the lack of the clear separation between public and private realms typical of Western societies effaces the boundary between individual characters and the societies in which they live, leading to a situation in which "*the story of a private individual destiny is always an allegory of the embattled situation of the public third-world culture and society*" (Jameson 1986, 69, Jameson's emphasis).

Jameson particularly emphasizes that the individual stories of the protagonists of postcolonial fiction tend to parallel the collective experience of anticolonial struggle and eventual independence. Noting the applicability of Jameson's notion to *In the Castle of My Skin*, Michael Harris suggests that Lamming's novel, though written during the colonial period, can be seen to trace "the entire colonial history of a West Indian island through decolonization and independence" (Harris 1992, 161–62). Readers such as Paquet have emphasized the allegorical nature of Lammings texts, as well (Paquet 1982). However, as Simon Gikandi has emphasized, *In the Castle of My Skin* is anything but an idealized vision of communal bliss. Indeed, the book emphasizes G.'s fundamental inability to "inherit his history and cultural tradition" or to feel at one with his community (Gikandi 1992, 77). G. feels alienated from those around him from the very beginning, and every step he takes, especially through the colonial education system of Barbados, serves further to alienate him from his friends, family, and neighbors. Lamming's book, by interweaving private and public elements, seeks to critique and strike a blow against this kind of alienation, but it in no way implies that a sense of solidarity between individual and community is unproblematic in Barbados or other colonial sites.

In the Castle of My Skin begins with G.'s ninth birthday, which we assume, based on Lamming's biography, occurs in 1936. To this point, G.'s childhood has been anything but an idyll in an island paradise. As he puts it, narrating in first person, "It was my ninth celebration of the gift of life, my ninth celebration of the consistent lack of an occasion to celebrate" (9). This particular birthday is also not a cause for celebration in that it is marked by a damaging flood that sweeps through his village and forces the cancellation of G.'s much-anticipated birthday party. This flood, which takes on almost mythical proportions, will ultimately come to be regarded by many of the villagers as the beginning of the end of a long era in which conditions in the village have remained virtually unchanged for generations. Meanwhile, the disappointment of the cancelled party is only one of many that G. will suffer amid the poverty of his upbringing living with his mother in a colonial village that is completely dominated by the white landlord, Mr. Creighton. As Supriya Nair notes, economic conditions for the black working and peasant class of Barbados were particularly harsh in the 1930s, due both to recent drops in sugar prices and to the general collapse of Western capitalist economies in the Great Depression (Nair 1996, 94).[1] Much of G.'s sense of deprivation thus arises from the material impoverishment suffered by his mother and himself as they struggle to make a life for themselves in Creighton's Village, Barbados, which offers them few economic opportunities.

But much of this sense of loss also arises from the young G.'s sense of loneliness and isolation, introducing the theme of alienation that runs throughout the text. G. notes, early on, that his life, from the very beginning, has been marked by "an almost total absence of family relations" (12). Though his mother provides a stable center, the other members of his family have been absent since his birth. His grandmother is in Panama; his grandfather is dead; and his uncle is in America. His father, significantly, is not mentioned in this list. Earlier, in fact, G. declares that his father "had only fathered the idea of me" and that he had really been fathered by his mother (11).

Absent fathers are, indeed, a recurrent image in the book. Not only is G.'s father completely missing from his life, but his mother, when asked about her own father, hastily explains that he died before she was born. Given her extremely light skin, it is likely that her father was white, perhaps even the father of the current Mr. Creighton. G., however, is careful not even to wonder about the origins of her light skin (277). He also seems relatively uncurious about his own father, but it is clear that his lack of a paternal figure contributes to his alienation, while at the same time serving as an image of the difficulty of establishing a viable and stable identity in the colonial environment of Barbados, which itself, as it were, has no father, but only a Mother Country. Indeed, the only truly paternal figure in Creighton Village is Creighton himself, demonstrating the paternalistic nature of colonialism itself. In a similar way, the only source of inherited cultural pride offered to G. in his upbringing arises from the secondary, colonized status of his homeland. Barbados, G. is taught, should be pleased to be known as "Little England" and as "the oldest and purest of England's children . . . the pride and treasure of the Empire" (37–38).

G. does derive important sustenance from the communal cultural traditions of the poor villagers, but, as he grows older, he becomes more and more estranged from the life of the village. As he attends the village school, he comes to believe that education, which in this school means mastering the language and knowledge of the British colonial rulers of Barbados, is the key to a better and more prosperous life. Later, when he goes to high school, thus joining the privileged few, he is even further alienated from his village. Much of the book, in fact, focuses on colonial schooling and on the way the British-dominated curriculum distorts the history and culture of the Caribbean in an attempt to convey the ideology of empire to its students. Thus, G. is faced early on with a central dilemma of the colonial subject: to succeed and to receive recognition of this success from official authority, he must learn to master discourses that are designed to demonstrate his own fundamental inferiority.

History and historiography are central to this educational process and are, in fact, major topics of *In the Castle of My Skin*, which is designed largely to counter colonialist accounts of the Caribbean past. In an excellent reading of the book, Supriya Nair demonstrates the centrality of this challenge to Lamming's novel, relating Lamming's project in the book to Frantz Fanon's insistence that seizing control of historical representations should be a central concern of anticolonial liberation movements (Nair 1996). This project has, in fact, been central to the work of postcolonial writers all over the world.[2] It does, however, take on a particular urgency in the Caribbean, where indigenous traditions were suppressed more thoroughly than in Africa or India and where colonial rule lasted far longer than anywhere else, with the exception of Ireland. The history of the Caribbean was thus more thoroughly dominated by colonialist accounts and for a longer period than were the histories of Africa or India.

In his description of the village school, G. notes that it consists of a courtyard with three corners occupied by a church, the school building itself, and the home of the head teacher, "three shrines of enlightenment that looked over the wall and across a benighted tenantry" (35). The school, in short, reproduces the colonial situation itself, with the students acting as subjects of religious and political power emanating from the metropolitan center of England. Throughout *In the Castle of My Skin*, Lamming illustrates the ways in which both religion and education were used as crucial reinforcements for British colonial rule in Barbados. Tiffin notes that religion is depicted in the book as "the foremost agent in the perpetuation of the ignorance of ancestry and history, that which continues deprivation by encouraging acceptance of it" (Tiffin 1986, 259). Granted, Christianity may bring some solace to the poor of Barbados by assuring them of a better life in the next world, but this solace is used primarily to teach patience and obedience and thus to reinforce the existing colonial system. As the mother of one of G.'s schoolmates, who happens also to be a Sunday School teacher, explains, "There is nothing for us to do . . . but rejoice in our bondage" (72).

Significantly, when the students of the village school gather in the courtyard, it is described as resembling a large ship packed with cargo. Given that the students are black, the implication that the school is reminiscent of a slave ship is clear, providing powerful reminders that the students' ancestors were brought to Barbados not as protected children but as brutalized slaves, robbed of their humanity in order to provide cheap labor for English-owned plantations. The school, with its message of British pride, does not, of course, emphasize this fact. Indeed, in the distorted vision of history promoted in the school, the experience of slavery is effaced altogether. The boys in the school thus have virtually no knowledge of this aspect of their history.

As the school officially commemorates the birthday of the former Queen Victoria, the boys overhear some old people discussing the fact that Victoria was a good queen because she freed the people of Barbados in the nineteenth century.[3] The puzzled boys have no idea what the people are talking about and are advised by their teacher to ignore the remarks of the old people concerning emancipation. When one boy insists that an old woman had specifically spoken of the phenomenon of slavery, the teacher merely responds that the woman is getting "dotish" and assures the boys that there has never been such a thing as slavery in Barbados (57). The teacher's claim is an outright lie: Barbados, colonized by the British in 1635, had been used since that time primarily for growing sugar cane on plantations that, from colonization until emancipation more than two hundred years later, had been manned primarily by slave labor brought from Africa.

By suppressing the historical memory of slavery, the colonial rulers of 1930s Barbados seek both to efface the brutality and inhumanity on which their rule is founded and to break any sense of cultural and historical connection between the people of Barbados and their African ancestors. They also seek to suppress all memory of the fact that the slaves of Barbados (as in many parts of the Caribbean) carried on a remarkable series of determined rebellions in their effort to gain freedom, an effort the memory of which could provide important sustenance to the anticolonial resistance movement of the twentieth century.[4] This official attempt to efface the historical record is countered in the text by oral histories offered by old people such as those who discuss Queen Victoria at the school. Based on personal memory, these oral histories are clearly presented in the text as more reliable than the written histories detailed in the children's schoolbooks.

Also important in this regard is the village shoemaker, who offers his shop as a gathering place where the local men can discuss social, political, and historical issues from the perspective of the people of Barbados rather than that of the colonial rulers of the island. Among other things, the shoemaker directly challenges the distortions of history promulgated in colonial schools, complaining that black political and cultural leaders such as Marcus Garvey are never mentioned in these histories and that the black teachers in these schools seek to deny their own African cultural heritage: "If you tell half of them that work in those places they have somethin' to do with Africa they'd piss straight in your face" (104).

In *In the Castle of My Skin*, G.'s lack of any memory of his father clearly parallels the broader lack of historical knowledge on the part of the young people of Barbados, though G. himself is only vaguely aware of this fact. Lamming, on the other hand, is intensely aware of it and has made it a central concern of his writing. For example, in an essay on the role of the Caribbean intellectual in the face of a long legacy of cultural domination by the West, Lamming insists that one of the central responsibilities of the Caribbean intellectual is to call attention to the special nature of Caribbean history:

I don't think there had been anything in human history quite like the meeting of Africa, Asia and Europe, in this American archipelago we call the Caribbean. But it is so recent since we assumed responsibility for our own destiny, that the antagonistic weight of the past is felt as an inhibiting menace. And that is the most urgent task and the greatest intellectual challenge: how to control the burden of this history, and incorporate it into our collective sense of the future. (Lamming 1994a, 92)

On the surface, this situation seems little different from that which obtains in Europe in the modern era, where a constant urge for innovation leads to a persistent drive to overcome the past and a tendency, as Karl Marx notes in *The Eighteenth Brumaire*, to feel that "the tradition of all the dead generations weighs like a nightmare on the brain of the living" (Marx and Engels 1978, 595).[5]

Crucial to this project, for Lamming, is the search for productive ways of drawing upon the African past to help envision a viable Caribbean future. This project, however, is a highly complex one. European colonization virtually exterminated the native populations of most Caribbean islands, leaving them with no indigenous cultural traditions upon which to draw. These populations, in the quest for cheap labor, were then replaced by African slaves, making African culture the closest thing to an indigenous, anticolonial cultural tradition in the Caribbean. But, as Lamming points out in his essay, "The Occasion for Speaking," Caribbean access to African traditions is highly secondary, both because of the distance from Africa and because the Caribbean remained under the colonial domination of Europe for so long. Lamming notes that the West Indian is a "peripheral man" in relation to the cultures of both Africa and Europe (Lamming 1992a, 34). Thus, though residents of the Caribbean share the colonial past of Africa, they cannot derive cultural strength from traditional African culture in the same way that Africans can. Instead, colonialism, which began in the West Indies and continued longer there than anywhere else, is "the very base and structure of the West Indian's cultural awareness" (Lamming 1992a, 35).

This sense of marginality to all of the various cultural traditions in which they participate helps to explain the special concern with questions of identity that haunts Caribbean literature, a concern that, among other things, is reflected in the prominence of the bildungsroman as the central form of the Caribbean novel. Thus, Michael Gilkes prefaces his study of the novels of Wilson Harris by noting that "the crisis of identity is a peculiarly Caribbean theme, amounting, at times, almost to an obsession" (Gilkes 1975, x). *In the Castle of My Skin*, like all of Lamming's writing, seeks to make a contribution to the project of developing a viable postcolonial Caribbean identity that escapes the domination of colonial past. Indeed, Michael Harris argues that Lamming's first novel and V. S. Reid's *New Day* are especially important in Caribbean culture because "they represent the earliest attempts to portray West Indian people as having a tradition and culture of their own" (Harris 1992, 161).

In much of his writing, Lamming suggests that West Indians can draw upon a sense of solidarity with other Third-World peoples in their fight to develop a viable postcolonial cultural identity. After all, the Caribbean is a unique crossroads of Third-World cultures; it has ethnic and cultural links not only to Africa, but to India and China, given that large numbers of indentured Chinese and Indian laborers were brought in to work on Caribbean plantations after the abolition of slavery. Thus, West Indians, despite the fact that all of their cultural identities are in a sense borrowed and indirect, belong in a central way to "that massive peasant majority whose leap in the twentieth century has shattered all the traditional calculations of the West" (Lamming 1992a, 36). Thus, "the West Indian, though provincial, is perhaps the most cosmopolitan man in the world" (37).

The curriculum of the village school in *In the Castle of My Skin* is designed precisely to prevent the students from developing any sense of participation in this cosmopolitan Third-World identity. And the participation of the school's black teachers in this suppression represents a strong indictment of the complicity of the black educated middle classes in the ongoing British domination of Barbados and other colonial possessions. Lamming thus anticipates the later warnings of Fanon of the potential for disaster in postcolonial African nations if those nations, in independence, simply replace the ruling European colonial bourgeoisie by an indigenous one, while leaving the basic class structure of the societies still in place. In particular, Fanon argues that the postcolonial bourgeoisie lack the historical energy that had enabled the European bourgeoisie to defeat their feudal-aristocratic predecessors and sweep into power in Europe in the seventeenth to nineteenth centuries. The postcolonial bourgeoisie of Africa and the Caribbean tend to be mere imitators of their Western masters, who themselves had already become decadent long before the time of decolonization. According to Fanon, the postcolonial bourgeois class thus:

> follows the Western bourgeoisie along its path of negation and decadence without ever having emulated it in its first stages of exploration and invention. . . . It is already senile before it has come to know the petulance, the fearlessness, or the will to succeed of youth. (Fanon 1968, 153)

Fanon is writing here primarily of Africa, but his own Caribbean background as a native of Martinique may have contributed to this insight. After all, as Lamming points out, the indigenous bourgeoisie of the Caribbean, by the time of independence, had been far more thoroughly entrenched than their counterparts in Africa. Indeed, Lamming notes that, by the late 1950s, the colonial Civil Service in Barbados and Trinidad had been manned primarily by "natives" for decades (Lamming 1992a, 35). Importantly, however, this experience did little to prepare the islands for independence, and actually seemed to result in a diminution of the movement toward independence by creating a class of leaders so thoroughly infused with British values (and so privileged under the British colonial system) that they had no reason to agitate for independence.

The principal figure of this phenomenon in *In the Castle of My Skin* is the tellingly named Mr. Slime, who starts out as a teacher in G.'s village school, then moves on to become a business and political leader in the village. Among other things, he founds a "Penny Bank and Friendly Society," into which he encourages the villagers to deposit their meager savings, toward the eventual dream of gaining ownership of the land on which they have long lived as tenants of the landlord, Creighton. Meanwhile, Slime himself gains power and influence to the point that the villagers begin to suspect he is on the way toward replacing Creighton as the dominant figure in village life.

But, in keeping with Fanon's warnings, the rise of Slime hardly represents an unequivocal boon for the people of the village; indeed, rather than help them purchase their own land, he begins using the money deposited in his bank to acquire the land for himself. Together with his partners, Slime begins to purchase one parcel of land after another, then to demand that the long-term inhabitants vacate the premises. Not surprisingly, one of the first to go is the self-educated shoemaker, whose reading and political awareness make him a potential rival for Slime. The shoemaker is thus forced to vacate the premises he has occupied for twenty years. When men come to remove his rickety building from the site, the structure collapses in a heap, leaving the shoemaker with nothing.

Even more telling and poignant is the story of Pa, an old man who is forced by Slime's land-acquisition scheme to leave his lifelong home in the village.[6] Pa and his wife, Ma, the oldest couple in the village, are featured in several chapters of the book, serving as bearers of local oral tradition. Late in the book, however, Ma dies, followed soon afterward by Pa's eviction, which will force him to live in the Alms House, a "charitable" institution regarded by the locals, including Pa, as the worst possible fate, worse even than prison (253). Pa's personal tragedy, meanwhile, is also representative of the passing of a way of life, as the traditional culture of the village collapses beneath the weight of the modernizing forces represented by Slime.

Indeed, the inevitable forward movement of history is a major theme of *In the Castle of My Skin*. Despite the attempts of the village school to suppress the facts of history, history itself frequently intrudes into the relatively insulated worlds of the school and the village. One day, for instance, classes are suddenly dismissed after a strike in the nearby city leads to violent clashes between workers and police that spills into the village itself, leading to a violent situation in which an angry mob nearly murders Creighton. Labor relations in Barbados are, in fact, central to the novel, which makes clear the role of the colony as a cheap source of labor for international capital. The police and other officials consistently support the employers in their battles against labor, while the workers are hampered in their efforts to organize by the betrayal of their own would-be advocates, such as the unscrupulous Mr. Slime. The labor strife to which Lamming calls attention was one of the major events of the history of Barbados in the 1930s, and was in fact part of a larger phenomenon that was central to the history not only of the Caribbean but of Great Britain and the United States in that decade.[7] Yet, official accounts of Western history tend to ignore, or at least minimize, the importance of this working-class activism. It is significant that Lamming, as part of his project to develop an alternative history, calls attention to precisely those aspects of experience that official accounts typically suppress.

Major changes also come to Barbados as a result of the seemingly distant outbreak of World War II. A course of military training is instituted in G.'s high school, and the reality of the war is brought home to Barbados when a large merchant ship, anchored off the island, is torpedoed. But modernity marches on, and the disruption of life in G.'s village due to economic changes, already under way before the war, continues. Just as G. must inevitably advance from childhood, to adolescence, to young adulthood, so too must Barbados move from its traditional colonial society toward the new world of independence.

One marker of this forward historical movement involves the book's various hints that Great Britain, the dominant force in Barbados for hundreds of years, is slowly being replaced as an outside influence in Barbados and the rest of the Caribbean by the United States. Much of this new American influence simply involves the replacement of British colonial domination with American neocolonial domination. Thus, Lamming, in his introduction to the book, makes clear his understanding of the threat posed to the Caribbean by the spread of an American capitalist system that seems determined to devour everything in its path: "Sometimes the twilight darkens and threatens to obliterate all memory in the tidal wave of capitalist consumerism. America spreads itself like a plague everywhere, capturing the simplest appetite with the fastest foods and nameless fripperies the advertising industry instructs us are essential needs" (xlv–xlvi).

On the other hand, cultural contacts between the Caribbean and African Americans also provide potentially new perspectives that might enable West Indians to develop a genuinely new postcolonial consciousness. Late in the book, G.'s longtime friend, Trumper, returns to the island for a visit after an extended stay working in the States. Among other things, Trumper's experiences with African Americans and his exposure to African American leaders such as Paul Robeson have given him a new racial consciousness and a better understanding of what it means to be black and poor in a world dominated by white capitalists. He thus begins to develop a sense of his collective identity as a working-class black man, an identity that transcends the hierarchies based on color (with lighter skin serving as a marker of higher status) that he and the other boys had unconsciously absorbed in their colonial childhoods.[8] He also makes trenchant observations about the nature of life in America, particularly of the way in which the fast pace and constant innovation that inform American capitalism lead to a fundamental sense of unreality (284).

Trumper's discovery of his racial heritage potentially provides a link to the African heritage of Barbados and to the larger context of global resistance to the neocolonial domination of the nonwhite Third World by the white capitalists of the First World. G. listens carefully to Trumper's stories of America, but does not yet have the experience fully to comprehend them. As the book closes, however, G. is about to broaden his experience considerably, as he prepares to depart for Trinidad to take a teaching job. Presumably, he (like Lamming himself) is on the way to gaining a wider experience of the world that will enable him better to understand the role of race in the global system of politics and economics. Though an increased consciousness of race is crucial to the lessons that G. still needs to learn, Lamming, in a way that is once again reminiscent of the work of Fanon, understands that this race consciousness must not be allowed to obscure the fundamental importance of class. Lamming notes, in his introduction, that the "overwhelming torment of race has made it difficult for Afro-Americans to perceive how central is the conflict of class in the ultimate liberation of black countries" (xliii).

Lamming seeks, throughout *In the Castle of My Skin*, to call attention to class and to avoid falling into the trap of obscuring the reality of class through a focus on race, although race is an obvious locus of colonial oppression. In his treatment of America, meanwhile, he warns that nominal independence from colonial rule does not necessarily mean liberation for the Third World, but may, in fact, merely lead to the replacement of British political domination by American cultural and economic domination. In its understanding of such issues, and its general treatment of the economic, cultural, linguistic, and historical foundations of colonialism and its successor, global capitalism, *In the Castle of My Skin* is a major contribution to the literature not just of the Caribbean but of the Third World. It should come as no surprise that militant postcolonial writers, such as the Kenyan novelist Ngugi wa Thiong'o, have seen Lamming's writing, which arises "from the centre of those struggling against the empire" as a crucial inspiration for their own work (Ngugi 1993, 6).

Historical Background

Barbados is an island of about 166 sq. mi. (430 sq. km) on the eastern edge of the West Indies. The total population is about 260,000, of whom approximately 8,000 live in the capital of Bridgetown, which is also the island's chief port and commercial center. About 86 percent of the population is of primarily black African descent, 10 percent of Asian or mixed race, and 4 percent of white European extraction. Historically, the island's most important product has been sugarcane, and sugar is still the most important crop. However, Barbados, with excellent beaches and a warm, pleasant climate, is a favorite tourist destination, and tourism is now the island's largest industry, representing nearly one-fourth of the gross domestic product. Banking and manufacturing are growing in importance, as well. Barbados is an independent nation with a parliamentary form of democratic government, but it remains a member of the British Commonwealth and recognizes Queen Elizabeth II of England as its monarch. Education is compulsory to age sixteen, and the literacy rate is approximately 99 percent.

Though probably initially inhabited by the Arawak Indians, Barbados was apparently uninhabited when first visited by the British in 1605. British settlers first came to colonize the island in 1627, bringing in large numbers of African slaves to work the large and productive sugar plantations that were soon established on the island. By 1655, Barbados was more densely populated than most regions in Europe. Slavery continued to dominate the island's economy for the next two hundred years, though the slaves of Barbados frequently rebelled against the brutal and dehumanizing treatment they consistently received. Slavery was officially abolished throughout the British Empire with the Abolition Act of 1833, largely because the rise of modern industrial capitalism was beginning to render the use of slave labor

increasingly unprofitable. In any case, slavery actually continued to be practiced in many parts of the empire, including Barbados, for several years
beyond 1833. Meanwhile, indentured labor had been used in the colony
since the seventeenth century as a supplement to slavery, and, subsequent
to abolition, plantations formerly manned by slave labor were operated
through the increased use of indentured laborers, many of whom were imported from China and India. In addition, plantation owners converted all
of their land to sugarcane and virtually ceased the production of food crops
in Barbados. Virtually all food had to be imported and, in order to buy this
imported food, former slaves were forced to work on the plantations. As a
result, the production of sugarcane in Barbados actually increased sharply
in the decades after abolition.

Barbados was the administrative center of the British Windward Islands
through much of the nineteenth century, but became a separate colony in
1885. Under the influence of both Garveyism and socialism, an active labor
movement arose in Barbados in the 1920s and 1930s, as popular leaders
such as Clement Payne served as effective advocates for the working-class
people of the island. Attempts to repress this labor movement (including
the arrest and eventual deportation of Payne) resulted in a violent workers'
rebellion in 1937, though the subsequent beginning of World War II tended
to break the momentum of the labor movement, which was beginning to
agitate for independence from British colony rule. This momentum was
never really regained after the war, and the moderate socialist Grantley Adams
remained dominant in the politics of Barbados from 1937 to 1961. However, Barbados continued to move toward independence as the British began systematically to dismantle their empire. Barbados, along with nine
other British Caribbean colonies, was a member of the West Indies Federation from 1958 to 1962, but internal disagreements made it impossible to
realize the initial plan to make this federation an independent state. Full
independence for Barbados as a state in its own right was proclaimed on
November 30, 1966, ending 330 years of continuous British colonial rule.

Errol Barrow, who originally rose to prominence at the beginning of the
1960s through his effective advocacy for the island's sugar workers, became
the first prime minister as the leader of the labor-oriented Democratic Labour
Party (DLP). Since 1966, the DLP has alternated in power with the Barbados Labour Party (BLP), which had been founded by Grantley Adams.
Adams's son, Tom Adams (like his father, a British-educated former winner
of the Barbados Island Scholarship), was the prime minister as the BLP
leader from 1976 until his death in 1985. Barrow regained power in 1986,
but died in 1987 and was succeeded by the new DLP leader, Lloyd Sandiford,
who generally continued Barrow's policies. Sandiford retained power in the

1991 elections, introducing a number of economic austerity measures in an attempt to improve the country's struggling economy. The BLP, with Owen Arthur as prime minister, returned to power in 1994. In 1996, Barbados challenged American hegemony in the Caribbean when it became the first Caribbean nation to enter into a mutual trade and investment agreement with Cuba. This agreement also abolished the need for visas for citizens traveling between the two countries. For an excellent history of Barbados, see Beckles 1990.

Notes

1. For an excellent discussion of the poverty of the peasantry of Barbados (and elsewhere in the Caribbean) during this period, see Williams 1984.

2. See, for example, Booker and Juraga 1997 for a discussion of African postcolonial historical novels.

3. This elaborate celebration stands in sharp contrast to G.'s earlier cancelled birthday party. It is also a good example of the use of spectacle to impress colonial subjects of the greatness of the British Empire, a practice that began in Victoria's reign. For discussions of this phenomenon, see Cannadine 1983 and Booker 1997.

4. For a discussion of these slave rebellions, see Beckles 1984. For a discussion of the relevance of this phenomenon to the modern independence movement, see Taylor 1995.

5. The central literary expression of this modern sensibility is the view of Stephen Dedalus, in James Joyce's *Ulysses*, that "history is a nightmare from which I am trying to awake" (Joyce 1986, 28). Significantly, Lamming employs this quotation as the epigraph to his introduction to *The Pleasures of Exile* (Lamming 1992a, 9).

6. The figure of Pa is based on Lamming's own grandfather, who was evicted from his home under similar circumstances.

7. Supriya Nair (1996) provides an excellent brief account of the historical events behind the labor unrest described in Lamming's novel (94–97). For a more detailed, contemporary account of conditions in the Caribbean, see Lewis 1939. For a discussion of the global context of these events, see Carby 1988.

8. Note, for example, G.'s discussion of the adjective "black" as a term of abuse, as seen in the way G. and the other boys mock their friend, Boy Blue, because he is the blackest of them all (127).

Chapter 3

Paule Marshall:
The Chosen Place, the Timeless People

Though written largely in the tradition of European realism, *The Chosen Place, the Timeless People* (1969) is a complex and impressive novel that addresses a number of issues that are crucial to Caribbean culture. The novel is particularly concerned with relationships between the Caribbean and the United States in the postcolonial era. Most of the major characters are from the United States, but the novel is set in the mid-1960s on the fictional Bourne Island, which Marshall constructs as a kind of amalgam of the Caribbean—or even of the Third World—as a whole. The principal plot line concerns a project, sponsored by an American research institute, to help develop "Bournehills," the most "backward" and impoverished end of the island. The American characters come to the island to lay the groundwork for this project, and their attempts to understand the social, cultural, and economic conditions that impede the modernization of Bournehills serve as a sort of primer on the problem of development in the Third World. In particular, Marshall details the historical background that has led Bournehills into its current state, while suggesting that an inability to understand this background has led to the continual failure of development projects in the region.

Marshall makes clear the almost allegorical status of Bournehills as a sort of representative Third-World site. Saul Amron, who leads the American research team, is an anthropologist who has considerable experience doing field work in the Third World. Thus, when he first sees Bournehills, it looks oddly familiar, reminiscent of all the other underdeveloped places he has seen throughout the Western hemisphere:

It resembled them all, not in physical detail so much, but in something he sensed about it as his eyes, half-closed against the glare, roamed slowly over the patchwork hills to the sea and back again. Bournehills, this place he had never seen before, was suddenly the wind-scoured Peruvian Andes. The highlands of Guatemala. Chile. Bolivia . . . Mexico. . . . And the spent cotton lands of the Southern United States. (99–100)

In a similar way, the characters themselves, while carefully detailed as individuals with distinctive characteristics and personal histories, are representative of larger social and historical phenomena. Indeed, as Barbara Christian notes, these characters together represent "the major actors populating much of the 'underdeveloped' world today" (Christian 1991, 299). Thus, Marshall moves beyond the individualism of much Western fiction to explore not merely single characters in isolation, but interactions among characters within a broad social context. As Christian puts it elsewhere, the book focuses not on "the way the world affects an individual psyche," but on "how our many psyches create a world" (Christian 1980, 135). Saul, for example, is to an extent the prototypical American social scientist, studying the Third World in a genuine effort to provide assistance, but limited in his success by a fundamental inability truly to understand the phenomena he studies. In addition, he is Jewish, a fact that partly explains his sense of affinity with oppressed peoples, despite the obstacles to understanding presented by his own American middle-class background. Saul is accompanied on the trip to Bourne Island by his research assistant, Allen Fusco. The son of an Italian father and an Irish mother, Allen is a sort of representative of European ethnicity in America. Though bright, personable, and good-looking, Allen, largely because of his ethnic background, has never felt quite at home in America. His sense of radical alienation, of being an outsider wherever he goes, is also furthered by the fact that he is apparently homosexual, though he himself does not appear fully aware of that fact. Even more than Saul, then, Allen identifies with the people of Bournehills; indeed, by the end of the novel he decides to make the area his permanent home, hoping that the inherent hybridity of the local culture will prove congenial to his own mixed nature.

If Saul and Allen represent the fact that even successful, white, middle-class Americans can be outsiders, then Saul's wife, Harriet, is the ultimate insider, the descendant of an old New England family that originally made its wealth largely through the slave trade and other exploitative operations in the West Indies. A wealthy woman with powerful connections, Harriet is entirely unable to identify with the people of Bournehills. Though she makes a few efforts to communicate with the locals, she feels desperately out of place in Bournehills, partly because of her growing realization that the people there are not particularly impressed by her breeding and background, thus leaving her without the sense of empowerment that her class position has always given her. Despite her life of wealth and privilege, she is in many ways the least alive of the characters, the least able truly to participate in life, especially when it involves genuine emotional connections to other people. This fact is symbolized by her drowning (perhaps by suicide, though that is left unclear in the text) at the end of the book.

Structurally opposed to Harriet is Merle Kinbona, their host in Bournehills. Merle is the daughter of Clara, a poor, black manual worker, and Ashton Vaughan, a prominent white man, Clara's employer. The liaison between Ashton and Clara, of course, follows in a long line of forced alliances between colonial planters and their women slaves, and Ashton in this sense is specifically described as resembling his great-grandfather, Duncan Vaughan, a wealthy planter known for his dalliances with the slaves who worked his sugar estate in early nineteenth-century Bournehills. Ashton leaves no other heirs, so Merle has inherited what was left of the declining family estate, much of which she has subsequently given away in small parcels to her neighbors in Bournehills. She has also been able to pursue her education in England, where she became involved in a sexual liaison with a manipulative, rich white woman.[1] Subsequently, she married an African graduate student there and had a child. Her husband, learning of her earlier liaison with the white woman, has left her, returning to Africa with their daughter. Merle is thus an embodiment of a common Caribbean predicament, caught between England and Africa but not really belonging to either. Damaged by this experience, Merle seems highly neurotic and has periods when she is virtually catatonic, yet it is she, not the rational Harriet, who in the end seems more capable of dealing with life and the challenges it offers.

Another important character from Bournehills is Vereson Walkes, known to the locals as "Vere." An ambitious young man, Vere returns to Bournehills (on the same plane that carries the three Americans) after a stay in the United States, where he worked as a migrant farm laborer. Brutally exploited in the States, he barely survived the ordeal, though he did manage to accumulate a small amount of money. Seeking a way to distinguish himself, he spends the money in Bournehills on a used car, an Opel, product of the combined technology of Germany and the United States. He lovingly restores the car and enters it in an annual road race, which he leads for a time. Then he loses control of the car and is killed in a crash, a clear suggestion of the negative impact of Western technological "progress" on the people

of places like Bournehills. Of the numerous other characters from
Bournehills, the most important is Lyle Hutson, an attorney. A poor boy
who won a scholarship to study in England, he has now been thoroughly
conscripted by the system of global capitalism, whose interests he serves,
while looking down upon his former neighbors. He is a figure of the corrupt postcolonial bourgeoisie, as described by Frantz Fanon.[2]

Marshall's sweeping evocation not only of the society of Bournehills, but
of the way that society participates in a larger global system, is highly reminiscent of Georg Lukács's arguments that the novels of early nineteenth-
century European realists, such as Walter Scott and Honoré de Balzac, were
particularly effective because of their ability to present the various aspects of
society as parts of an integrated "totality." In particular, Lukács argues that
this process of totalization, whatever the attitudes and ideologies of the
authors, counteracts the tendency of capitalism to compartmentalize human experience into disconnected and incompatible fragments. For Lukács,
this leads to a radical sense of alienation and painful psychic disorientation
on the part of the human beings who must live this fragmented life, so that
the ability of novels to project an alternative wholeness can have an important therapeutic function, while at the same time providing an implied criticism of capitalist fragmentation.

One of the principal aspects of this phenomenon, for Lukács, is the ability of the great bourgeois realist novels of the early nineteenth century to
maintain an intimate connection between the public and private spheres.
This gradual decline in a sense of this connection, Lukács argues, was one
of the most important signs of the growing decadence of the European
bourgeoisie after their historical rise to power in the seventeenth and eighteenth centuries, supplanting the aristocracy as the ruling class of Europe.
Since literature, to a large extent, reflects prevailing developments in society
at large, European novels themselves begin to lose any sense of connection
between private and public life, declining, as the nineteenth century proceeds, into a decadent depiction of personal, private life as entirely separate
from public, political life.

In this sense, *The Chosen Place, the Timeless People* can be seen as an
attempt to counter this decadence, recalling the early nineteenth-century
bourgeois novels that Lukács recommends as models for twentieth-century socialist writers. Here, Marshall's novel is highly reminiscent of the
work of the South African novelist Nadine Gordimer, who, in works such
as *Burger's Daughter* (1979) and *A Sport of Nature* (1988), effects a similar connection between public and private experience.[3] Both Marshall and
Gordimer, of course, write in modes that are heavily influenced by Western realism, though it is certainly important to recognize that they can

both also be considered Third-World writers. The Third World, lacking the capitalist development of Western Europe and North America, also suffers from less alienation and fragmentation of experience, so that one might expect Third-World writers to be capable of connecting different realms of experience in ways that First-World writers cannot. It is for this reason that Fredric Jameson urges Western scholars to study the works of Third-World literature, which typically feature protagonists whose personal experience allegorically reflects the historical experience of their societies as a whole.[4] And Jameson's model, however controversial, resonates with historical reality. As Fanon notes, in the process of decolonization, "individual experience, because it is national and because it is a link in the chain of national existence, ceases to be individual, limited, and shrunken and is enabled to open out into the truth of the nation and of the world" (Fanon 1968, 200).

For Lukács, the great realist novelists achieve their connection between public and private realms primarily through the technique of "typicality," that is, through the creation of characters who are both distinct individuals and "typical" representatives of large historical forces, thus embodying private and public energies in a single figure. For example, he praises writers such as Walter Scott and Leo Tolstoy for creating "characters in whom personal and social-historical fates closely conjoin" (Lukács 1983, 285). The relevance of this notion to *The Chosen Place, the Timeless People*, the characters of which are so obviously the result of identifiable historical forces, should be obvious.

In addition, it is important to note that, for Lukács, these historical forces are dynamic and that, in the best realist historical novels, the characters are not simply the static result of existing conditions, but continue to grow and evolve in response to ongoing historical change. Ultimately, in fact, the true importance of writers such as Balzac and Scott lies, for Lukács, in their ability to capture the sense of dramatic historical transformation that underlay the revolutionary rise to power of the bourgeoisie, as symbolized most vividly in the French Revolution, but as represented most fundamentally in a gradual cultural revolution that saw bourgeois ideas and values rise to dominance in the West, along with the rise of capitalism as the dominant economic system.

The emphasis on history in *The Chosen Place, the Timeless People* thus suggests an additional way in which Lukács's theoretical work is relevant to Marshall's novel. On the other hand, the historical experience with which Marshall's novel deals is not that of the triumphant European bourgeoisie of the Enlightenment, but of the oppressed people of Bournehills, the exploitation of whose ancestors in fact fueled the European bourgeois cultural revolution. The European bourgeoisie were able to overcome the traditional rule of the aristocracy largely because of the vast amounts of wealth they derived from colonies such as those in the West Indies, where the indigenous people were largely exterminated and where inexpensive labor was supplied by imported African slaves.[5]

Because of this historical experience, Bournehills is consistently depicted by Marshall as trapped in the past, unable to move into the future. Not only do the inhabitants seem to resist all outside attempts to modernize their lives, but they seem almost fixated on the past. In particular, they cling to the one positive historical memory they have, that of the long-ago Pyre Hill Revolt, in which the now-legendary Cuffee Ned led his fellow slaves in a rebellion against their British masters. Marshall draws upon numerous elements of Caribbean history and legend in constructing the legendary history of Cuffee Ned. Denniston notes that the most direct source may be the Berbice Rebellion of 1765, led by Kofi-Akan, still a national hero of Guyana (Denniston 1995, 101). Spillers, meanwhile, suggests that Marshall's fictional rebellion draws upon a variety of historical slave rebellions, ranging from the Haitian Revolution of 1791 to North American revolts such as those led by Nat Turner and Denmark Vesey (Spillers 1985, 162).[6] Indeed, the revolt of Cuffee Ned, like so many elements of the book, has a rather allegorical quality. In the novel, Marshall describes the rebellion as "the experience through which any people who find themselves ill-used, dispossessed, at the mercy of the powerful, must pass" (286–87).

The Pyre Hill Revolt ultimately failed, but Cuffee Ned and his followers fought long and well, and this example of heroic collective resistance remains crucial to the cultural identities of the inhabitants of Bournehills. Indeed, references to Cuffee Ned and his rebellion constantly punctuate the speech of the locals, while an elaborate reenactment of the Pyre Hill Revolt remains central to the annual celebration of carnival on the island.[7]

However, though the memory of this revolt clearly helps the oppressed inhabitants of Bournehills to maintain a sense of dignity and self-worth, this kind of fixation on the past ultimately impedes the ability of the people to move forward into the future. By continually rehearsing the past, the residents of Bournehills avoid ever really dealing with it, and the critical treatment of this fixation resonates with themes that Marshall herself has identified as central to her fiction: "the importance of truly confronting the past, both in personal and historical terms, and the necessity of reversing the present order" (Marshall 1973).

The status of Bournehills as a land trapped in the past is figured in the book in a number of ways, one of the most vivid of which is conveyed through the contents of Merle's private room, a sort of sanctuary where she sometimes withdraws from the world. Saul, who has developed an intimate relationship with Merle that involves sex but is primarily a matter of friendship and solidarity, enters the room to check on her when he becomes concerned about her health. There, he sees a museum-like collection of objects from the past that perfectly symbolizes Bournehills as a whole. In addition to various pieces of furniture and other memorabilia from the colonial era, there are a number of drawings and prints depicting scenes from that period, including representations of the sumptuous lifestyle enjoyed by Merle's planter ancestors and scenes of the suffering experienced by the African slaves who were also her ancestors.

Saul, observing this scene, realizes how expressive it is of Merle's personality. But he also understands that it expresses the personality of Bournehills as a whole:

> Like the room it, too, was perhaps a kind of museum, a place in which had been stored the relics and remains of the era recorded in the faded prints on the walls, where one not only felt that other time existing intact, still alive, a palpable presence beneath the everyday reality, but saw it as well at every turn, often without realizing it. (402)

In addition, Saul understands that the history that pervades Bournehills is not simply a local phenomenon but part of a larger event. Bournehills, he muses, "might have been selected as the repository of the history which reached beyond it to include the hemisphere north and south" (402).

Having come to this realization, Saul finally begins to understand why so many development projects have failed in Bournehills. The weight of the past is simply too heavy, and any attempts by advanced capitalist countries like the United States to modernize the region are interpreted by the locals merely as an extension of the long and baleful history of exploitation of the people of Bournehills by such countries. It is no accident, for example, that Saul's research is funded primarily by the United Corporation of America, a huge conglomerate that made much of its initial wealth through exploitation of the West Indies and that clearly hopes to develop the region in the interest of making additional profits there. As a result, Saul suddenly realizes that programs such as the one in which he is engaged are doomed because they do not address the fundamental historical problem of Bournehills. Indeed, he concludes that only a violent catharsis, something "on the scale of Cuffee's" can move the region beyond this crippling past and into a better future (402).

In this sense, Saul's insight (and Marshall's) closely resembles the controversial insistence of Fanon that such cleansing violence is probably necessary throughout the formerly colonial world to prevent the continuation, in new forms, of the colonial past.[8] In opposition to Gandhi and other proponents of nonviolent resistance to colonialism, Fanon, in his long essay "Concerning Violence," argues that the long history of violence wrought upon colonial peoples by their European masters (of which slavery can be taken as an extreme example) can be overcome only by violent revolt on the part of the former victims of colonialism. "Colonialism," Fanon writes, "is violence in its natural state, and it will only yield when confronted with greater violence" (Fanon 1968, 61). Without a violent catharsis, Fanon concludes, the end of colonialism does not automatically bring an end to exploitation, and "for 95 per cent of the population of underdeveloped countries, independence brings no immediate change" (75).

Such a catharsis does not appear to be in the offing for Bournehills, where the most cathartic activity would appear to be the local carnival, an annual blowing-off of steam that ritualizes some of the violent impulses described by Fanon, while keeping them safely contained in relatively harmless forms.[9] This underlying violence might explain part of the sheer terror experienced by Harriet when she is swept up by a crowd of carnival revelers in one scene, though it is also clearly the case that her terror here results partly from the realization that these revelers are oblivious to her white skin and her illustrious family background, those markers of privilege and power that have served her so well throughout her life (293–97).[10] Indeed, the carnival slogan, "All o' we is one," bespeaks precisely the kind of solidarity and collective effort that is needed to pull Bournehills out of its lethargy and that has been so long lacking in the region.

However ritualized and contained, the carnival does nevertheless contain some potentially powerful energies, as Harriet perhaps senses in this scene. Similarly, despite the historical paralysis that seems to have descended on Bournehills, Marshall does suggest that there is some hope for the future. She cannot draw upon the experience of historical victory that provided the impetus for the great bourgeois novels of the early nineteenth century, because the poor people of Bournehills have experienced no such victory, except in the fleeting instance of the Pyre Hill Revolt. But she does invest her book with important utopian dimensions that prevent it from being a mere lament for the hopelessness of the underdeveloped world of a kind associated with writers such as V. S. Naipaul.

The carnival itself, with its free mixing of classes and races, is an important utopian image. However, probably the most important utopian scene in the book occurs after the local sugar mill, still run by the old British firm of Kingsley and Sons, breaks down, leaving the people of Bournehills with no way to process the sugarcane they have labored so long and hard to produce. In a sense, this dilemma merely calls attention to the historical stasis of the region, still engaged, almost out of habit, in the production of a once-lucrative crop that is no longer very profitable. But at least, the text give us to understand, they have a sense that they are doing *something*. When the mill breaks down, they are at first thwarted, denied even the symbolic achievement of producing an annual sugar crop. However, spurred on by Allen and Saul, some of the local leaders manage to rouse the people into an impressive collective effort, banding together to organize a few rickety vehicles to transport their cane across the island to another mill at Brighton. This effort, we learn, is the first major successful cooperative effort among the people of Bournehills since the days of Cuffee Ned, whose spirit once again seems to animate the region (405).

The lessons learned in this collective effort will very possibly be of great value to the people of Bournehills in the future. Saul has learned a great deal from the effort as well, realizing that the development of Bournehills must be undertaken primarily by the people who live there, not by outsiders such as himself, whose efforts merely perpetuate the underdevelopment and dependency of the Third World.[11] Thus, in the wake of the drowning of Harriet, he decides to return to the United States and resume his former teaching career, concentrating this time on training students from the Third World to return to their homes with the technical skills needed to help their neighbors improve their lives and move out from beneath the domination of foreign companies and organizations.

In this sense, Saul's future students will follow in the footsteps of Merle's African husband, Ketu Kinbona, who passed up an opportunity to pursue more glamorous subjects in England in order in order to study agriculture, expertise which he perceived to be critical to the progress of Africa, where he always intended to return. Meanwhile, Merle decides more literally to follow in Kinbona's footsteps and travel to Makarere, Uganda, where he teaches at the university. There, she hopes to renew her relationship with her daughter and bring her relationship with her husband to a more graceful and civil end, thus putting to rest that difficult episode from her past. At the same time, she hopes to renew her sense of connection with African history and culture, presented in the book as important sources of inspiration for the people of Bournehills. Thus, like Bournehills itself, Merle prepares finally to move forward, which is made clear in that she must sell the contents of her "museum" (along with the ancient Bentley once owned by a

British colonial governor of the island) in order to finance her trip to Africa. Free of this collection of the detritus of the past, she will be able to move forward. Indeed, as the book ends, she is already making plans for her life after she returns from Africa, including a possible run for political office to try to shake the complacent bourgeois politicians of the island out of their malaise.

This hopeful ending, combined with the thoughtful treatment of so many serious and important issues, helps to make *The Chosen Place, the Timeless People* a positive and important contribution to both Caribbean and African American fiction, reinforcing Christian's declaration that Marshall's works have been crucial to "the tradition and literature of African American women and the third world," despite the fact that they have received relatively little critical recognition (Christian 1991, 289). The book is honest about the problems of the Third World and about the terrible suffering the people there have experienced and continue to experience. But, as Denniston notes, Marshall finally "provides in this novel a vision of hope as she transforms suffering into creative, responsive, and responsible action" (Denniston 1995, 125).

Historical Background

See chapter 2 for Barbados and chapter 18 for Grenada, where much of *The Chosen Place, the Timeless People* was written. However, Marshall's novel clearly seeks to engage the history of the Caribbean as a whole, for which one should consult such works as Eric Williams 1984 or Rogozinski 1994.

Notes

1. The depiction of this exploitative lesbian relationship, together with the suggestion that Allen is tormented by his homosexuality, has led some to see *The Chosen Place, the Timeless People* as homophobic. However, the relationship between the British woman and Merle is really a matter of class, not gender. Spillers thus notes that the grounds for the exploitative relationship are well established, and in ways that have nothing to do with homophobia (Spillers 1985, 173n). Note also that the heterosexual Harriet, when she discovers the affair between Merle and Saul, becomes just as manipulative as the British woman in her efforts to eliminate this "unthinkable sexual rival" (Denniston 1995, 199).

2. See Fanon 1968. See also chapter 3 for a discussion of Fanon's notion that the postcolonial bourgeoisie merely carry on the legacy of colonialism by mimicking their European predecessors and thus perpetuating existing systems of exploitation after nominal independence. There are numerous scenes and

motifs in Marshall's novel which suggest this phenomenon, leading Saul to conclude that "the middle class is the same the world over" (74).

3. For a discussion of the relevance of Lukács's theories of realism to the novels of Gordimer, see Booker 1998a, 136–37.

4. For Jameson's theory of "national allegory" in Third-World literature, see Jameson 1986. See also the discussion of this theory in chapter 3 of this volume.

5. For a particularly eloquent description of the role played by Caribbean colonies in the French Revolution and in the rise of the bourgeoisie as a whole, see C.L.R. James's *The Black Jacobins* (1989).

6. Note also the mention in Michelle Cliff's *Abeng* (1984) that, in Jamaican history, Cuffee was the name of a commander of a Maroon army (a regiment of escaped slaves), who battled against the British. Thus, in contemporary Jamaican dialect, the word "cuffy" signifies an upstart.

7. Cuffee Ned was eventually captured and executed, though rumors persist in Bournehills that his spirit rose again and still inhabits the island.

8. See Earl Lovelace's novel, *Salt* (1996), discussed in chapter 19, for a similar suggestion that the past must be dealt with before the postcolonial states of the Caribbean can move forward into a productive future. Lovelace, however, does not insist that this process must involve violence.

9. For more on the importance of carnival as a motif in Marshall's novel, see Gikandi (1992, 187–91).

10. John Cooke suggests that this scene represents "a ritualistic transformation of power: the unmasking of the West" as the islanders celebrate "their Pan-African heritage" (Cooke 1980, 14).

11. For a similar skeptical vision of the impact of "foreign aid" programs on the Third World, see the Sengalese film, *Guelwaar* (1993), directed by Ousmane Sembène.

Chapter 4

Merle Hodge:
Crick Crack, Monkey

Crick Crack, Monkey (1970) narrates the growth and maturation of its pro-
tagonist/narrator, Tee (Cynthia Davis), from early childhood into adolescence. As such, the book is clearly related to the genre of the bildungsroman,
one of the central genres of Caribbean fiction. However, *Crick Crack, Monkey* enjoys a special place in the genre. For one thing, the book was the
first major bildungsroman by a postcolonial woman writer in the Caribbean and thus reflects a realm of experience not previously represented in
Caribbean literature. As Simon Gikandi notes, the book was "the first major
novel by a Caribbean woman—in the period after independence—in which
the writer assumed the consciousness of her subject and gave it expression"
(Gikandi 1992, 203). The autobiographical orientation of the book allows
it to explore the private experience of its protagonist in vivid detail. At the
same time, this private experience occurs within a public context, the description of which allows Hodge to explore a number of crucial issues involving the figuration of race, class, and gender in colonial and postcolonial
Trinidad.

As is typical of the bildungsroman, *Crick Crack, Monkey* pays a great deal
of attention to the education of its protagonist, in this case her literal education in the colonial schools of Trinidad. But Hodge's description of Tee's
experience in the colonial educational system of postwar Trinidad goes well
beyond a mere depiction of Tee's gradual accumulation of knowledge and
maturity. For one thing, the book details the island's dual educational system: One set of "EC" schools, run by the government, is directly aligned
with the Anglican Church; another set of "RC" schools is run by the Catholic
Church. For reasons they do not themselves entirely understand, the stu-

dents in each of the school systems regard the students in the other system as their enemies, and each group of students conducts an ongoing war against the other. Hodge's depiction of the educational system thus demonstrates the strong influence of the legacy of colonial missionary work, both by showing the religious orientation of much education and by indicating the extent to which Trinidad's colonial heritage tends to fragment the society of the island, dividing the inhabitants among themselves on the basis of religious rivalries inherited from Europe that have little to do with Trinidad itself.

In addition, Hodge's narrative demonstrates the extent to which this system continued to be dominated by British points of view. Indeed, the EC schools Tee attends prior to high school seem to be much more concerned to impress their students with the greatness of the British Empire than to endow them with any useable skills. This British-oriented education is largely irrelevant to Trinidadian life, a point brought home in one episode, in which a teacher punishes the entire class because most of them are unable to spell "sleet" or even to say what "sleet" is (67). Such practices suggest to the students that their own experience is somehow secondary and inferior, unworthy of formal acknowledgement in schoolbooks. Indeed, the formal glorification of Britain in her schooling instills the young Tee with such a sense of insecurity and inferiority that she at one point invents an imaginary personage, Helen, who is her white alter ego. Unlike Tee, Helen resembles, in her appearance, behavior, and experience, the proper British girls they read about in their schoolbooks. Tee, in fact, comes for a time to regard Helen as the "Proper Me," while Tee herself is Helen's "shadow hovering about in incompleteness" (62).

Tee's experience here clearly resembles that of Hodge, who has remarked elsewhere in a radio interview that she and her black schoolmates in colonial Trinidad

> never saw ourselves in a book, so we didn't exist in a kind of way and our culture and our environment, our climate, the plants around us did not seem real, did not seem to be of any importance—we overlooked them entirely. The real world was what was in books. (qtd. in Gerschel 1988, 78)

To an extent, of course, Hodge is describing here the predicament of all colonial subjects, who are consistently marginalized and made to feel less authentic than their colonial masters, who control the machinery of cultural representation (schools, publishing, films, etc.) through which authenticity is defined. In writing *Crick Crack, Monkey*, Hodge clearly sought to counter the colonialist bias of the British fiction she and her fellow students had read in school. As she herself puts it, Trinidad and other colonized territories were "occupied by foreign fiction. Fiction which affirms and validates our world is therefore an important weapon of resistance" (Hodge 1990, 206).

This vision of literature as a weapon in the contest for cultural identities is typical of postcolonial writers. However, Hodge's (and Tee's) sense of marginality and inauthenticity is related to her gender, as well. Ketu Katrak, in a comparative study of *Crick Crack, Monkey* and Bessie Head's *Maru*, notes the critique of the British colonial educational system in the work of male writers such as Kenya's Ngugi wa Thiong'o. She argues, however, that such critiques tend to ignore the crucial component of gender, a factor that makes the experience of female students in colonial schools even more problematic than that of male students. Katrak argues that women postcolonial writers, such as Hodge and Head, demonstrate that "a gendered educational system placed women in complex, sometimes worse positions than in precolonial times in relationship to their own communities" (Katrak 1995, 62).

By the 1950s, when Hodge herself was attending colonial schools in Trinidad, an emergent anticolonial nationalist movement was beginning to develop a distinctive Trinidadian cultural identity. Trinidadian writers such as C.L.R. James, George Lamming, Sam Selvon, Ralph de Boissière, and V. S. Naipaul were developing growing literary reputations, and their works were largely peopled by nonwhite, Trinidadian characters. But these writers were all male, and the most important of their characters were almost invariably male, as well. In addition, as Gikandi emphasizes, the nationalist movement itself had a strongly masculine orientation. In 1970, when *Crick Crack, Monkey* was first published, this orientation still reigned supreme in both Caribbean literature and Caribbean postcolonial political discourse. Her strongly feminine perspective thus represents an important new voice in Caribbean fiction, a voice that would soon be joined by such women writers as Erna Brodber, Zee Edgell, Michelle Cliff, and Beryl Gilroy. For Gikandi, the work of such women "not only recenters them in history as custodians of an oral tradition, but also functions as an indicator of sources of domination that might have been lost or repressed in both the colonial text and male-dominated nationalist discourse" (Gikandi 1992, 201).

The very fact that *Crick Crack, Monkey* was written by a woman and that it focuses on feminine experience lends the book a special force. Tee's attempt to develop and maintain a sense of her own identity amid the attempts of those around her to thrust identities upon her takes on a special character because of her gender. Granted, Tee's life is dominated by strong female figures, by the struggle between her two aunts—the working-class Tantie and the middle-class Beatrice—to define her in their own images. But these women play such crucial roles partly because Tee's own mother, presumably her central female role model, dies in childbirth as the book begins. The very fact that Tee begins her narration at the moment of her mother's death suggests the extent to which this death represented a crucial turning point in Tee's life. In addition, Tantie and Beatrice are able to dominate Tee's sense of her own identity because most of the positive role models that Tee might have in the society as a whole are male, giving her little access to alternative identities beyond those proposed for her by her aunts. Indeed, as a child, the only alternative she can imagine is the "proper" (white, British) self represented by Helen.

It is clear that Tee, in the later adult position from which she narrates the book, has nevertheless managed to transcend the identities offered by her aunts, allowing her to look back upon her childhood experience with a certain critical distance. As Gikandi points out, Tee is the fictive "author" of the text, the very writing of which represents a creative and independent attempt to explore and express her own subjectivity, which had previously existed only as "the projection of other people's desires and intentions" (Gikandi 1992, 210). But this project is a complex and contradictory one as the adult Tee, consciously aware of the meaning of her childhood experience, attempts to relate this experience from the point of view of a childhood self that lacked such awareness.

Tee's alienation from the official value system of her colonial society is crucially complicated by her gender, and this alienation is embedded in the very texture of the book's language. Nevertheless, the book's overt thematic emphasis is less on gender than on class, a category that is, in colonial Trinidad, inextricably intertwined with race, as well. For example, the educational system is fragmented not only on the basis of religion but also on the basis of class. The system is strongly hierarchical, with different schools corresponding to the status of different layers of Trinidad society. When Tee, after much anticipation, first starts school, she finds that the regular government school has no openings. She is thus forced to attend a small, independent, Anglican-oriented school run by Mr. and Mrs. Hinds. Even the young Tee seems aware that Mr. and Mrs. Hinds are incompetent teachers and that there may be something wrong with the indifferent instruction offered in this school. Mrs. Hinds spends most of her time sewing and ignoring her students, while Mr. Hinds, a devoted Anglophile, spends most of his time trying to convince his students of the superiority of all things English, arguing that the only way they can become anything other than uncultured "piccaninnies" is by learning to emulate their English betters.

Hinds's glorification of England is so total that Tee begins to confuse his description of the Mother Country with descriptions of heaven she has received in her religious training: "And now at school I had come to learn that Glory and The Mother Country and Up-There and Over-There had all one and the same geographical location. It made perfect sense that the place where my mother had gone, Glory, should also be known as The Mother Country" (30). This identification is reinforced in her Sunday-school education, which centers on the study of Bible verses, accompanied by illustrations featuring "children with yellow hair" communing with a pale Jesus (30). Meanwhile, the language of these Bible verses consistently equates blackness with sinfulness and whiteness with salvation, further contributing to Tee's sense of inferiority.

As Tee grows older, she finds that she is often regarded as inferior not merely to her island's British rulers, but also to middle-class Trinidadians. As she moves up in the school system, she finds that she and the other former students of the Hines school are consistently looked down upon. Indeed, when she eventually wins a scholarship to the prestigious St. Ann's High School, Tee finds that she is essentially ostracized there because she has not come to this point through the proper educational channels. No one at St. Ann's seems impressed that Tee has won a scholarship despite her inferior training. Though she now lives with Aunt Beatrice and her bourgeois family and has even been christened a Catholic, Tee finds that her background still accompanies her and affects the way she is treated by her teachers and schoolmates.

The motif of class is principally treated in *Crick Crack, Monkey* in the opposition between Tee's working-class, paternal aunt, Tantie, and her bourgeois, maternal aunt, Beatrice. After the death of their mother, Tee and her brother, Toddan (Codrington), are sent by their father to live with his sister, Tantie. The father then goes to England to seek work. The children are happy with their aunt, who is poor, but who has a strong vitality. She is a passionate woman who sometimes rages against the children, but who clearly loves them and treats them as if they were her own. She is also able to meet their basic needs, though there is little room for luxuries. To an extent, in fact, she teaches them to scorn the luxury and pretentiousness that might be associated with the bourgeois lifestyle of Beatrice, whom Tantie refers to as "The Bitch" because of her arrogance and her ongoing effort to win custody of the children and thus save them from what Beatrice sees as the degradation of life in Tantie's "niggery" household.

But, as Narinesingh notes, life in this household in fact has a "rich, solid texture" marked by a strong "generosity of heart" that contrasts sharply with the "veneer of gentility and respectability" that characterizes Beatrice's household (Narinesingh 1981, viii, xiv). Tantie eschews bourgeois propriety, employing a lively and colorful speech that is laced with colloquialisms and profanity. She is unpretentious in her dress and personal habits, and has little concern that either she or the children live up to standards of conduct inherited from the island's British rulers. She also accepts her working-class neighbors as equals, and has no objection when the neighbors befriend local East Indian children. Beatrice, on the other hand, is desperate to establish herself as a proper bourgeois in the British mold and to rid herself of all vestiges of her African past. She is horrified to see her niece and nephew playing with "coolie children" while living with Tantie (11). More importantly, she is distressed by Tee's dark skin, inherited from her father, a man of whom Beatrice never approved because of his lowly origins. Beatrice virtually worships Elizabeth Carter, her white British ancestor, and regards Tee's father as inferior because he has no such heritage. This attitude, of course, makes Tee ashamed of her own family background:

> I began to have the impression that I should be thoroughly ashamed; for it seemed to me that my person must represent the rock-bottom of the family's fall from grace. Sometimes when I was alone in the living-room Elizabeth Carter's indistinguishable portrait grew features, a pair of eyes that frowned angrily and a mouth that was pursed together with disapproval. (18)

Beatrice, of course, does nothing but exacerbate this sense of class and racial shame. Excoriating Tee for speaking like a market woman instead of using proper English, she warns the girl that she must work all the harder to present an acceptable appearance despite her dark skin (83). Tee, whose grandmother, Ma, is in fact a market woman, is overcome by shame and hopes desperately that Beatrice and Beatrice's daughters will not discover this horrible fact (84). Gradually, Tee herself comes to regard her former habits as "ordinary" and "niggery," and hopes somehow to be able to overcome her early upbringing.

In an influential reading of *Crick Crack, Monkey*, Marjorie Thorpe suggests that the world of Tantie (and of Ma, Tantie's mother) is one of "belonging and security," where the children are free to be their true selves, while Beatrice's world, based on mimicry of the British, is one of "alienation and displacement" (Thorpe 1977, 37). There is much in the book to support this binary reading, and it is certainly true that Tantie's world, with strong roots in African culture, is treated as more authentic than the British-inspired bourgeois world of Beatrice. On the other hand, Tantie's world is still a colonized world, and Tee develops her initial sense of insecurity and inferiority while living with Tantie. Thus, as Gikandi argues, the structure of the book is considerably more complex than a simple polar opposition between Tantie's Trinidadian, working-class authenticity and Beatrice's bourgeois mimicry of the British. In particular, Tee experiences limited choices in either world, modeling her behavior and language after Tantie while living with Tantie, then beginning to adopt Beatrice's attitudes and speech patterns when she goes to live with her. Thus, for Gikandi, the true value of the novel lies not in privileging the Creole culture of Tantie over the colonized culture of Beatrice, but in its ability to "sustain both the creole and colonial cultures as opposed sites of cultural production which the 'modern' Caribbean subject cannot reconcile or transcend entirely" (Gikandi 1992, 213).

From this point of view, it is important to recognize that Tee never feels entirely at home in the world of Tantie and that, after exposure to Beatrice's world, she becomes fundamentally estranged from the world of her childhood. Beatrice's attitude, of course, is not merely hers. It is the official stance of Trinidad's colonial society, reinforced by church, school, books, newspapers, and virtually all of the other official sources of information with which Tee comes into contact. It is little wonder, then, that Tee, after she goes to live with Beatrice when she starts high school, begins to accept this attitude as her own, despite her happy memories of her time with Tantie and despite her own sense of guilt at coming to regard Tantie and her circle as inferior. Thus, her shame at being associated with Tantie's black, lower-class world is compounded by the additional shame of coming to realize that she is beginning to look down on her beloved aunt. This situation is perfectly encapsulated in a scene in which Tantie and several others come to Beatrice's home to pay Tee a visit. Beatrice and her daughters make themselves scarce, not wishing to have any commerce with such lowly people. But Tee finds herself uncomfortable in this circle as well and is greatly relieved when they finally depart, while at the same time being ashamed of her relief (106–07).

Tee's transformation indicates the power of the ideological forces that surround her in colonial Trinidadian society, urging her to think of all things white, British, and bourgeois as good and proper, and all things black, African, and working-class as shameful and degraded. Importantly, she is not merely influenced by these ideological forces; she, as a subject, is literally created by them. Particularly useful as a description of this process is Louis Althusser's notion of "interpellation," or the "hailing of the subject"—the process through which individuals are formed as subjects by powerful forces working in the interest of the prevailing ideology of a given society. For Althusser, individual subjects are not preexisting entities that can subsequently be influenced by the attitudes and opinions they encounter in society. On the contrary, individual subjects come into being within a pre-existing ideological framework. As a result, individual subjects do not create ideas so much as ideas create individual subjects. Thus, "the category of the subject is only constitutive of all ideology insofar as all ideology has the function (which defines it) of 'constituting' concrete individuals as subjects" (Althusser 1971, 171).

In Tee's colonial situation, however, the process of interpellation is significantly more complex than it might be in the metropolitan center of Britain, from which the most powerful interpellating forces in Tee's society emanate. This process, to be fully effective, requires that the individual subject accept the prevailing ideology as his or her own. The ideological forces described by Althusser define and construct subjects by broadcasting, in subtle and even invisible ways, signals that tell individual subjects what they are supposed to be like. The message, "This is our society's official attitude," alternates with and is ultimately indistinguishable from the message, "This is you." But in Trinidad and other colonial societies, the official ideology defines Britishness; it encourages Trinidadians to desire to be like the British, but it also warns them that they are fundamentally inferior to the British and can never fully attain Britishness no matter how hard they try. The message, "This is our society's official attitude," alternates with the message, "This is us, but this can never be you."

Complex cultural interchanges (and Anglicization of certain members of the indigenous bourgeois elite) notwithstanding, the radical racial and cultural duality of the colonial situation is such that there can be no chance that the bulk of the Trinidadian population would ever mistake the position and attitudes of the British bourgeoisie for their own. To put it in Althusserian terms, interpellation occurs when the individual subject is created in the image of official ideology, not when that ideology proclaims the subject an alien (and inferior) "other." Thus, even the most Anglicized members of Trinidadian society cannot be truly British, and they know it, which only serves to increase their contempt for the less Anglicized elements of the population, which they associate with their own colonial inferiority. The racial contempt of Mr. Hines for the "piccaninnies" in his classroom can be related to his sense of shame at his own blackness, which prevents him from being British. And Beatrice's contempt for Tantie and the Creole society she represents can be traced

to the fact that Tantie reminds Beatrice of her own fundamental difference from the British bourgeoisie she so slavishly imitates.

That Beatrice's pomposity is actually an expression of insecurity can be
seen from her reaction, late in the book, to the news that Tee's father is
sending for Tee and Toddan to come join him in England. Beatrice, suddenly reminded that this man, for whom she has expressed such contempt,
is now a resident of the "Mother Country," reverses her attitude and is
proud to be associated with such a man and his family. And Beatrice is not
alone. Her imperious daughters begin to look on Tee with "mute awe" and
brag to their friends that she is their cousin (109). And Mrs. Wattman, the
teacher at St. Ann's who has snubbed Tee throughout her time in the school,
suddenly takes an interest in the girl, questioning her about her upcoming
trip and gazing on her with a "besotted expression" of envy (110). As Frantz
Fanon would emphasize, individuals such as Beatrice and Mrs. Wattman
are not full-fledged bourgeoisie, but mere imitators of their European bourgeois masters, perpetually doomed to second-rate status within the bourgeois class (Fanon 1968).

For her own part, Tee looks forward to the trip to England as a way out
of the dilemma in which she finds herself in Trinidad, trapped in the animosity between her two aunts and ashamed of her own embarrassment at
her association with the Creole, working-class side of her family. Before she
departs, she pays one last visit to Tantie and realizes that she now feels
hopelessly alienated from Tantie's world: "everything was changing, unrec-
ognizable, pushing me out. This was as it should be, since I had moved up
and no longer had any place here" (110–11). Tee knows full well that she
can never return to the home of her youth, partly because her movement
from the world of Tantie to the world of Beatrice represents not merely a
change of class, but a temporal shift that recapitulates the historical movement of the colonial world from tradition to modernity, with the consequent increase in material opportunity and decrease in psychic wholeness.

Removal to England represents an additional step forward into modernity and therefore will do nothing to alleviate Tee's sense of alienation, whatever other opportunities it might offer. One can anticipate that, in England, Tee will experience racial and cultural prejudices that will merely
exacerbate her complex sense of shame. In any case, England is not really
neutral territory to which she can escape and thus learn to come to terms
with the opposition between her aunts. On the contrary, England itself is
the real source of that opposition and of the modernizing forces that have
destabilized both Tee and her colonial society.

Hodge's choice of the bildungsroman form as a venue for the exploration
of these issues is an ideal one, despite the fact that this genre is in many

ways quintessentially European. Franco Moretti, in *The Way of the World*, argues that the bildungsroman became an important genre in European literature of the late eighteenth and nineteenth centuries because the youthful perspective of young protagonists encountering a new world provided a perfect analogue to the historical experience of the newly dominant bourgeoisie and to their modern world view, with its emphasis on change and innovation. Using Goethe's *Wilhelm Meister's Apprenticeship* as a paradigm, Moretti notes that the "classical" bildungsroman, arising at the end of the eighteenth century, told the story of a protagonist who became a mature adult subject through the process of integration into the society around him. For Moretti, however, this classical form of the bildungsroman was extremely short-lived. The genre's central need for closure, when the *bildung* (development) is completed and the individual becomes a successful and mature adult subject, is fundamentally incompatible with capitalism, in which this final and definitive stabilization of the individual is impossible. "Maturity," Moretti argues, is strictly possible only in a precapitalist world and is "hardly compatible with modernity'" (Moretti 1987, 27).

Put differently, Moretti argues that the fragmentation of human life under capitalism makes it impossible to sustain the smooth integration of private and public spheres that is central to the classical bildungsroman. Indeed, as the nineteenth century progressed, individual desire and social demand came to be widely regarded in the West as fundamentally opposed. In the highly unstable, postrevolutionary society of nineteenth-century France, when the bourgeoisie were still struggling with the aristocracy and the Catholic Church for political and ideological dominance, this opposition led to the development of bildungsromans, by writers such as Balzac and Stendhal, in which the protagonist ends the text fundamentally estranged from society, typically declaring contempt for all the society represents. But, in the stable, well-established bourgeois-dominated society of nineteenth-century England, the opposition between private and public spheres led to the opposite situation in which individuals do enter society, but only at the expense of the surrender of their individual identities.

In the French bildungsroman, integration into society fails; in the English bildungsroman, such integration is experienced as a loss of personal identity. On the other hand, as Moretti notes, comfortable integration into society is not a problem in traditional precapitalist societies. It should thus come as no surprise that, in traditional oral cultures such as those that existed in Africa before the advent of capitalism, the "initiation story" was a central cultural form (Julien 1992, 95). However, it is clear that, in the colonial world, in which traditional society is disrupted and ideological domination is imposed from without, the comfortable integration of public and private realms Moretti associates with the classical bildungsroman (or that one might associate with the African initiation story) cannot occur. In *Crick Crack, Monkey*, Tee lives in a colonial society dominated by British models that are designed to convince her of her own inferiority and that define her as an outsider, excluded from full integration into society, even through the sacrifice of her individuality. And the main opposition to these British models comes from an anticolonial nationalist discourse that is dominated by masculine images, again marginalizing Tee. As a result, while Tee clearly cannot surrender her individuality in exchange for social acceptance, as in the nineteenth-century English bildungsroman, she also lacks a position from which to establish her identity in opposition to her official society, as in the nineteenth-century French bildungsroman.

Such considerations of the difficulties faced by the colonial subject help to explain why the bildungsroman, which fundamentally deals with the development of individual subjectivity, would be such a prominent genre among postcolonial writers, especially women. They also explain why postcolonial bildungsromans tend to end in problematic and open-ended ways, with no closure achieved. As Tee heads for England, her problems are anything but solved—because there simply is no solution available. The ending of *Crick Crack, Monkey*, in which the protagonist neither enters society nor decides to battle against it, but simply leaves, is quite typical of the postcolonial bildungsroman, as can be seen by examples such as James Joyce's *A Portrait of the Artist as a Young Man*, in which young Stephen Dedalus leaves colonial Ireland to try to become a poet in France, or George Lamming's *In the Castle of My Skin*, in which G. leaves Barbados for a teaching job in Trinidad.

Crick Crack, Monkey is even more typical of the female postcolonial bildungsroman. Both Stephen Dedalus and G. go away in search of career opportunities, but Tee's situation at the end of Hodge's novel is even more unsettled than that, partly because she is so young, still in high school. Indeed, female postcolonial bildungsromans tend to end with their protagonists still in adolescence, thus expressing the lack of closure and resolution associated with the attempt to develop a stable, feminine identity in a masculine, colonial world. Tee's experience, for example, is strikingly similar to that of Tambudzai, the protagonist of *Nervous Conditions* (1989), a postcolonial bildungsroman by the Zimbabwean writer Tsitsi Dangarembga. Other bildungsromans by Caribbean women writers, such as Zee Edgell's *Beka Lamb* (1982), Michelle Cliff's *Abeng* (1984), and Jamaica Kincaid's *Annie John* (1985) show a similar lack of resolution, leaving their protagonists before adulthood.

That such later writers would produce works that resemble *Crick Crack, Monkey* might partly indicate Hodge's influence as the founder of the Caribbean female postcolonial bildungsroman. But, more importantly, it indicates the extent to which Tee's experience is not eccentric but typical of girls and young women in a colonial Caribbean world moving toward independence. Thus, Hodge, Edgell, Cliff, and Kincaid are all involved in a similar project of exploring viable identities for women in the postcolonial Caribbean, just as postcolonial writers in general are involved in an attempt to develop new cultural identities that escape the domination of the colonial past.

Historical Background

The neighboring islands of Trinidad and Tobago together constitute a single republic, with the former island representing well over 90 percent of the total area of 1,980 sq. mi. (5,129 sq. km) and the total population of just over 1.2 million. The capital and largest city of the republic is Port of Spain, in northern Trinidad, a cosmopolitan city with a population of about 50,000. Approximately 45 percent of the population of the republic is of African descent, about 40 percent is of East Indian descent, and the remainder is of a mixture of European, Middle Eastern, and Chinese descent. English is the official language, but a form of French patois is widely spoken. Trinidad possesses sizable petroleum reserves, and petroleum products represent the republic's most important exports. The islands also produce sugar, cocoa, and bananas, as well as enjoy a large tourist industry, spurred by the subtropical climate and widespread fame of Trinidadian cultural institutions such as calypso music and the carnival. As a whole, the republic enjoys one of the highest standards of living in the Caribbean. Eight years of education are compulsory, and the literacy rate is about 96 percent.

Trinidad was discovered on July 31, 1498 by Christopher Columbus, who gave the island its current name. However, archeological records indicate that it had been inhabited for thousands of years by that time. When Columbus arrived, he found the island inhabited by Amerindians, principally the peaceful Arawaks in the south and the more warlike Caribs in the north. Though the Caribs, in particular, fought fiercely against European colonization, the Spanish eventually established their domination of the island, and the native Amerindian population was virtually exterminated by a combination of war, enslavement, and disease.

Spanish control of the island remained somewhat problematic, however, as evidenced by the so-called Arena Massacre of 1699, when the remaining

Amerindians revolted against attempts to force them to convert to Christianity, killing a number of priests, as well as the Spanish governor and most of his men. Retribution against the rebels was swift and brutal. Nevertheless, true colonization of the island was delayed until the 1780s, when the King of Spain issued the Cedula of Population, which offered free grants of land to any Catholics friendly to Spain who would settle on the island.

Most of the settlers who came in response to the Cedula were French, and most brought African slaves with them. A creolized French became the dominant language on the island and still affects local dialects to this day. In 1797, the British attacked Trinidad and the Spanish governor, Chacon, surrendered the colony without a fight. The island became a British colony and was soon fortified by the construction of a number of defensive forts. The capital, Port of Spain, was burned to the ground in the Great Fire of 1808, but the new British governor, Sir Ralph Woodford, soon rebuilt the city and began to develop the rest of the island.

After the end of slavery in the 1830s, the island's white rulers brought in large numbers of indentured laborers from China and, especially, India, to work their plantations, adding significantly to Trinidad's ethnic mix. In 1889, Trinidad and Tobago were joined as an administrative unit, largely because the sugar-based economy of Tobago had collapsed in 1884, making the smaller island unable to survive on its own. Unrest among the nonwhite population of Trinidad, aware of their second-rate status under the colonial system, grew through the nineteenth century, culminating in the Water Riots of 1903, when the Red House, the seat of the colonial government, was burned to the ground after the governor attempted to impose new taxes on water.

Oil was discovered in south Trinidad as early as 1857, and by the mid-1920s, oil had replaced sugar and cocoa as the island's main exports. By 1936, Trinidad was the leading oil exporter in the British Empire, though harsh working conditions in the oil fields led to strikes and riots among workers in 1937, an experience that helped the working people of Trinidad gain a sense of their own collective power, which soon developed into a strong nationalist anticolonial movement. This movement was suppressed during World War II, when the cultural, economic, and social fabric of the island was powerfully altered by the presence of large numbers of American troops on bases established on the island by the United States.

After the war, the independence movement regained its momentum. In 1956, Dr. Eric Williams led the formation of the People's National Movement (PNM), the political party that would subsequently lead the fight against colonial rule. Trinidad and Tobago was a central part of the West Indies Federation from 1958 to 1962, with Port of Spain serving as the capital of the federation. After the collapse of the federation on August 31, 1962, Trinidad and Tobago became an independent nation, with Williams as the first prime minister. Queen Elizabeth II, however, remained the titular head of state until 1976, when Trinidad and Tobago dissolved its formal ties with Britain and established a new republican form of government, though remaining a member of the British Commonwealth.

Williams remained in power until his death in 1981, though he and his policies grew increasingly unpopular with black militants on the island. The PNM remained in power until 1986, when the national Alliance for Reconstruction became the ruling party. The PNM regained power in the next election, however, and remained in power through the 1990s. For more on the history of Trinidad and Tobago, see Rennie 1973 and Eric Williams 1984.

Chapter 5

Sam Selvon:
Moses Ascending

In his first novel, *A Brighter Sun* (1952), Sam Selvon employs essentially standard English in his narration but has the characters speak in Trinidadian dialects, enacting a dialogue between these two styles that refuses to privilege the literary language of the narrator over the vernacular tongue of the characters. Selvon never uses dialect as "improper" or as a comic device to show the lack of sophistication of his characters. Indeed, language becomes comic only in scenes such as that in which Tiger, the protagonist, attempts to speak a literary form of English that is incongruous in his cultural context. In *The Lonely Londoners* (1956), meanwhile, Selvon takes an important step forward in his use of dialect, having the third-person narrator speak in essentially the same dialect as the protagonist, Moses Aloetta, a black Trinidadian in London. *The Lonely Londoners* is a comic and satirical work, but Moses's language is not a target of the book's satire. It is, in fact, a clearly appropriate venue for the presentation of Moses's particular view of London as a resident who nevertheless remains a racial and cultural outsider. Moses's dialect is a literary construct; rather than attempt simply to reproduce any particular Trinidadian dialect, Selvon chooses to construct a representation of a Trinidadian dialect that allows him to reflect, in a very effective way, Moses's thoughts and feelings.[1]

Moses Ascending (1975), the sequel to *The Lonely Londoners*, takes Selvon's use of different languages and dialects to a new level of complexity.[2] Mervyn Morris notes, in his introduction to *Moses Ascending*, that the book employs a "surprising combination of styles: archaic and modern; formal, often stilted, Standard English and casual Trinidad slang, academic phraseology and non-

Standard grammar; pseudo-literary affectations, clichés, foreign expressions, all tumbled together with splendid indecorum, and the detail often wrong." Further, Morris notes, this complex stylistic mix is supplemented by a diverse "range of reference" that includes "allusions to English classics, Greek mythology, Trinidad calypso, international pop songs, Roman history, British Empire history, Trinidad carnival, the titles of novels or films, and so on" (Morris 1984, xi).[3]

This complex and often incongruous mixture of styles and materials is used to considerable comic and satiric effect in Selvon's text, while at the same time suggesting important intercultural dialogues that are representative of the multicultural nature of London society in the 1960s. Much of the book's mixture of styles derives from Moses's ambition to be a writer, which causes him to attempt to mimic a variety of styles of literary English, while still reverting to his natural Trinidadian dialect in moments of stress. Indeed, it is easy, and to some extent justifiable, to interpret Moses and his literary pretensions as the satirical objects of the book's comic mixture of languages. Moses can certainly be ridiculous as he pompously constructs his cliché-ridden prose within a context in which he accepts any number of stereotypes about the literary life, attempting to model himself after "bona fide writers," who construct "pure" art that avoids any contaminating engagement with political reality and who refuse to compromise their art by descending into "cheap journalese" (103).

However, Moses's mangling of literary English, whether he is aware of it or not, can also be taken as a parody of the English literary tradition and of the pretensions of literary language as a whole. For example, he directly compares his relationship with Bob to that between Robinson Crusoe and his man, Friday, obviously relishing in the reversal of roles that leaves him, the Caribbean native, in the role of master, and Bob, the white Englishman, in the role of subaltern slave. Indeed, Moses's description of their relationship even directly echoes the style of Defoe's prose at points, as when he describes his efforts to educate his poor, benighted servant and break him of his savage ways (45).[4] By the end of the book, however, Bob is dominant in the household, while Moses has been relegated to living in a corner of the basement. Moses's attempts to play master to Bob's slave are thus revealed as ridiculous posturing. At the same time, Selvon's comic reinscription of *Robinson Crusoe* also potentially reminds us that there was already something ridiculous about Defoe's original descriptions of the Crusoe-Friday relationship and of his descriptions of non-Europeans (they are essentially all "savage cannibals") as a whole. In the same way, Selvon potentially calls our attention to the fact that many of the great classics of English literature, from Shakespeare's *The Tempest* to Joseph Conrad's *Heart of Darkness*, are overtly racist.[5]

Michel Fabre concludes that *Moses Ascending* represents "a unique attempt, along the lines of postmodern fiction, to unite the iconoclastic techniques of the West with the iconoclastic techniques of the calypso in order to liberate Trinidadian fiction by negating the monopoly of the 'great tradition'" (Fabre 1988, 220–21). In this same vein, Morris concludes of *Moses Ascending* that "the whole novel is largely a response to the assumption that the culture of Europeans is superior to the culture of others, whether Africans, Asians or Caribbean people" (1984, x). And Mark Looker notes that "behind the garbled and incongruous allusions to Western culture . . . lies Selvon's evisceration of culture as museum piece or as social *accoutrement*" (Looker 1996, 179).

There is, then, a very serious side to the comic confrontation of styles that constitutes the linguistic matrix of *Moses Ascending*. This novel thus adds new dimensions to Selvon's work, recalling the richly dialogic texture of works such as James Joyce's *Ulysses*, while anticipating postmodernist works such as Thomas Pynchon's *Gravity's Rainbow* and postcolonial works such as Salman Rushdie's *Midnight's Children*. Granted, *Ulysses*, *Gravity's Rainbow*, and *Midnight's Children* are all massive works, achieving their encyclopedic effects through the sheer accumulation, page after page, of diverse cultural materials. By comparison, *Moses Ascending* is a seemingly lightweight work in more ways than one, consisting of 140 pages of light farce. On the other hand, that Selvon can create such impressive comic and dialogic effects in such a short and seemingly slight book may make his achievement all the more remarkable.

Various critics have recently placed works such as *Ulysses*, *Gravity's Rainbow*, and *Midnight's Children* in the tradition of Menippean satire, strictly speaking, an ancient Greek genre, especially as delineated in the work of the Soviet literary theorist, Mikhail Bakhtin, who has, in this and other ways, elaborated a complex theory of the novel as a uniquely "dialogic" genre. Bakhtin notes that Menippean elements underlie an important strain in the development of the novel, which often derives its energies from complex, carnivalesque confrontations among different styles and materials. Bakhtin's theory of the novel, which places great emphasis on the productive effects of dialogues among different styles within the same text, is of obvious relevance to *Moses Ascending*. Indeed, though he does not mention Bakhtin directly, Looker probably has Bakhtin in mind when he notes that, in this novel, "Selvon creates a dialogic form which has the narrator in constant colloquy with his material, with the reader, and by extension with society at large" (Looker 1996, 168).

Bakhtin's theory of the novel is founded on language; he argues that one of the distinguishing features of the novel is its use of the various language styles used in society as objects of literary representation. For Bakhtin, the novel incorporates the various "languages" of society into its own discourse, setting them into dialogue with one another: "Diversity of voices and heteroglossia enter the novel and organize themselves within it into a structured artistic system. This constitutes the distinguishing feature of the novel as a genre" (Bakhtin 1981, 300). Importantly, the different styles or "languages" in a novel are derived directly from the world at large. Far from being mere literary affectations, they carry specific sociopolitical connotations, each language representing an entire world view. Bakhtin's key concept of "heteroglossia" refers not just to the different styles of language used by different groups in society, but to the various points of view that constitute the entire social, cultural, and ideological context of the novel. In the novel, the languages interact in a dynamic way, typically with the development of an opposition between "high" languages and "low." The dialogue in the novel thus dramatizes ideological struggles in the society as a whole, with the confrontations between "high" and "low" languages being particularly reminiscent of class struggle.

Part of Bakhtin's project is to suggest the utility of the novel as a mode of literary expression in the attempt to build a new socialist culture in the postrevolutionary Soviet Union, despite the widely acknowledged status of the novel as the quientessential literary mode of the bourgeois culture that the Soviets were seeking to supplant. Bakhtin's theories suggest the utility of the novel as a postcolonial genre, as well. He sees the novel is unique in its contemporaneity, which involves a close connection with extraliterary genres, as well as a direct connection to the extraliterary world of everyday life. This contact endows the novel with an almost infinite generic flexibility, allowing it to adapt to a variety of new situations. In addition, the novel is able to change and evolve by parodying and challenging the previously accepted conventions and standards of the genre. Thus, the novel, which had risen to prominence in Britain as the quintessential literary expression of the world view of the newly emergent bourgeoisie, can also be used in the service of postcolonial projects that seek to challenge the hegemony of the European bourgeois literary tradition.[6]

The opposition between "high" and "low" languages that for Bakhtin informs all human societies is particularly strong in a colonial society such as Trinidad, where the dominant English language, emanating from the metropolitan center, interacts with local dialectical variants. And *Moses Ascending*, with its complex mixture of languages and styles, from street slang, to Trinidadian dialect, to literary English, enacts such dialogues in a particularly obvious way. In the best tradition of the novel as envisioned by Bakhtin, Selvon's novel challenges the conventional hierarchy of these styles, suggesting that the "low" styles of the book are at least as appropriate and authentic as the "high" literary style to which Moses aspires. And the comic irreverence with which Selvon enacts this deconstruction of hierarchies is reminiscent of Bakhtin's use of the medieval carnival as a metaphor for the intermixture of "high" and "low" cultures that he sees as central to the richly dialogic texture of the novel.

Given the importance of the carnival to Trinidadian culture, Bakhtin's use of the carnival as a metaphor for the interaction among languages in the novel indicates an additional way in which his work might be relevant to this culture.[7] In addition, the complexity of the carnival metaphor helps us to appreciate the complexity of *Moses Ascending*. The carnival, however seemingly transgressive, involves an officially sanctioned and purely temporary suspension of rules and order that is clearly designed to allow a blowing off of steam that will ultimately work to the advantage of the status quo.[8] In this vein, the failure of Moses's attempts to rise in British society, however comic, has a dark side that comes close to suggesting the hopelessness of all such projects.

Reading *Moses Ascending* through Bakhtin does a great deal to indicate the potential gravity of this book, which seems at first glance to be a light entertainment, a farcical account of the comic misadventures of the now middle-aged Moses as he attempts to rise to British bourgeois respectability. Moses, from this point of view, is revealed to be a sort of "picaro," the kind of roguish antihero whose point of view, for Bakhtin, is often used in the novel to deflate the pretensions of "high" culture. Such heroes are often themselves the butt of their own humor, but their aberrant and marginal perspectives shed new light on the dishonesty and pretentiousness of more respectable members of society, as well. For Bakhtin, novels featuring such protagonists are an extremely effective form of satire. In them,

> hypocrisy and falsehood saturate all human relationships. The healthy "natural" functions of human nature are fulfilled, so to speak, only in ways that are contraband and savage, because the reigning ideology will not sanction them. This introduces falsehood and duplicity into all human life. (Bakhtin 1981, 162)

Selvon, through Moses, sets about his exposure of the falseness and vulgarity of British bourgeois values from the very beginning of the novel, in which Moses decides to become a property owner, knowing the hallowed status afforded property in this capitalist society. But Moses must make this attempt within the context of a growing racist hostility to non-European immigrants by the white natives of London, who feel increasingly threatened by the Africans, Asians, and West Indians they now find in their midst. Thus, the best he can do is acquire, from a West Indian who is returning home to Jamaica, a dilapidated "mansion" in a deteriorating neighborhood. He can afford this decaying hulk, which is scheduled for demolition in three years' time, because he rents out most of it to tenants, who are less fortunate than himself. He installs himself in the "penthouse" (i.e., the top-floor flat) and begins to pursue a life of leisure that leaves him free to cultivate his literary aspirations. Meanwhile, his assistant, Bob, does the actual day-to-day work of running the boarding house. In other words, in true capitalist fashion, Moses makes an initial investment of capital through purchase of the house, then plans to live off of the labor of others.

But Moses, after moving into his new home, immediately discovers that the pursuit of his bourgeois ambitions will require him to deny his own identity. Thus, one of his first goals is to distance himself from his former associates among the black West Indian immigrants of London. But it is not so easy to escape the past. Just as he is settling in, his old friend, Galahad, now a militant black power advocate, drops in for a visit, hoping that Moses, now seemingly prosperous, will be willing to make a donation to the cause. When Moses shows a decided lack of racial solidarity, Galahad reminds him that, to the white population of London, he is still a black man, house or no house (11–12).

Moses, of course, knows that Galahad is right, though he fantasizes that, in a capitalist London where virtually everything has been reduced to the status of a commodity and is thus for sale, it might be possible to purchase at least a simulation of whiteness. He thus envisions a time when, in addition to wigs and other appearance-altering products, it might be possible to buy "a complete new face. . . . But the greatest invention will be when you can walk in black as midnight and emerge as pure and white as the driven snow" (16). This fantasy of becoming white shows Moses's awareness of racism, but it also shows a lack of solidarity with the other nonwhite characters in the book. Thus, it is not surprising that his descriptions of Galahad and the other black power advocates with whom he becomes involved in the book are highly satirical. Indeed, in keeping with the carnivalesque energies that drive the text, *Moses Ascending* deflates pretentiousness and self-seriousness of any kind—or any color.

Still, we should be aware that it is Moses who tells the story, and that his description of these militants as something of a curse and embarrassment comes partly from his desire to distance himself from them as part of his attempt to succeed on the terms of white British society. Despite their rhetoric of black solidarity, they are perfectly willing to take advantage of Moses by moving their headquarters into his basement, despite his objections. They are even willing to let Moses remain in jail after he is mistakenly arrested during one of their demonstrations, feeling that the publicity surrounding his unjust arrest will help their cause. Further, despite their anticapitalist rhetoric, the black power militants are more than willing to enjoy the fruits of capitalism. Thus, BP, the American Black Panther representative who comes to speak to the brothers in London, rides about town in a Mercedes and eventually absconds with the Party treasury.

Of course, Moses, with his bourgeois ambitions, is hardly a sympathetic observer of the Black Power Party. And even Moses is forced to admit, especially in his acknowledgement of the persecution of the Party by the London police (and of his own fear, as a black man, of police brutality), that Galahad and the other members of the Party have some legitimate political points. Indeed, after the police attack a peaceful meeting and arrest many of the participants, Moses himself becomes outraged and bails them out. He thus reveals the generous side of his nature, though he does not become committed to their cause, despite their extravagant expressions of gratitude for his help. Meanwhile, the Party remains ensconced in his basement despite his desire to remove them.

Of course, if the Party exploits Moses by moving into his basement, we should recall that they are able to do so not because of his support for the cause, but because he first installs Brenda, a beautiful young member of the Party, there. And he puts Brenda up in the basement only because he hopes to use her as an unpaid housekeeper and because both he and Bob are hankering for some "black pussy," having both been limited strictly to "white pussy" during their lives in England. In short, turnabout is fair play, and the Party's exploitation of Moses is enabled by his attempt to exploit Brenda.

Moses's vision of Brenda as a sexual object again suggests his lack of a sense of racial solidarity with other blacks, but at least he is consistent, tending to regard women of any color merely as sexual objects throughout his appearances in Selvon's fiction. In this, he participates in a motif that runs throughout Selvon's work, in which West Indian men, feminized by their subaltern positions within the colonial system, seek empowerment through sexual exploitation of women.[9] In Selvon's novels of immigrant life, this usually means white women, the sexual mastery of whom provides West Indian men with a measure of revenge for their own depersonalization and objectification by white British society, as well as a measure of validation of their own manhood. As Moses himself sardonically points out, "those who cry Black Power loudest usually have a white woman in tow, whether as lifeline or whipping-boy I leave to you" (121).

But Brenda, despite Moses's description of her as a "little thing," is not so easy to dismiss as a mere sexual object. Only about eighteen, she may be naïve, but she does have strong political commitments and, unlike Moses, is working hard to try to achieve justice for Britain's black population. And she is smart enough to turn the tables on Moses, taking advantage of his desire to take advantage of her by using it to secure his basement for the use of the Party. She is perfectly willing to use her sexuality as a weapon in the struggle for racial justice, but that is a different matter than having her sexuality exploited by others for their purposes. It is clear, for example, that Brenda knows very well what she is doing when she initiates a sexual relationship with Bob, thereby encouraging him to become one of the Party's few white supporters.

In a similar way, Moses attempts to exploit the illegal Pakistani immigrants who flow through his house, which they use, despite his objections, as a temporary stopping-off point. Moses seeks to envision himself as culturally superior to (i.e., more British than) the Pakistanis in much the same way that he attempts to envision himself as the sexual master of women. His descriptions of the Pakistanis, which consist of the same Orientalist stereotypes that the British had long applied to Asians, would seem to align him with the official power structures of white Britain. He only decides to include the "Pakis" in his memoirs because he believes they will lend an air of exoticism, but he seems to confuse Muslims with Hindus and Sikhs, and accepts most of the standard British clichés about oriental behavior, as when he admits that "it would not of surprised me to find one of them climbing up a piece of rope, or blowing a flute and bringing out a king cobra from a basket" (86).

Again, however, Moses is not in a position of genuine power, despite his vision of himself as aligned with the metropolitan center against the colonial margins. It is obvious that Moses, as a postcolonial subject, is in a position far more similar to that of the Asians than that of the British.[10] In addition, the Pakistanis, following in the footsteps of Brenda, elude his control and force him to do as they ask, rather than the other way around. It is certainly clear that they are unimpressed by his British airs. In one telling scene, Moses reveals his sense of linguistic superiority to the Pakistanis (some of whom genuinely appear not to speak English) by asking one of them (whom he simply refers to as "Paki") if he "speakee English?" Paki's reply is succinct and to the point: "Fuck off" (69).

That Moses tends to be unable to assign individual names to the Pakistanis indicates his British belief that, first, they have long, weird-sounding names, and, second, they all look alike. Indeed, he goes through most of the text believing that one of his tenants, Faizull Farouk, is actually two different people, one named Faizull and one named Farouk. On the other hand, Moses is somewhat aware of such tendencies, noting that he need not bother to make fine distinctions between various kinds of Asians because "English people so stupid that the whole lot of Orientals and Blacks is the same kettle of fish as far as they are concerned" (51).

Paki, meanwhile, proceeds to explain his position in a style that is a sophisticated mixture of literary English and American slang, complaining that he "should not have to suffer the proximity of disbelievers," but acknowledging that "you pays your money and you takes your choice" (69). By contrast, Moses, in this same scene, begins narrating in Trinidadian dialect, as when he notes that he went to look for Faizull during the conversation with Paki: "I . . . try the door, but it was lock. I bang, but nobody won't answer" (69). This reversal of roles, with Paki speaking the language of the metropolitan center and Moses speaking the language of the colonial margins, suggests Moses's lack of power and control in their encounter. Or at least it suggests Moses's sense of not being in control, since the entire encounter is related to us by Moses, making it difficult to tell whether we are really meant to believe that Paki speaks in this fashion or whether Moses, narrating the episode after the fact, is simply playing with the style to make a point. Indeed, this fundamental uncertainty runs throughout the text. Moses, as narrator, speaks in a variety of styles and registers, and it is often difficult to tell whether these variations should be attributed to Selvon (thus indicating Moses's fundamental linguistic instability) or to Moses himself (thus indicating his substantial facility with style).[11]

The multiple styles of Moses's narration can, to a first approximation, be attributed to his own multicultural background and to his attempts to "lift" himself by developing the kind of sophisticated literary style that he believes white British society will respect. And this stylistic multiplicity can have a number of implications. One might, for example, interpret Moses's continual shifting among styles as a sign of the growing fragmentation of his own personality amid the postmodern context of London.[12] In *The Lonely Londoners* (1956), having been in England for only a few years, Moses still speaks almost entirely in his original Trinidadian dialect. In *Moses Ascending*, having been in England for more than two decades, that dialect is diluted, and he tends toward more "proper" English, even when he does speak in dialect. But he is now perfectly capable of speaking in the Queen's English, at least if he has time to think about it and construct his sentences carefully. Thus, when he is grabbed by a policeman during the black power demonstration, he admits that, "If I had had time I would of said, 'Unhand me, knave,' but instead I say, 'Let me go, man, I ain't done nothing'" (36).

Moses's attempts to master literary English can be seen as an attempt to solidify his position in British society. Unable to acquire physical whiteness, he tries for the next best thing, aspiring to the economic and cultural achievement of a white Englishman. In particular, Moses seeks to learn to use the English language like a proper Englishman. Having installed English as the official language all over the Empire, the British had long regarded their own superior mastery of the English language as a key sign of their intellectual superiority to their colonial subjects, ignoring the obvious fact that, for these subjects, English was an acquired second (or third, or fourth . . .) language, while the British themselves seldom achieved any extensive facility in the native languages of their subjects. This strategy was highly successful, and colonial subjects all over the world sought to master the English language as a validation of their cultural and intellectual ability. Compare, for example, the poignant story of the Indian Hari Kumar in Paul Scott's *The Jewel in the Crown* (1966), who attempts to overcome his subaltern status as a colonial subject by learning to speak impeccable English with a flawless upper-class accent and intonation, spurred by his father's fantasy of having a son who, over the telephone, would be indistinguishable from an Englishman. Kumar, who even Anglicizes his name to Harry Coomer, succeeds in learning to speak the Queen's English, but discovers that he is still not accepted as an Englishman. Further, and tragically, he is now so Anglicized that he is not accepted as an Indian either, leaving him adrift in the world without any cultural anchor for his personal identity.

The myth of British linguistic superiority was, of course, particularly effective in the Caribbean, where Britain's colonial subjects typically had no access to alternative indigenous languages, but were forced to accept English as their only language. It is not surprising, then, that Moses the aspiring author seems uncritically to accept the notion that, in order to be a literary success, he needs to learn to write proper British English.[13] After all, like Scott's Kumar, he realizes that, even if he cannot be a white Englishman, he can learn to speak and write like one. Indeed, he is specifically reminded of this fact early in *Moses Ascending* when he first encounters Brenda, who comes to him as an emissary from the Black Power Party. Though her parents are from Jamaica, Brenda was born and raised in Britain, and, despite her Afrocentric politics and appearance, she speaks impeccable English. "If I did shut my eyes," Moses muses, "I would of thought it was a nordic talking, the accent was so high" (17).

Moses can himself achieve some rather high accents, typically when he attempts to mimic literary language. In fact, his entire narration enacts a complex dialogue with the British literary tradition, not only through style, but through specific allusions. More often than not, however, Moses's attempts to write in literary English either descend into cliché or end up comically mixed with contemporary slang and Trinidadian dialect. Thus, he explains his education of Bob, noting that "whilst I was indoctrinating him, I also learn a lesson myself, which is that Black and White could live in harmony, for he was loyal and true, and never listened to all that shit you hear about black people" (5). Similarly, Moses's attempts to use a sophisticated vocabulary often appear quite forced and unnatural, as when he informs us that, upon moving into his new house, he "ensconced" himself on the top floor (3), or when he suggests that it would be "catholic" if he could provide a reasonable explanation for a seemingly unprovoked attack on a peaceful black power meeting by London police (94).

All in all, Moses's attempts to deploy English in a sophisticated literary manner is a colossal failure, and Brenda's critical description of his style as jumbled and confused is probably justified, even if her criticism, at least as relayed to us by Moses, is itself rather garbled. Indeed, Brenda accurately perceives the oral nature of Moses's narrative style when she notes that "you should stick to oral communication and leave the written word to them what knows their business" (105). This criticism, especially coming from Brenda, whom he hopes to impress, cuts Moses to the quick, which he explains by again resorting to cliché, complaining that he left her "with a heavy heart" because she was "hurling contempt and defamation on my usage of the Queen's language, which had always been my forte, as I have tried to show" (105).

Brenda's criticism of Moses's writing is followed by a quick succession of other defeats, as well. Caught in a compromising position with Jeannie, Bob's new wife, Moses, out of guilt, moves to Bob's old room and allows Bob and Jeannie to move into the penthouse. Moses is then forced to cede even this new room to the Party, after Brenda threatens to reveal his various indiscretions if he does not cooperate. Moses thus winds up in a dusty corner of the basement, moving aside stacks of novels by George Lamming and James Baldwin in order to make space for himself. Yet, despite such defeats, Moses, in keeping with the carnivalesque spirit of the novel, remains irrepressible to the finish. He thus ends his narration not in a mode of despair, but by plotting his revenge on Bob in the mangled literary English that has served him throughout, planning not only to inform Jeannie of her husband's continuing liaison with Brenda, but also to "arrange for

both of we to catch Master Robert in *flagrento delicto*, when I will fling
down the gauntlet" (140).

Notes

See chapter 4 for historical background.

1. Clement Wyke, in his book-length study of Selvon's style, notes that in
The Lonely Londoners, Selvon employs a narrative voice that uses a "mixing and
alternation of standard and dialectical elements which allow the narrative point
of view to accommodate the shifting voices of the storyteller" (Wyke 1991,
38). See also Fabre 1982.

2. See Ramraj 1983 for a comparison of *The Lonely Londoners* and *Moses
Ascending*.

3. Though it reaches a new level in *Moses Ascending*, this complex combination
of materials is central to Selvon's technique from the beginning. Simon Gikandi,
for example, notes the appearance of "disparate elements" in *A Brighter Sun*. Gikandi
then suggests that this diversity reflects Selvon's "indebtedness to the calypso aesthetic, especially its melodic lines, which come loaded with words and phrases that
appear to be unrelated and to have no value in themselves," but which, on closer
examination, initiate interesting dialogues (Gikandi 1992, 116–17).

4. For more of Selvon's dialogue with Defoe's text, see Baugh 1988.

5. Moses himself sometimes mocks the high accents of the educated British,
as when he notes that "in this world you must not *heng* your hand too high"
(3).

6. See Brennan 1990 for a discussion of the usefulness of the novel as a
form for the expression of the national consciousness of an emergent postcolonial
nation.

7. For Bakhtin's discussion of the carnival, see, especially, Bakhtin 1984. On
the carnivalesque aspects of *Moses Ascending*, see Dickinson 1996.

8. On the temporary nature of carnivalesque subversion, see Eagleton (1981,
148).

9. Compare, for example, the attempts of Tiger, in *A Brighter Sun* (Selvon
1952), to assert his domination of his wife, Urmilla, seeking to demonstrate his
manhood through an exercise of masculine power in his own household, sometimes to the extent of employing physical violence to prove his relative strength.

10. Moses seems at least partly aware of this fact, which would account for
the confusing "welter of emotions" that he feels toward the Pakistanis (88).

11. Edward Baugh (1988) concludes that Moses's various blunders are unconscious on his part, but highly conscious on the part of Selvon.

12. See Jameson 1991 for a discussion of the fragmentation of individual
identities as a key symptom of the postmodern condition.

13. Moses's seeming acceptance of the myth of British literary superiority can
be seen in the level of shock he experiences when he learns that Bob, a white
Englishman, is illiterate (128).

Chapter 6

Michael Thelwell:
The Harder They Come

Although Michael Thelwell is the author of only one novel, he enjoys a prominent place in contemporary Caribbean and African American culture. His novel, *The Harder They Come*, is one of the most important works of Caribbean literature. Thelwell has also made important contributions as a teacher (at the University of Massachusetts in Amherst) and as a civil rights activist. He has written a number of short stories (many focusing on the American Civil Rights movement) and essays. The most important of the essays is probably "Modernist Fallacies and the Responsibility of the Black Writer," which is included, along with several other essays and stories, in the volume *Duties, Pleasures, and Conflicts* (Thelwell 1987). In this essay, Thelwell lambastes modernist literature for its fascination with technique and consequent disengagement from historical reality. He urges black writers to adhere to a realist aesthetic in their representation of black experience. Thelwell very effectively follows his own advice in his short stories and in his only novel, which powerfully evoke the realities of black experience in the United States and in his native Jamaica.

The Harder They Come is based on the 1972 Perry Henzell film of the same title, which, though set in the 1960s, was based on the real story of notorious Jamaican gunman Ivanhoe "Rhygin" Martin, who became something of a popular hero in Jamaica in the late 1940s after a highly publicized shoot-out with police made him a cult figure among the poor and dispossessed of the island. Thelwell details the process of adapting the film, which was the first genuinely Jamaican film, to novel form in his essay "*The Harder They Come:* From Film to Novel." In this essay, Thelwell describes his initial hesitation to undertake the project, at the request of Grove Press, for fear that a novelization of the film would trivialize its artistic and political message. After all, the film crucially relies on visual images of urban Kingston and on a powerful *reggae* soundtrack to convey the texture of Jamaican working-class reality. In addition, the film, as a film, is able to address head-on one of its own central themes, the cultural imperialism involved in the impact on Jamaica of North American film. Eventually, however, Thelwell was persuaded that a novel based on the film had the potential to supplement, rather than degrade, the film's messages, especially as he felt that the novel, as a genre, had important potential for the expression of "the articulation of shared cultural experience" in Jamaica and the rest of the Third World (Thelwell 1991, 145).

Thelwell himself describes the vision that motivated his writing of the novel:

> It was my intention that it be not a novel about Jamaica but a Jamaican novel: that is, an artifact naturally and organically derived from the cultural sensibilities, references, experiences, and political perceptions of the people, recognizably anchored in their historical experiences, and expressed in a language, informed by the metaphors, imagery, proverbial lore, narrative forms, styles, and traditions of the indigenous classes. (Thelwell 1991, 149)

In pursuit of this project, Thelwell adheres quite closely to the plot of the film, no doubt partly as an expression of respect for the film's achievement.

As one might expect, the novel includes a bit more background information on Ivan Martin and his historical context, beginning in Book One with an account of his childhood in the care of his grandmother in rural Jamaica that is not included in the film. This first book is entitled "The Hills Were Joyful," in an obvious allusion to the novel *The Hills Were Joyful Together* (1953) by Roger Mais, one of Thelwell's most important predecessors in the realistic depiction of the plight of the Jamaican working class, along with other Jamaican proletarian writers such as Andrew Salkey and Vic Reid.

Thelwell describes the rural environment of Ivan's childhood in essentially utopian terms, in a conscious effort to present the positive virtues of the traditional values of this community, values that are strongly rooted in the communal practices brought from Africa on slave ships generations earlier. Thelwell notes that, by the time he was writing the novel, it had become fashionable to believe that "life in technologically poor, rural communities of black people was an unbroken gothic tapestry of ignorance, depravity, pathology, futility—an unrelieved impoverishment and depravity of mind and a coarseness of spirit" (Thelwell 1991, 149). Thelwell, without idealizing or romanticizing traditional Jamaican rural life, counters this woeful vision with reminders that rural Jamaicans, while generally poor in material ways, were at least able to feed themselves by working the land, while their organic connection to this land—and to the communal social fabric provided by their neighbors—provided them with a sense of identity, belonging, and stability unavailable even to the most wealthy in the more modern world of global capitalism.

Ivan, as a child, can be certain not only of the love and support of Miss Amanda, his grandmother, but of an extended network of friends and acquaintances. Thus, the old and ailing Miss Amanda takes great comfort in the fact that, should Ivan ever need help that she is unable to provide, there are any number of adults in the community who feel "obliged by custom and friendship to come to his aid" (36). The close-knit nature of communal life in rural Jamaica is represented by Thelwell in a number of ways, as in his detailed description of important cultural gatherings, such as the corn shelling contest at the home of Maas' Nattie, where the locals gather to help the old man shuck and shell his newly harvested corn, part of a larger network of agricultural practices in which anyone who "had a major project needing many hands" could count on his friends and neighbors to pitch in, with the implication that the favor would be returned when needed (47). This gathering is important not only for the work that gets done, but for the cultural interchange that occurs, as the various participants sing, tell stories, and generally catch up on the details of each other's lives.

Another important cultural practice presented in *The Harder They Come* is the elaborate funeral of Miss Amanda, which mourns her passing, memorializes her life, and celebrates the ongoing vitality of the group even as individuals necessarily die. This event goes on for nine days and provides a final image of the traditional communal culture of rural Jamaica before Ivan, now fourteen years old, sets out on his journey to urban Kingston to seek his mother, who is working there but with whom, in the first of many images of the alienating effect of city life, Ivan and Amanda had lost contact some time before. The culture shock of Ivan's migration from the country to the city will subsequently be a central theme of the book, though it is important to note that signs of modernity had already been for some time creeping into Ivan's rural environment, as in his acquisition of a transistor radio, to which he listens with rapture, dreaming of being a singer himself and hearing his own songs on the radio.[1]

Book Two of the novel begins approximately at the beginning of the film, as Ivan, after his grandmother's death, travels to Kingston via a symbolically (though rather comically) harrowing bus trip that provides him with his first introduction to the vicissitudes of modern life. This journey, reminiscent of mythical descents into hell, removes Ivan from the stability of his urban community and deposits him in the midst of the noise, confusion, and poverty of an urban Kingston, leaving him lost and disoriented. Ivan's experience in this sense can be usefully described in terms of the concept of "cognitive mapping," recently emphasized by the cultural critic Fredric Jameson as a key to understanding the sense of rootlessness and confusion that seems an integral part of life in the postmodern world of global capitalism. In traditional societies, Jameson argues, individuals understood what was expected of them and had a firm sense of their place in the order of things. In our contemporary world, however, individuals have been uprooted from these traditional moorings and now find themselves afloat in a vast and mysterious system they can neither understand nor escape.

In particular, Jameson derives his concept from Kevin Lynch's book, *The Image of the City*, a classic work on the disorienting effects of urban environments. As Jameson points out, Lynch notes that "the alienated city is above all a space in which people are unable to map (in their minds) either their own positions or the urban totality in which they find themselves" (Jameson 1991, 51). But Jameson, of course, has something larger in mind than mere physical difficulty in finding one's way around in modern cities. For Jameson, this cognitive disorientation also involves the ideological problem of no longer being able to understand one's relationship to "that vaster and properly unrepresentable totality which is the ensemble of society's structures as a whole" (51).

Ivan's experience in Kingston obviously involves both of these forms of cognitive disorientation. In the confusing sprawl of urban Kingston, Ivan is quite literally physically lost and cannot find his way around, but he is also ideologically lost, understanding neither the workings of the social system of Kingston or of the large global system of which it is a part. Further, he has no effective way to gain this understanding. For one thing, while the more experienced denizens of Kingston certainly know the local ropes better than the newly arrived Ivan, they, too, have little real understanding of the larger system of global capitalism that holds them so firmly in its grip. For another, in the alienated context of the city, Ivan cannot count on the help and support that were so crucial to the communal existence of his childhood.

Ivan learns this latter lesson the hard way. Immediately after arriving in Kingston, with all of his worldly possessions in tow, he receives an offer from a boy with a pushcart to help him transport these possessions to the home of his mother. Though the boy expects to be paid, his offer of help makes perfect sense to Ivan, who is accustomed to such cooperative efforts.

Ivan thus gladly accepts the offer, only to be robbed of his possessions when the boy sends Ivan off on a side errand, then escapes with the pushcart into the noise and confusion of the city, leaving Ivan alone in this inhospitable terrain with only with a small amount of cash and the clothes on his back.

In Kingston, the naïve Ivan, now fourteen years old, has a number of new experiences, including seeing Rastafarians for the first time.[2] The book is powerful in its presentation of the squalor and poverty of Kingston, while at the same time making clear that the plight of the poor is not due to historical necessity but to the manipulations of a rich upper class of Jamaicans and foreigners, especially Americans, who exploit the poor and make huge profits from them. Ivan finally manages to locate his mother, but he finds that she is in no position to provide much help. Living in poverty and squalor, she is also ill and in fact soon dies. Ivan is left to his own means, struggling to make an honest living, but finding that there are few opportunities open to him.

In one extremely telling segment, Ivan wanders through a neighborhood of rich, suburban homes, hoping to find work as a servant or gardener. In most cases, he can get no nearer to the homes than the locked front gates that close off their well-manicured lawns, patrolled by vicious guard dogs, from the street. At one home, he finds the gate unlocked and wanders inside, eventually coming upon a rich woman reclining on the verandah. This woman is a black Jamaican, but Ivan, intensely aware of the class difference between them, finds it impossible to feel that he and she have anything in common: "She was not white. But he couldn't think of her as black either, though there was not much difference in their color. *He* was black. *She* was rich" (171). Class, in Jamaica, clearly supercedes race. Predictably, the woman treats Ivan rudely and orders him off the premises. He persists in asking for work, declaring that he is willing to do anything. She still refuses. Starving and desperate, he asks for ten cents to buy food, whereupon the woman lectures him on the shame of a healthy boy like himself begging for handouts when he is perfectly able to work (172).

This complete lack of sympathy or understanding is typical of all of the middle- and upper-class people Ivan meets in Kingston, though he does experience occasional moments of kindness from other poor people like himself. After nearly starving, he finally makes his way to the church of the Reverend Cyrus Mordecai Ramsey, a Pentecostal Baptist preacher to whom his mother had referred him earlier. Here, he learns of the death of his mother and manages to get taken on as an assistant to Longah, the church handyman. He also develops a fondness for Elsa, an orphan who has been brought up by Ramsey.

Ramsey, a sort of comprador preacher who is sponsored by a home church in Memphis, Tennessee, is a typical example of religious blindness to social reality.³ Presumably ministering to the souls of Jamaicans, he offers them little more than occasional escape from suffering through church rituals that at least carry some vestiges of the communal cultural practices of an earlier era. But he offers nothing that might help alleviate this suffering at its source in social and economic inequality. He also heartily disapproves of Ivan's fascination with the African rhythms of the new *reggae* music that has recently become so popular on Kingston radio. He actively discourages Ivan's relationship with Elsa as well, presumably because of Ivan's inclination toward this "devil's music" and other forms of sinfulness. There are, however, also hints in the text that the preacher harbors his own sexual feelings for the girl.

Ivan works for Ramsey, stays in the shack attached to the church, and meanwhile begins to run with the urban youth gangs of Kingston, which are the only sources of communal activity in the city. But this alternative society of outcasts can provide only a weak echo of the traditional communal life Ivan left behind in the country. Roaming the nighttime streets in an attitude of contempt for authority, these gangs in fact take their inspiration from the American films they watch in Kingston's theaters. Their models are not black political leaders like Marcus Garvey, but white American movie stars like Humphrey Bogart and James Cagney.

Thelwell introduces this motif partly because the historical Ivan Martin was known to be fascinated by American Westerns. But he also introduces it because the extent to which the urban youth of these gangs are held in thrall by American films is itself historically accurate and suggests one of the major forms taken by American cultural imperialism in the Caribbean, even when most Caribbean islands were still European colonies. One might compare here (despite Thelwell's expressed contempt for Naipaul) V. S. Naipaul's insistence in *An Area of Darkness* that he had no particular sense of being dominated by British culture when he was growing up in British colonial Trinidad in the 1930s and 1940s, largely because American culture was even then a more potent presence:

> The Americans made the real automobiles, as they made the real films and produced the best singers and the best bands. Their films spoke universal sentiments and their humour was immediately comprehensible. American radio was modern and marvellous and at least you could understand the accent. (Naipaul 1968, 189)

Thelwell's Ivan, like his historical model, is himself greatly taken by American films, especially Westerns, despite the seeming preference of most gang members for gangster films. Indeed, Ivan's first trip to a movie theater is one of his most memorable experiences in the new world of Kingston, and serves as a sort of microcosm of many of the book's larger themes. Ivan approaches the Rialto Theater in an attitude of awe and excitement, but the narrative suggests that there might be something inauthentic about the images dispensed by the theater: "A marketplace of dreams, it was designed to appear fabulous, more magical, more impossibly brilliant than the illusions it dispensed so cheaply" (143).

When Ivan enters the theater, he discovers that the impressive façade of the building is just that, a false front that belies the relative modesty of the interior, which is merely a roofless courtyard (145). Nevertheless, he is enthralled by the images projected on the theater's screen, images which themselves recapitulate the history of colonial and neocolonial domination in Jamaica. The show begins to the strains of "God Save the Queen," accompanied by a giant technicolor image of the Union Jack waving on the screen, followed by shots of redcoated soldiers and the Queen herself. This reminder of the more than three hundred years in which Jamaica was under British control is then followed by a double feature of two American films (a gangster film and a Western), thus providing a reminder of the way in which British rule, by the 1960s, has been supplanted by American popular culture as the most powerful outside force in Jamaica.

During the time Ivan stays at the church, he takes every opportunity to watch such films and clearly begins to model himself on their white heroes.[4] Then, his stay at the church comes to an abrupt end after Ramsey, infuriated by the ongoing relationship between Ivan and Elsa and by Ivan's continuing fascination with *reggae* music, orders Ivan to vacate the premises once and for all. Ivan, preparing to leave, goes to Longah's work shed to fetch the bicycle that he himself has constructed from scrap. When Longah refuses to let Ivan take the bicycle, the two men fight. Ivan ends up slashing Longah with a knife, essentially in self-defense after Longah attacks him with a broken bottle. In another of the book's embedded allegories of class-based oppression, Ivan is subsequently arrested and brought before a pompous judge, the Honorable Justice Josephus V. O. Allen. Ramsey maliciously testifies to Ivan's wickedness, and Allen sentences Ivan to receive eight lashes of the tamarind switch.

This barbaric sentence is a relic of the British colonial justice system, which quite generally employed techniques of physical punishment.[5] As Michel Foucault notes, these techniques can be associated largely with the era of feudal-aristocratic rule in Europe (Foucault 1978). They had been largely abandoned back in Europe with the advent of the modern era of bourgeois rule, but continued to be widely practiced in the colonial world, where "the agents of government speak the language of pure force" (Fanon 1968, 38). Ivan, already injured in the fight with Longah, barely survives the beating, recuperating with the help of Elsa, who leaves the abusive preacher to be with Ivan. In the meantime, Ivan finally gets a chance to make a recording in the studio of Mr. Hilton, a local music magnate, so things seem to be looking up.

Unfortunately, this opportunity is not as lucrative as it might first appear. Though Ivan's performance is impressive, and his song is clearly a potential hit, Hilton refuses to release the record unless Ivan signs over all the profits from the record to Hilton's company in exchange for a one-time payment of a mere fifty dollars. Ivan at first refuses the deal, but eventually returns and accepts it when his need for cash becomes desperate. Hilton then releases the record but, in an apparent effort to teach Ivan some humility, instructs his minions not to push the record, thus ensuring that it will not be a hit.

This episode, based on the actual early experiences of *reggae* star Jimmy Cliff, who plays Ivan in the Henzell film, is another of the reminders in both the book and the film of the economic exploitation of the poor by the rich in Jamaica. Hilton, in fact, is one of the key figures of this exploitation in *The Harder They Come*. He is first introduced *in flagrante* with a white woman tourist in his luxurious mansion, and he is presented throughout as a selfish capitalist opportunist who follows North American models in his willingness to employ any manner of unscrupulous business practices in order to squeeze additional profit out of his various enterprises.

Interestingly, the *reggae* motif was originally introduced into the film for the economic reason that Island Records offered to help finance the making of the film in return for being able to use it as a showcase for Cliff's music. As Thelwell notes, however, this commercial intervention actually resulted in a significant enrichment of the film and his own novel, helping both better to tell their stories from the perspective of working-class Jamaicans. *Reggae*, Thelwell argues, is "the natural music idiom of the ghetto" that expresses "in its lyrics the defiant, class-conscious, highly political sensibility and experience of the rude-bwai youth culture of the poor" in Jamaica (Thelwell 1991, 143–44). Strongly linked to the Rastafarian movement, *reggae* music (best known in the United States through the recordings of *reggae* superstar Bob Marley) features highly politicized lyrics while drawing upon traditional African musical forms, thus providing working-class Jamaican youth with a rallying point for resistance to oppression. But this

characteristic of *reggae* makes Hilton's business activities all the more repre-
hensible in that he attempts not only to exploit his working-class artists and
other employees but to co-opt and commodify the emerging *reggae* sound
for his own profit, with no appreciation of the extent to which this music
might serve as an authentic form of Jamaican cultural expression and social
protest.[6]

Indeed, Hilton's business largely involves an attempt to strip *reggae* of its
power as a tool of resistance and to reduce it to a mere economic commodity. In this sense, his activities clearly mirror those of the police superinten-
dent, Ray Jones, who attempts to regulate and control the local ganja (marijuana) trade, both for his personal profit and as a means of containing the
subversive potential of the drug, which is central to the practices of
Rastafarianism. Jones's strategy is simple. Feeling that the ganja trade, with
its potentially subversive links to Rastafarianism, cannot be stopped altogether, he seeks instead to "control and direct it" (246). His strategy thus
greatly resembles that associated by Foucault with bourgeois societies of the
West in the nineteenth century, which, Foucault argues, sought not to repress sexuality in the manner described by Freud, but to administer and
control sexual energies for their own purposes (Foucault 1980). In the process, Jones not only makes a considerable amount of money, but also establishes a network of informers and other connections that is valuable to him
in his other police work.

Here, Jones's strategy recalls Foucault's emphasis on the importance of
surveillance and information gathering to modern bourgeois techniques
of power (Foucault 1978; 1980). In fact, Jones, trained in the United
States, is an emblem of modernization, which in this case means the increasing cultural and economic domination of Jamaica by North America.
His "regulation" of the ganja trade is designed largely to ensure that the
trade is controlled not by Jamaicans, but by North Americans, who make
most of the profit from the trade, while Jamaicans do most of the work
and take most of the risk. His attempts to control the ganja trade, highly
reminiscent of the practices of power that Foucault associates with the
modern "disciplinary" era of bourgeois rule, can be taken as a sign of
increasing modernization in Jamaica, but also as a reminder that this
modernization does not necessarily accrue to the advantage of the Jamaican people (Foucault 1978).

Meanwhile, Ivan himself, realizing that he is not likely to be able to
survive on the proceeds of his recording career anytime soon, becomes extensively involved in the ganja trade. His acquaintance, Jose (one of Jones's
informers), gets him in touch with Ras Peter (also known as Pedro), an
expert ganja preparer. Ivan then works with Ras Peter to bring freshly har-

vested ganja into Kingston from the surrounding hills for processing and marketing in the city. Meanwhile, Elsa cares for Man-I, Ras Peter's young, sickly son, whose mother was killed in a recent attack by the army on the ganja growers.

Through Jose, Ras Peter and Ivan pay protection money to Jones, who is thus able both to skim off much of their profit and keep track of their activities. Ivan, meanwhile, begins to realize that the real money in the ganja trade is being made on shipments to North America, which yield profits in the millions, while he and Ras Peter are struggling for a few meager dollars. Angry and needing their money for necessities such as medicine for Man-I, Ras Peter and Ivan eventually refuse to pay Jose the protection money. In retaliation, Jose and Jones arrange for the police to arrest Ivan, not realizing that Ivan is now carrying a pair of pistols for protection. In the resulting shoot-out, Ivan kills several policemen and escapes, news reports of which lead to his fame as a desperado. Hilton rereleases Ivan's record, which rises to the top of the charts, while Ivan, now generally known by his boyhood nickname, "Rhygin," becomes a near mythical figure, reported to be involved in virtually all subsequent criminal acts in Kingston.[7]

But Ivan's individualist rebellion, informed by no coherent political vision, is doomed to failure. As with the youth gangs that attempt to model themselves on the stars of American gangster films, Ivan continues to model himself after Western heroes. His rebelliousness is thus safely contained within the ideology of global capitalism and poses no real threat to the capitalist system. Eventually, Ivan conceives a plan to escape to Cuba, that one Caribbean bastion of legitimate opposition to capitalism, but it is not to be. Elsa, desperate to get help for the rapidly declining Man-I, reveals Ivan's whereabouts to Ramsey, who immediately conveys the information to the police. Ivan is quickly located by the police, then shot down in a final gun battle in a scene that he himself compares to something from a movie, even as he goes to his death. The news of Ivan's death is broadcast over the radio, and his career ends where it began, in the media.

To an extent, then, *The Harder They Come* is a story of failed rebellion against neocolonial capitalist domination. Ivan, as the protagonist, attempts to combat this domination by participating in a variety of forms of resistance: he runs with gangs that express their contempt for authority; he performs *reggae* music with explicitly political overtones; he participates in the ganja trade; and he becomes a notorious outlaw, battling police with his twin six-guns. Yet, none of these forms of rebellion are able to strike genuinely damaging blows against the capitalist system he seeks to oppose, partly because of his own lack of awareness of who his real enemies are. The traditional society of Ivan's youth is obviously unable to resist the historical momentum of capitalist modernity. The gangs largely enact clichés adopted from American film; their petty crimes are little more than echoes of standard capitalist business practices and in any case constitute little more than a social nuisance that simply justifies the use of additional official power in the name of law and order. The main impact of Ivan's *reggae* music seems to be the further enrichment of Hilton and his capitalist empire. Similarly, the ganja trade serves largely to enrich North American drug dealers, while providing Jones with a tool for the extension of his police power. And Rhygin's six-guns are no match for the automatic rifles wielded by the police and military and supplied by the U.S. government.

Yet, *The Harder They Come* is not entirely pessimistic about the possibility of resistance to the power of neocolonial capitalism. It is not at all clear, for example, that the potentially subversive power of Ivan's music (which continues to play on the radio even after his death) is completely contained within the ledgers of Hilton's corporate empire. However much the distribution of *reggae* might be controlled by record companies and the broadcast media, this music continues to speak to the poor and disenfranchised of Jamaica in ways that are anything but in the interests of capitalists such as Hilton. Meanwhile, though the youth gangs in which Ivan participates seem unable to mount any genuine resistance to capitalist exploitation and domination, the Rastafarians who circulate through the novel (and the film) are less easily contained within Western cultural categories. Though perhaps lacking in practical specifics, the alternative utopian energies of Rastafarianism provide a reminder that it is possible to envision a society in which social relationships are not simply defined by the individualist antagonism of social relationships under capitalism. At the same time, the Rastafarians offer a black cultural identity that derives much of its force from non-Western sources, especially traditional African culture.

If nothing else, the very existence of the film version of *The Harder They Fall*, with its overt critique of the mind-numbing effect of American films on Jamaican audiences, suggests that it is possible to make films that go beyond and even directly oppose the Hollywood norm. In the same way, Thelwell's book demonstrates that it is possible, within the traditionally Western bourgeois genre of the novel, to construct a work that is powerfully critical of Western bourgeois ideology and particularly of the neocolonial domination of Jamaica and other Third-World societies by global capitalism. He seeks to find in his novel an authentic mode of Jamaican cultural expression from within, rather than merely describing Jamaican culture from the outside. And he does so not merely in the content, but also in the style of his novel.

Thelwell rejects the pretentious artifice of the modernist novel, confining himself instead to a straightforward realism that can be "read by the 'unlettered' masses with something approximating the enthusiasm with which they had greeted the film. A novel that Rhygin himself might want to read" (Thelwell 1991, 147). Designed to be a Jamaican novel for an audience of primarily Jamaican readers, *The Harder They Fall* makes extensive use of the creolized English of Jamaica, especially in the dialogue of the characters.[8] Thus, the very language of the book tends to contain an element of resistance to domination by the metropolitan centers of Britain and North America. If nothing else, this strategy, which clearly makes the book more accessible to Jamaican readers than to British and North American ones, is a potential lesson in cultural relativity, reminding North American and British readers that their access to the written word is not absolutely superior to that of their Third-World counterparts. Perhaps more importantly, Thelwell's effective mixture of standard English and Jamaican dialect demonstrates that standard English is not necessarily superior to such dialects as a literary language. The book thus makes a positive contribution to Jamaican cultural identity by reminding Jamaicans of the beauty and literary power of their own particular version of English.

The Harder They Come is powerfully effective in its description of life in neocolonial Jamaica and in its careful delineation of the role of international capitalism in the continuing poverty of the Jamaican masses. Various forces, including official corruption, popular culture, and traditional Christian religion (most of which are heavily influenced by foreign, especially American, pressures), are specifically identified as crucial to the oppression of the Jamaican poor. On the other hand, the poor do have some resources, and they are able to convert many of these forces into sources of resistance, as exemplified by the development of *reggae* music and the Rastafarian religion. Thelwell develops all of this material in a consistently realistic mode, though the book also makes sophisticated use of linguistic effects, such as authentic Jamaican dialects, and literary techniques, such as multiple points of view and the use of *reggae* rhythms as a structural device, in presenting its points.

Historical Background

Jamaica, with a land area of 4,232 sq. mi. (10,962 sq. km) and a total population of more than 2.5 million, is easily the largest and most populous of the former British islands in the Caribbean. The capital city, Kingston, with a total population of about 600,000, is the largest of the former British cities in the Caribbean. Spanish Town (population about 90,000) and

Montego Bay (population about 70,000) are also among the most populous cities of the formerly British areas of the Caribbean. The population of Jamaica is mostly (about 76 percent) of black African descent; 15 percent of the population is of mixed African and European descent, while people of primarily European, East Indian, and Chinese descent make up the remainder of the population. Though the mostly mountainous island of Jamaica produces bauxite and other mineral products, its principal exports are agricultural products such as sugarcane, coffee, and bananas. Tourism is also an important industry. English is the official language, though most Jamaicans also speak a distinctively Jamaican creole form of English. The literacy rate is approximately 98 percent.

The island of Jamaica was sighted by Columbus in 1494; it was conquered by Spain in 1509, when Spanish settlement began under a license from Columbus's son. The Spanish virtually exterminated the native Arawak population, maintaining control of the island until 1655, when it was captured by the British, who gained official control of the island in a treaty established in 1670. Port Royal was the capital and major city in the late seventeenth century; it was also an important base for pirates, such as Sir Henry Morgan, who brought considerable wealth to the area. Spanish Town became the capital in 1692, when Port Royal was largely destroyed by an earthquake.

In the eighteenth century, Jamaica was used primarily for the production of sugar on large plantations worked by African slave labor. During this century, numerous slaves escaped into the wild areas of the interior and established fugitive settlements, often joining the Maroons, slaves who had escaped earlier, largely during the confusion surrounding Spain's loss of control of the island. Sugar production declined in the nineteenth century due to the abolition of slavery and to changes in British tariff laws that made sugar production less lucrative. The resultant economic hardship, combined with the hidebound policies of the British-controlled government of Governor Eyre, led to demonstrations in 1865. Under the leadership of Paul Bogle and George William Gordon, these demonstrations became a full-scale rebellion, the so-called Morant Bay Uprising. The rebellion was brutally put down; over 400 rebels were killed; 600 were flogged. Bogle and Gordon were hanged and have subsequently become recognized as national heroes. As a result of the rebellion and the issues to which it brought British government attention, Eyre was recalled and Jamaica became a Crown Colony, ruled directly from Britain.

Under the Crown Colony, the capital was moved to Kingston, which gradually grew to central prominence on the island, though it had to be rebuilt after being largely destroyed in an earthquake in 1907. Banana production was encouraged as a supplement to the flagging coffee and sugar industries, and a general program of development was implemented. The vast majority of the people of Jamaica remained dismally poor, however, and were particularly hard hit by the impact of the Great Depression of the 1930s, a phenomenon made even worse when a blight destroyed most of the island's banana production. By 1938, labor unrest spread across the island (and throughout much of the Caribbean), sometimes leading to violence as the colonial authorities sought to repress the organization of workers. Norman Manley, at the head of the People's National Party (PNP), and Alexander Bustamante, at the head of the Jamaica Labour Party (JLP), soon emerged not only as labor leaders but as leaders in a growing independence movement.

As elsewhere in the Caribbean, this independence movement was to some extent derailed by the coming of World War II, though a new constitution, dictating universal suffrage and a measure of Jamaican self-rule, was established in 1944. Economic conditions improved somewhat during the 1950s as Jamaica gradually moved toward independence, which was granted in 1962, with Bustamante becoming the first prime minister of the new nation. Economic development continued through the 1960s, but did not keep up with population growth. In addition, the growing economic gap between the island's mostly black workers and the mostly white managerial class led to increasing social tensions. The Black Power movement, influenced by the Civil Rights movement in the United States, rose to the forefront of militant social protest, to some extent drawing upon the distinctive black nationalism of the Rastafarian movement that had begun in Jamaica during the difficult days of the Depression and that gained increasing worldwide attention in the late 1960s and the 1970s, largely due to the prominence of *reggae* superstar Bob Marley.

Michael Manley, son of Norman Manley, became prime minister in 1972, heading the party founded by his father. Though Manley was almost entirely white, his socialist policies reached out to the poor black population of Jamaica. He and other PNP leaders often adopted the dress and manners of the black lower classes, and they made a special effort to reach out to the formerly marginalized Rastafarians. Manley established increasingly close relations with the Castro government in Cuba. In 1974, he announced his intention of making Jamaica a socialist state and declared his plan to begin the nationalization of Jamaica's largest industries and most valuable resources. This plan was largely put into effect between 1974 and 1978, while Manley and his PNP government won a sweeping reelection in 1976. A new spirit of hope and optimism energized the common people of Jamaica, which moved to the forefront of

Third-World politics. However, Jamaica's white upper classes grew increasingly wary of Manley's policies. Meanwhile, frightened by Manley's initial successes, capitalist enterprises began to withdraw from contacts with Jamaica, isolating the island and leading to a downturn in the economy. By 1980, economic conditions led to the defeat of the PNP in general elections. Edward Seaga, now leading the JLP, became the new prime minister.

The Seaga government, with close ties to the Reagan administration, brought Jamaica back into the capitalist fold and drew large amounts of foreign aid from the United States. In 1983, the JLP won all sixty seats in the Jamaican Parliament via questionable elections in which the PNP refused to participate because of their obvious unfairness. But the tide of public opinion was increasingly with Manley and the PNP, who swept back into power in a landslide victory in the 1989 elections. Manley, in his second term, pursued more moderate policies and moved more cautiously toward social justice, while attempting to maintain contacts with the United States. Ill health forced him to retire in 1992, handing over the reigns of government to his lieutenant, P. J. Patterson. Patterson, reelected in the 1997 elections, has continued Manley's new, more moderate policies, with an emphasis on private economic development, though with little success. On Jamaican history and politics, see Barrett 1997, Holt 1992, Payne 1995, and Stephens 1986.

Notes

1. In a later scene, Ivan returns to the country after several years in urban Kingston, only to find that his traditional society has been largely destroyed by the impact of modernity. Ivan, realizing that he quite literally cannot go home again, is despondent when he finds that noise, pollution, and commodification have come even to the country.

2. The Rastafarian religion, which has its roots in the Jamaican anticolonial struggles of the 1930s, holds that Ethiopian Emperor Haile Selassie, also known as Ras Tafari, was in fact the second incarnation of Christ. Rastafarianism is thus an offshoot of Christianity, but with important African influences added. At the same time, the movement is as much cultural and political as it is religious and clearly draws its energies from attempts of working-class Jamaicans to establish a sense of their own cultural identities apart from those thrust upon them by their colonial rulers and, later, by global capitalism and the postcolonial bourgeoisie of Jamaica. On Rastafarianism and its political implications, see Barrett 1997, Chevannes 1994, Turner and Ferguson 1994, and Waters 1989.

3. Among other things, Ramsey's attempts to promote conventional Protestantism can be seen as an attempt to counter the potentially subversive power of Rastafarianism.

4. The more politically aware Rastafarians are also fascinated by American film in *The Harder They Come*, but at least they have the insight to side with the Indians rather than the cowboys (205).

5. For an extended discussion of techniques of colonial power, see Booker 1997.

6. On *reggae* and its political potential, particularly its links to Rastafarianism, see Cooper 1996, King and Jensen 1995, Potash 1997, and Waters 1989.

7. The Jamaican term "rhygin," probably taken from the English "raging," indicates aggressiveness, vigor, and passion.

8. This strategy can be understood in terms of the concept of "national language." See Edward Kamau Brathwaite 1984.

Chapter 7

Zee Edgell:
Beka Lamb

Beka Lamb was published in 1982, the year after the colony of British Honduras became the independent nation of Belize. The book, which was the cowinner of the British Fawcett Society Book Prize, thus became the first published novel about Belize and the historical process through which the new nation was formed. The book might therefore be considered a historical novel; on the other hand, it details Belizean history through the eyes of its title character, focusing on her personal development, as well. Indeed, though it directly covers only a few months in the life of its fourteen-year-old protagonist, *Beka Lamb* can rightly be considered a bildungsroman, both because these months are crucial to the evolution of the consciousness of Beka Lamb and because, via numerous flashbacks, the book indicates Beka's development over a longer period of time.

The time period covered by the book, which occurs during the mid-1950s, is also a crucial one for British Honduras, the colony in which Beka lives. An emerging independence movement, which Beka's grandmother, Miss Ivy, adamantly supports, is gaining power that will eventually lead to decolonization and the establishment of the nation of Belize. Meanwhile, the very success of this independence movement leads to the imposition of increasingly repressive policies by the colonial government. Thus, one of the central events that runs through the text involves the arrest and imprisonment, on charges of sedition, of Prichad and Gadsden, two anticolonial activists supported by Miss Ivy and her circle. Moreover, the situation in British Honduras is further complicated by the fact of long-standing claims by neighboring Guatemala of sovereignty over the area. It is within this

complex political climate that Beka begins to gain an understanding of the
adult world around her.

Importantly, Beka develops this understanding in the midst of a historical crisis, though she herself is mostly unaware of this fact. For example, a
year before the main events described in the book, the home of the Hartleys,
a rich creole family with important connections within the colonial government, was stoned by demonstrators who subsequently marched on the British governor's house, as well. Told about these events by her grandmother a
year later, Beka is quite surprised to learn of the depth of anti-British feeling in the colony. To her, "things British had nearly always been things
best," and much of her official education has involved reminders of the
grandeur of the British Empire and the benevolence of the colony's British
rulers (54).

One of the central events related in *Beka Lamb* is the annual celebration
of the National Day to commemorate the defeat of the Spanish fleet by a
British force (consisting largely of black slaves) in the battle of St. George's
Cay just off the coast of Belize on September 10, 1798. The memory of this
important historical event is largely a matter of pride for the people of
British Honduras, despite the fact that the victory led to their colonization
by the British. It is thus a sign of their secondary, colonial condition that
their "National Day" actually commemorates the colonization of their nation by another. Further, as Granny Ivy notes to Beka, the Belizeans like to
remember the central role played by blacks in the battle, but like to pretend
that the "slavery part . . . hardly ever existed" (46).

But, given the tense political situation that obtains in the colony during
the events narrated in *Beka Lamb*, the National Day celebrated in the book
is a very special one. Occurring in the midst of Belizean agitation for independence, the holiday for once becomes a focal point not for celebration
but for protest. Indeed, Radison, the colony's British governor, is forced to
remain in his mansion, avoiding the normal festivities in Battlefield Park
for fear that his presence will cause the protests to erupt in violence. Meanwhile, this being the 1950s and the height of the Cold War, Radison attempts to capitalize on anticommunist feelings by branding the members of
the People's Independence Party as communists, thus hoping to make their
cause unpopular (146).

Given such episodes, it is clear that *Beka Lamb* is a highly political novel
that goes well beyond a mere evocation of adolescent experience. Politics
are so much a part of the texture of Beka's adolescent world that, when she
and Toycie Qualo, her best friend, play make-believe, Beka pretends to be a
politician. In fact, a central aspect of the book is its careful interweaving of
the personal experience of the title character with the public experience of

Belize. Meanwhile, this dialogue between public and private experience is carefully supplemented by an additional dialogue between tradition (largely inherited from Africa) and modernity (imposed on the colony by their European rulers, but also a central inspiration for the emergent independence movement). As Simon Gikandi notes, "what is unique about *Beka Lamb* . . . is Zee Edgell's ability to develop a tense dialectic between the subject on one hand, and her community and colonial society on the other hand, without falling back on the old and worn-out polarities of tradition and modernity" (Gikandi 1992, 221).

This project begins in the very first sentence of the book, which establishes the mixture of elements that will characterize its remainder: "On a warm November day Beka Lamb won an essay contest at St. Cecilia's Academy, situated not far from the front gate of His Majesty's Prison on Milpa Lane" (1). The basic thrust of this information, like many of Beka's childhood memories, is positive: we are greeted with the good news of Beka's success in the contest, while the setting on a "warm November day" suggests an almost idyllic climate. We will later learn, however, that the warm weather of British Honduras is hardly a boon to Beka, who has little tolerance for heat and in fact suffers a great deal from it. Moreover, we will learn that the colony is plagued by hurricanes; indeed, the central climactic event of the book will be a damaging hurricane in which Toycie is killed. None of this is indicated in the first sentence, of course, but Beka's personal victory is announced amid a framework, consisting of her Catholic school and the British colonial prison, that provides a simultaneous announcement of large and (to the young Beka) often mysterious institutional forces that surround her in her childhood. Indeed, the Catholic Church stands throughout the text as a dominant ideological force that imposes the terms of European civilization on the colony, with the military might of the British Empire (symbolized by the prison) always available as a backup should this ideological domination fail to hold sway.

In the second sentence, we quickly learn that Beka has not always been so successful and that her victory in this contest represents a new departure in her life. "It seemed to her family," we are told, "that overnight Beka changed from what her mother called a 'flat-rate Belize creole' into a person with 'high mind'" (1). Again, this sentence is rich with meaning. Not only does it suggest a sudden change in Beka's life, but it also indicates the extent to which her sense of herself is determined by the perceptions of others. After all, the sentence does not say that Beka herself actually changed; it only says that it "seemed" to her family that she had changed. And, finally, this change of perception is couched not in merely personal terms, but in terms of a rise in social class. Beka's newfound success elevates her from the status of a common, run-of-the-mill creole to a person whose intellectual achievements set her apart from the norm. Importantly, however, these achievements are defined in terms set not by Belizeans themselves but by the outside agency of the Catholic Church—with the clear implication that there is something inherently inferior about creoles who have not been thoroughly Westernized.

The opening passage then continues with a statement by Miss Ivy that "befo' time" Beka would have had no chance to win such a contest. Beka's change in status is thus directly related to a more fundamental change in historical conditions, a change that offers educational opportunities that would earlier have been unavailable to girls of her race and class. Among other things, this reminder introduces the crucial topic of gender into the book. Moreover, it introduces Granny Ivy's consistent concern with the differences between "befo' time" and the present, differences toward which Ivy is herself often highly ambivalent. Yet, she is the book's principal carrier of tradition and oral history, and it is primarily her storytelling that provides Beka with a sense of connection to the past world of her ancestors. This connection, given the unsteady political conditions in British Honduras, is growing increasingly tenuous, yet Miss Ivy endorses Beka's attempt to get a modern education and helps out with chores around the house so that her granddaughter will have more time to study (2). And, as a charter member of the People's Independence Party, Miss Ivy is a strong proponent of political change. She also supports modernization in general, and part of her political program involves demands for improvements in the local infrastructure to provide for better public safety (3).

Miss Ivy's understanding of the need for modernization is vividly symbolized in the text in a story she tells Beka concerning a circus that came to Belize once in her own childhood. The circus featured a polar bear, kept cool in the semitropical heat through the application of ice supplied by the local ice plant. Unfortunately, the plant broke down soon after the circus arrived, and the bear, deprived of ice, soon died from the heat. This event, which still brings tears to Miss Ivy's eyes decades later, is for her a symbol of the substandard and second-rate conditions that apply throughout the colony, where "nothin' lasts" and "tings bruk down" (16).

For Miss Ivy, modern European technology can be an important key to improving life in Belize. However, she understands that, as long as the area remains colonial, it will have access only to the leftovers of European modernity. For her, then, the key to genuine modernization is independence. In this, she strongly disagrees with Beka's father, Bill Lamb, who also supports modernization, but seems to feel that British rule provides the best framework within which to modernize Belize. He is par-

ticularly concerned about the threat of a Guatemalan takeover, regarding
ongoing British rule as the only way to ensure that Belize will not be
absorbed by its larger neighbor. Bill works as a bookkeeper for Blanco's
Import Commission Agency and is thus a figure of the colonial bourgeoisie, dedicated to working within the existing colonial system to try to
build a better life for himself and his family. Bill and Ivy thus carry on
frequent, sometimes heated, debates about politics, so that the texture of
Beka's home life is highly political.

Such ambivalence runs through the entire text of *Beka Lamb*, which presents British Honduras as a society on the verge of monumental changes,
the consequences of which will be both positive and negative. The loss of
any organic connection with the traditions of the past is one of the prices
paid by the people of the colony for increasing modernization. Thus, Granny
Straker, Beka's ancient great-grandmother is depicted as providing, through
her personal memory, one of the last remaining links with the past. When
Granny Straker dies, this link is lost, though her funeral supplies an occasion for an exercise not only in collective identity, but also in communal
memory:

> It was more than a funeral they watched. In a way, it was a small
> lesson in community history, and everyone, for those minutes, was
> a diligent scholar. Belizeans did not often articulate what they did
> know of their history, even amongst themselves. By and large, most
> people preferred to forget the time that had gone before. But on
> certain occasions, and especially at the funerals of the very aged,
> through the use of innuendos and euphemisms, a feeling was com-
> municated, and this was understood. (63)

This feeling, however, is short-lived, and the death of Granny Straker
signals another step toward the loss of such feelings altogether. Indeed, Beka's
mother, Lilla, explains to her soon after the funeral Granny Straker's own
recollection that the British colonial government, with the support of the
Catholic Church, had, in the "old days," insisted on the abandonment of
tradition in its effort to impose modern ways on the colony. Thus, "the
more you left behind the old ways, the more acceptable you were to the
powerful people in the government and the churches who had the power to
change a black person's life" (70).

Such abandonment of long-held traditions inevitably results in a certain cultural impoverishment. In keeping with the fundamental ambivalence of *Beka Lamb* toward the historical phenomenon of modernity,
though, Beka's mother reminds her that many of the traditional practices
squelched by the British were probably "harmful, health-wise and so on"

(70). Indeed, Lilla herself is generally a proponent of modernity, regarding the "old ways" largely as a matter of superstitions that stand in the way of progress, so that, left unchecked, "the old ways will poison the new" (66). Meanwhile, within the complex ethnic and cultural mix that is modern Belize, the opposition between modernity and tradition is also related to the identification of differences between ethnic groups. In particular, the creole population to which Beka and her family belong is largely characterized by having accepted modern practices at the expense of the loss of tradition. In contrast, the colony's Carib population, made up of the descendants of escaped slaves who had formerly come to the region in an attempt to flee the crippling consequences of European-dominated modernity, are characterized by a continuing reliance on traditions inherited from their African ancestors. As a result, the Carib and creole populations, despite their common African ancestry, tend to interact very little and to regard one another with suspicion.

The racial and ethnic divisions that characterize Belizean society thus arise not from any traditional animosities among Belizeans, but from oppositions directly caused by the experience of slavery and colonialism and the consequent historical movement from tradition to modernity. And this historical movement closely parallels the adolescent development of Beka herself: Increasing maturity and experience open up a new world of opportunities, but they also separate her from a childhood that has been largely happy. The element of loss that is associated with Beka's developing maturity is represented in narrative form primarily through the loss of her friend, Toycie, whose tragic death is actually the culmination of a whole series of personal tragedies. Toycie is an excellent student and a talented musician; she is also three years older than Beka, and it is clear that Beka looks up to her as an admired role model. Toycie's experiences thus demonstrate to Beka the potential injustices of the adult world in a particularly powerful way, introducing an element of personal crisis that parallels the public crisis in the society around her.

Toycie's downfall begins when she becomes romantically involved with Emilio Villanueva, the son of her guitar teacher. But neither Emilio's mother nor Miss Eila, Toycie's aunt and guardian, approves of the relationship, so Toycie, with the help of Beka, has to keep it a secret. Again, however, what at first seems to be a purely personal experience turns out to have powerful social and political overtones. Emilio, part Spanish and part Mayan, represents an element of the society of British Honduras that, among other things, is aligned in the minds of many with the Guatemalan attempt to claim the colony. And it is clear that the social unacceptability of the relationship between Toycie and Emilio is largely inspired by this politically-charged ethnic difference. Toycie, young as she is, sees Emilio only as a dashing young boy, an impressive swimmer and diver who seems to her a romantic figure. And neither she nor Beka, in their youthful innocence, is concerned with Emilio's ethnic heritage, despite the fact that they accept the aversion of most of their elders to Guatemalan rule.

The political innocence of the girls is demonstrated in the text in a key scene in which they examine the beautiful guitar given Toycie by Mrs. Leigh, the wife of a British colonial official for whom Toycie served as a baby-sitter and Miss Eila worked as a housekeeper. The guitar quickly becomes Toycie's most valued possession, and the two girls regard it almost with awe. Then they discover a label on the inside of the guitar indicating that the instrument was made in Spain. Beka is instantly alarmed, reminding Toycie that Guatemala's claim to Belize is based on rights inherited from Spain, which was once granted colonial control of the area by the pope. Mortified at the political incorrectness of the otherwise beautiful instrument, the two girls see no choice but to obliterate the Spanish label and substitute something else. Toycie suggests "England" as an alternative label, given that Mrs. Leigh was English, but Beka reminds her that the current British colonial governor has been harsh in his treatment of the People's Independence Party. In an innocent expression of national consciousness, Toycie thus decides to change the label to read "Made in Belize."

In the colonial environment of British Honduras, even the most seemingly innocent and private experiences have powerful political overtones. It should perhaps come as no surprise, then, that Toycie's seemingly idyllic relationship with Emilio leads to disastrous consequences. When the sisters at St. Cecilia's discover that Toycie is pregnant, they immediately expel her from school, despite the fact that she is such a good student and is nearing graduation. They then turn a deaf ear to all appeals on Toycie's behalf, in the name of morality and "conscience."

Sister Virgil, in fact, responds to these appeals with the imperious reminder that "the rate of illegitimacy is quite high" in the colony, with the obvious racist implication that the citizens of the colony tend toward immoral behavior. It is, of course, the Catholic Church that has made sex education, birth control, and abortion unavailable in the colony, thereby ensuring that the rate of illegitimacy will remain high. Beka may not be entirely aware of the full hypocrisy of Sister Virgil's haughty attitude, but she is certainly aware that an injustice has been done. She is also aware of the role played by gender in this injustice: though it is clear that Emilio is the father of Toycie's child, no one even considers expelling Emilio from his school because of the pregnancy.

Emilio himself reacts to Toycie's pregnancy with a cruel rejection, partly because the two partners have not actually had intercourse, and he is unaware that the sexual play in which he and Toycie have been engaged could cause pregnancy. He thus declares that he must not be the father, suggesting that she has had intercourse with someone else. Worse, he declares that he could never marry Toycie anyway, because even the extent of sexual activity in which she has engaged with him renders her unsuitable as a bride. As Toycie explains to Beka, "He could never marry anybody who played around with him like I did, because if I can do it before marriage, after marriage I would do it with somebody else and his mamacita would collapse if he married somebody that wasn't a virgin because she's so religious" (109).

Through Toycie's experience, Beka learns important lessons about both religious hypocrisy and masculine bias. Of course, Toycie herself is affected even more dramatically. Distraught, she "falls" from a bridge, with hints that she may have jumped. In any case, she is badly hurt and loses the baby. She also suffers a breakdown and is confined in the Belize Mental Asylum, euphemistically referred to as the "Sea Breeze Hotel." The staff of the asylum genuinely seems to want to help, but conditions there are nevertheless prisonlike, echoing the carceral imagery introduced via the British colonial prison mentioned in the first sentence of the book. Indeed, in a further reinforcement of this imagery, we learn that the asylum overlooks an area known as Barracks Green, where the German residents of the town had been incarcerated in a small concentration camp during World War II.

Soon afterward, Toycie, who is still confused and distracted despite occasional signs of improvement, is released from the asylum and taken into the countryside by Miss Eila. When the hurricane hits, Toycie wanders out into the storm and is killed by a falling mango tree. Her death is thus apparently accidental, though it may be that she wandered into the storm as a form of suicide. At any rate, just as the storm hits, Beka is finishing up her prize-winning essay, the essay that will open educational opportunities that had been closed off to the less-fortunate Toycie. The winning of the contest will ultimately represent an important turning point in Beka's life, among other things allowing her to surmount the tendency toward lying that serves in the text as a marker of her uncertain relation to the reality around her.

Beka's essay itself provides important thematic reinforcement to the theme of tradition versus modernity that runs through the entire novel. It is itself an exercise in history, which she plans to base primarily on the oral accounts provided by Mr. Rabatu, an extremely old man who had been one of the acolytes who went to Fort George to greet the first Sisters of Charity to arrive in Belize many decades earlier. Unfortunately, Mr. Rabatu can remember very little about the event except that the nuns wore veils in an effort to hide their feminine nature and thus prevent the local men, presumably unable to control their natural impulses, from becoming sexually excited by the white women. This memory leads Mr. Rabatu off into a digression about the increasing wantonness of women in the present day. Beka thus gets relatively little information from him and has to supplement his story with a study of written documents from the library. Among other things, she includes a great deal of historical information about social and economic conditions in the late nineteenth century.

Beka's essay thus suggests the gradual supplantation of traditional oral histories by more modern methods of historical narration, though it is important that Beka's written history serves to an extent to preserve the past. Tradition and modernity are not opposed in a simple way, but are involved in a complex dialogue. Meanwhile, Mr. Rabatu's account of the arrival of the veiled nuns suggests that the early Catholic missionaries to the area accepted the typical racist notion that nonwhite men are somehow irresistibly attracted to white women. Such notions were particularly prevalent in the colonial world and form the flip side of the notion, promulgated by Sister Virgil and the other teachers at St. Cecilia's, that nonwhite women are inherently promiscuous and therefore prone to having illegitimate children.

Of course, such stereotypes are part of the attempt by Europeans to assert their moral superiority and thus justify their colonial role at various sites around the globe. There is also clearly an element of sexual fantasy involved in these visions of the unrestrained sexual conduct that Europeans might expect to encounter in the colonial world. Such sexual fantasies were, in fact, a central part of the network of stereotypes that Edward Said has described as "Orientalism." Thus, Said notes that, "just as the various colonial possessions—quite apart from their economic benefit to metropolitan Europe—were useful as places to send wayward sons, superfluous populations of delinquents, poor people, and other undesirables, so the Orient was a place where one could look for sexual experiences unobtainable in Europe" (Said 1979, 190).

Said, focusing particularly on the Middle East but in ways that have implications for the non-European world as a whole, notes that European scholars and writers, especially from the nineteenth century onward, have tended to describe non-Europeans in rigidly stereotypical ways that have little to do with reality but are primarily designed to make Europeans feel good about themselves. For Said, in short, such stereotypes really say more about Europeans than non-Europeans. He concludes, in fact, that a central component of the European sense of identity is "the idea of European identity as a superior one in comparison with all the non-European peoples and cultures" (Said 1979, 7).

It is against the background of such demeaning stereotypes that a colonial subject such as Beka Lamb must attempt to develop a sense of her own identity. And the sexual element that was central to these stereotypes clearly makes this process even more complicated for a *female* colonial subject, especially one educated in Catholic schools that consistently remind her of the sinfulness of her own nature and of the necessity for overcoming this sinfulness.

It is little wonder, then, that Beka plans, after graduating from school, to leave the colonial environment of Belize. Indeed, she wants to get as far from Belize and into as different an environment as she possibly can. Miss Ivy, the Belizean nationalist, is greatly disappointed by this attitude, which she describes as "ungrateful" and attributes to Beka's colonial education, which teaches her to regard the outside world as superior to Belize (147). By the end of the book, however, Beka and her grandmother are on good terms, and Beka prepares to face the future. The book thus ends where it began. On the night that Beka wins the essay contest, as announced on the first page, she stays home alone while Miss Ivy attends an important political meeting. Alone with her thoughts, Beka observes a sort of private wake for Toycie, whose family had not been able to afford the public ceremony of a real wake. As the evening ends, Beka feels that she has appropriately mourned for Toycie and is ready to move forward.

Historical Background

Belize is a small republic on the Caribbean coast of Central America. It has a population of approximately 200,000 and a land area of about 8,870 sq. mi. (22,970 sq. km). Belize City (population 40,000), the capital until 1970, is the largest city and major port, though Belmopan is now the capital. Most of the interior is heavily forested, and the production of lumber, especially mahogany and cedar, is an important industry. Sugar, however, is the main export, while clothing, fruit, and fish are also produced and exported. Tourism has recently become the focus of the economy, especially "green" tourism, concentrated on beaches, coral reefs, and the rain forest. English is the official language, though the population consists of a rich mixture of peoples of African, Mayan, and Spanish American descent. The literacy rate is about 93 percent.

Belize was founded as a base from which British buccaneers attacked Spanish ships in the early seventeenth century. Spain and Britain fought for possession of the area until the definitive defeat of the Spanish in the battle of St. George's Cay in 1798 solidified British control. Since 1821, Guatemala has repeatedly stated its own claims to the area, a situation that continued to cause political tensions in Belize for the next 170 years. From 1862 to 1884, the colony was officially administered by the British governor in Jamaica. Belize then came under the rule of its own colonial government, until 1964, when the colony was granted internal autonomy by the British. In 1981, Belize gained full independence from Britain, and Guatemala officially recognized that independence, giving up its own claims, in 1991.

Because of its British colonial heritage and its English language, Belize has long been culturally and economically linked more to the Caribbean than to the rest of Central America. See Bolland 1988, Fernandez 1989, and Peedle 1999.

Chapter 8

Earl Lovelace:
The Wine of Astonishment

Earl Lovelace's *The Wine of Astonishment* (1982) is in many ways a paradigm of the postcolonial novel. It addresses, within the specific context of colonial Trinidad, many of the issues that have been crucial to the project of the postcolonial novel as a whole. Lovelace's book is centrally concerned with the various forms of oppression, based on class, race, and gender, that are suffered by the colonial subjects of Trinidad. It is also concerned with resistance to oppression, particularly with the ways in which the people of Trinidad have struggled to maintain a sense of their own cultural identity in opposition to the identities that are forced upon them by the colonial situation. Finally, this contest of identities is presented within a concrete historical context in which the opposition between colonizer and colonized often becomes an opposition between tradition and modernity. In *The Wine of Astonishment* (and in the more general case of the Caribbean as a whole), modernity is represented not only by the imperial center of metropolitan Britain, but by the United States, which, during and after World War II, becomes a major cultural and economic force that in many ways represents an alternative (though not necessarily a preferable one) to British colonial domination.

The Wine of Astonishment is set in the rural community of Bonasse, in the interior of Trinidad. The life of this community is very much centered in the Spiritual Baptist Church, which provides not only a spiritual, but also a cultural center for the people of the community. In this sense, *The Wine of Astonishment* indicates, as Torres-Saillant notes, "the intimacy of Caribbean letters with religion" (Torres-Saillant 1997, 86). But there is more than conventional religion at stake in Lovelace's depiction of this church. The forms of worship practiced in this church have strong roots in traditional African culture, and the members of the church see it as a specifically black alternative to the Catholic or Anglican churches, which they believe to be oriented toward "the whiteman and his brown tools." This charismatic church, with its emphasis on celebration, is meant to offer spiritual solace to those who suffer in the material world. Its singing, shouting, and speaking in tongues are designed, as the narrator points out, to "carry the Word to the downtrodden and the forgotten and the lame and the beaten, and we touch black people soul" (32). But the church also provides a central gathering place for the people of Bonasse, a social center where they can discuss "how the corn growing, how the children doing, for what price cocoa selling, and the men could know which brother they should lend a hand to the coming week, and the sisters could find out who sick from the congregation so we could go and sit with her a little and help her out with the cooking for her children or the washing or the ironing" (33).

This church is designed to help the people of Bonasse bear the suffering that is thrust upon them by their colonial condition. However, by providing a spiritual release and escape from the reality of poverty and oppression, the church provides a sort of safety valve that clearly decreases the likelihood that its members will take any concrete action to oppose poverty and oppression in the material world. To this extent, the church functions directly in the interest of Trinidad's British colonial rulers, who had, after all, actively encouraged the evolution of Christianity in their African and Caribbean colonies for this very reason. But the Spiritual Baptist Church is far more than an opiate of the masses of Trinidad. The church, by acting as a rallying point for the community as a whole, provides a potential focal point for the kind of collective action that is crucial to any effective political resistance. Moreover, this particular church has evolved according to its own logic outside of British control. It provides the people of Bonasse not only with a collective cultural identity, but with an identity that is specifically black and working-class and thus potentially anticolonial.

There is little wonder, then, that the British rulers of Trinidad found this church a threat to their authority. Indeed, the religious practices of the Spiritual Baptist Church were banned in Trinidad and Tobago by a colonial edict issued in 1917, supposedly because the worship services of the church were so loud that they represented a public nuisance and because these services were not truly Christian but were in fact conducive to heathen savagery. *The Wine of Astonishment* traces the impact of this historical ban on the fictional community of Bonasse, focusing especially on the years from the beginning of World War II up until 1951, when the ban was lifted. Narrated in Trinidadian dialect by Eva Dorcas, wife of Bee Dorcas, the minister of the town's Spiritual Baptist Church, the book details the attempts of the community to maintain a sense of its cultural identity amid this suppression of a central form for the expression of this identity, both through the exploration of alternative forms and through an attempt to keep the church going despite the law.

In particular, Bee, who functions in the text as a figure of patience and perseverance, tries to maintain the church by eliminating the specific practices of worship that are banned by the law, thus conducting the kind of subdued and "dignified" service of which the colonial administration approves. This approach, which essentially represents a de-Africanization of the church, at least allows the church to continue to function as a sort of community gathering place. However, this approach is acceptable to the government largely because it removes precisely the elements that made the church so dangerous as an alternative cultural practice in the first place. As a result, the former centrality of the church to the community of Bonasse is seriously diminished, and the community increasingly finds itself without a viable cultural center.

In the absence of an effective Spiritual Baptist Church, the community seeks other alternative cultural centers. Most obviously, the local store run by Buntin, one of the black men of the town, becomes a crucial gathering place. As Nigel Thomas points out, Buntin's shop is "a focal point of community nurturing, an unofficial education centre, comparable to the village squares in many West African communities" (Thomas 1991b, 2). Thomas further notes that Buntin is cast as a sort of "oral historian," who spends more time reminding his customers of their black cultural heritage than in conducting commerce. Meanwhile, the men of Bonasse gather in the store to discuss politics, crops, and many of the same topics they had formerly discussed in church. Nevertheless, a store is a place of commerce, and this shift from Bee's church to Buntin's store as a cultural center already suggests a growing impact of modernization, with its attendant tendency toward commercialization, commodification, and consumerism.

The ultimate fate of Buntin's store also provides a reminder of the unavailability of economic opportunity to the colonial subjects of Trinidad. Because he is black, Buntin is continually denied loans that might allow him to expand his business and remain more competitive with newer stores that are arising in the area, especially the store run by the Chinese shopkeeper, Chin. The situation becomes particularly critical during World War II, when the presence of a substantial military force in Trinidad brings an influx of dollars and commercialization. Chin, able to get proper financing, responds by expanding his store and stocking his shelves with new goods. Buntin, without financing, is unable to compete and finds his business rapidly going downhill. Instead of new goods on his shelves, he merely has pictures of black heroes such as Marcus Garvey, Joe Louis, Jack Johnson, and Haile Selassie. But, however valuable these heroes might be as a source of black cultural pride, they do little to help keep Buntin's shop afloat in the context of the newly commercialized Trinidad. As a result, Eva complains, "Buntin shop going to pieces. He giving credit and people not paying him, and Buntin don't even look like he care how his business go once the men come in his shop to talk stupidness about the war or Marcus Garvey" (75).

Indeed, the American presence in Trinidad during World War II is depicted throughout *The Wine of Astonishment* as an unequivocal cultural disaster for the people of Trinidad. The flow of dollars lures young men and women away from rural areas into centers such as Port of Spain, where the dollars are concentrated. This movement removes young people from their families and communities, leaving them rootless and alone in impersonal urban settings where those around them are not friends, neighbors, and relatives, but competitors for the same dollars. This environment, Eva notes, is characterized by "people going away from each other, becoming strangers to each other right here with each man fighting for himself" (74). Even worse, this new spirit of alienation and cutthroat competition is not confined to the city, but reaches all the way back to rural communities such as Bonasse, where the former sense of communal solidarity is replaced by "every man for himself" (78).

In the underdeveloped colonial context of Trinidad, this new spirit of capitalism hardly leads to triumphant success for most Trinidadians. Lacking the skills, training, and resources necessary for big-time business success, young Trinidadians struggle for dollars any way they can, which means that, at best, they work as servants or menial laborers. But it mostly means that young men become hustlers or thieves and young women become prostitutes. A central figure of this phenomenon is the hustler and war profiteer, Mitchell, who establishes important connections on the U.S. military base, where he serves as a native informant for a gullible American officer who decides to write a book about Voodoo and who believes whatever nonsense Mitchell feeds him. Mitchell parlays this connection into a thriving criminal enterprise, selling black-market goods (mostly stolen from the base), lending money, and generally flaunting his newfound wealth, feeling he has the right to make lewd sexual advances to women on the street because he can afford to pay them off if they complain (19).

This new "prosperity" also introduces new class divisions into a Trinidadian society already informed by violent class conflict, and especially by official aggression against the lower classes (Brathwaite 1975, 132). There are, after all, some young people (mostly young men) who are more educated and perhaps more talented than others. For these elite few, the opportunities offered by colonial society have always been greater, and this situation intensifies during World War II. As Eva notes, the entire direction of twentieth-century Trinidadian history, even in rural communities like Bonasse, has been toward the placing of a greater and greater premium on education, as the warrior is gradually replaced by the scholar as the "chief figure" in village society (46). Scholars play this central role because they are seen as potential leaders who can presumably help the entire community succeed within the increasingly complex context of modernity. On the other hand, in a motif that is central to much of Lovelace's fiction (especially *The Schoolmaster* [1968] and *Salt* [1996]), education tends to alienate this talented few from their rural, working-class roots, making it difficult for them to continue to feel that they genuinely belong to the community they are supposed to represent. This situation is exacerbated during World War II, when increased economic opportunities for the fortunate few introduce a growing economic gap between the educated and the uneducated.

In *The Wine of Astonishment*, this phenomenon is represented primarily in the figure of Ivan Morton, a village boy who shows great promise as a student, raising hopes that he can become an effective community leader. Unfortunately, Morton fails to make sufficiently high scores on his examinations and is thus denied a college education. He does, however, manage to get a job teaching in a Catholic school, though in order to do so he has to abandon his Spiritual Baptist roots and convert to Catholicism. This opportunistic conversion then becomes typical of all Morton's activities as he becomes more and more selfish in his ambitions, and less and less connected to the community from which he came. The high status enjoyed by scholars helps him to win the love of Eulalie, a beautiful local girl who is also being courted by the handsome and virile Bolo, a champion athlete. But Eulalie, despite her beauty, is dark-skinned and uneducated. Morton thus does not regard her as the kind of wife who would further his professional ambitions. When she becomes pregnant, Morton abandons her in order to marry another woman with lighter skin and better English grammar.

Most of the citizens of Bonasse, still looking to Morton for leadership, forgive him his abandonment of Eulalie, concluding that "Eulalie look for her own trouble." By the time of the disruption of Trinidadian society brought about by World War II, Eulalie has been forced into prostitution, and Morton has continued to move further and further from his roots. When he moves out of the house built by his father and into the mansion formerly occupied by the local British plantation owner, his transformation from man of the people to comprador bourgeois is complete. He denies not only his original religion and class position, but also his race. "We can't be white," he acknowledges in a conversation with Bee, "but we can act white" (13). Elected to represent the people of Bonasse in the island's legislative council, it is clear that Morton (who comes mockingly to be known in Bonasse as "Mr. Civilize") represents only himself, which he believes he can best do by representing the interests of international capital and ignoring the interests of his original constituency.

Bolo serves in *The Wine of Astonishment* as a counterpoint to Morton, not only in his rivalry for the hand of Eulalie, but also in his staunch refusal to sell out to capitalist modernization. Thus, as Maureen Warner-Lewis notes, Bolo and Morton are central figures in the text's meditation on leadership within the colonial context of Trinidad, a motif that is central to all of Lovelace's fiction (Warner-Lewis 1987). In *The Wine of Astonishment*, the patient Bee provides a third (and ultimately favored) alternative, pointing a way beyond the opposition between Morton's total complicity with colonial authority and Bolo's violent, and ultimately suicidal, resistance to it. Bolo is a champion stickfighter and thus, in an earlier age, would have occupied the central leadership role now occupied by Morton. As Lovelace notes in an interview in response to a question concerning the central role played by stickfighting throughout his fiction, Trinidadian stickfighting is a symbol of "warriorhood." However, in this highly ritualized form, the warrior "is not the war machine that you see in Western tradition. It would be more correct to see him as an artist" (Thomas 1991a, 13). Stickfighting remains an important cultural practice in Trinidad, and a champion like Bolo remains an influential figure, despite the growing emphasis on education and modernity. During World War II, however, this situation changes dramatically when the British colonial administration, presumably for "security" reasons, bans the annual carnival, another central form of Trinidadian cultural expression, and a principal venue for crucial Trinidadian cultural practices such as steel band competitions, calypso competitions, and (of particular importance in *The Wine of Astonishment*) stickfighting competitions.

Bolo is thus dealt another blow to his dignity and self-respect, denied the chance to practice the art that makes him someone truly special, despite the fact that, by profession, he is but a lowly coconut picker. At one point during the war, he attempts to resurrect his identity as a champion by enacting pantomimes of the stickfight in Buntin's store, accompanied by the singing of his friend, Clem. Bolo soon realizes, however, that this show, performed largely for drunken crowds of outsiders, is a perversion of his art, an example of the very sort of commodification that traditional cultural practices such as stickfighting are meant to oppose.[1] He concludes that he is making a clown of himself and refuses to continue the performances. The more easygoing Clem continues to perform his music, but gradually shifts from traditional stickfighting tunes to more marketable calypso tunes, much in demand by the hustlers and American soldiers who begin to frequent Buntin's store. Eventually, Clem moves to the Port of Spain to try his luck as a full-time calypso singer, with the clear implication that he will succeed only if he tailors his music to suit the needs of the capitalist market.

The lonely Bolo becomes more and more alienated and bitter. For a time, he attempts to lead the people of Bonasse in active resistance to colonial authority. Thomas thus compares him to the Mau Mau rebels of Kenya (Thomas 1991b, 5). When Corporal Prince, a colonial policeman, is sent to Bonasse to enforce the suppression of the Spiritual Baptist Church during the war, Bolo essentially declares war, urging the locals to kill the policeman as an act of defiance. When Prince raids the church and finds Bee leading a traditional Spiritual Baptist ceremony, he arrests the minister and the entire congregation, marching them off to jail. Bolo, who had been present at the service, suddenly appears, stops the procession and challenges Prince to arrest him if he thinks he is man enough. Prince, though a powerful man, is certainly no match for Bolo in a fair fight. But Prince, as a colonial policeman, is backed by a huge apparatus of power that Bolo cannot hope to resist on his own. Bolo knocks Prince to the ground, but is immediately set upon by the nine baton-swinging policemen who accompany the corporal. Bolo is badly beaten, then taken off to jail and later sentenced to three years in prison.

When Bolo emerges from prison, he is a deeply embittered figure who begins to bully and terrorize the citizens of Bonasse, partly as an expression of his contempt for their failure to join him in resisting Corporal Prince and other manifestations of repressive colonial authority. When the war ends, the carnival is reinstated and Bolo, though now perhaps past his prime, seems to have a chance to resume the practice of his former art. The impact of modernity, however, is not so easy to reverse, and the stickfighting competition at this first postwar carnival turns into a mere travesty of the important cultural rite that it once was. An inexperienced seventeen-year-old boy is badly hurt in one fight, leading Bolo to enter the ring to challenge the winner. But no one will challenge the formidable Bolo, who realizes that the warrior spirit that once animated the competition has been lost. Enraged, Bolo destroys the drums that provide the musical accompaniment to the competition. Subsequently, he becomes a feared figure in Bonasse, roaming the streets and frequently the local joints in a constant search for trouble.

There is a strong element of sacrifice in the abusive behavior of Bolo, who is clearly presented in the text as a figure of Christ, despite his violence (Cary 1988, 107–108). In particular, Bolo's behavior seems designed to provoke the locals into banding together to oppose his reign of terror, thus regaining some of their former sense of community. He finally manages to trigger a final confrontation when he abducts the two daughters of Primus, a local citizen remarkable for his conciliatory attitude and refusal to voice any resistance to authority. Bolo holds the two young women essentially as hostages, challenging the villagers to try to rescue them. Bee attempts to organize the people of Bonasse to rescue the women, but few of them are willing to face Bolo. Meanwhile, Primus goes to the police for help. In a final, cataclysmic scene, Bolo is heartbroken to find himself confronted not by the united people of Bonasse, but by a group of colonial police, marking still another failure of Bonasse to function as a genuine community. Bolo refuses to submit to the police and is shot and killed, as is the younger of the two women.

In *The Wine of Astonishment*, men, from Morton's abandonment of Eulalie to Bolo's abduction of the two daughters of Primus, frequently use women as tools in their own attempts to restore a sense of masculine pride that has been denied them by their predicaments as colonial subjects. The quest for a cultural identity that is the central subject of the book is, in fact, consistently presented as a quest for a masculine identity, while the colonial identity thrust upon Trinidadians by their colonial rulers is consistently presented as feminine. There is, in fact, a masculinist bias in the attitudes of most of the citizens of Bonasse, as can be seen from the tendency of the majority to blame Eulalie, rather than Morton, for her pregnancy.

The book, with its female narrator, is to an extent critical of these attitudes, and Eva notes that the community should, in fact, have been more sympathetic to Eulalie (46). Similarly, Eva is sad to see the village girls turning more and more to prostitution, but she does not condemn them. In fact, she is sympathetic to their plight, which attributes directly to the American presence in wartime Trinidad (30). Eva's own strength in the face of adversity can be taken as a sort of feminist statement. She is, as Marjorie Thorpe notes, "cast in the tradition of those clear-thinking, resolute and spiritually resilient mother-figures who have always peopled the world of Caribbean fiction" (Thorpe 1982, ix). On the other hand, despite her strength, Eva herself is hardly a figure of feminist resistance. Indeed, she is a rather traditional, nurturing female figure. For example, when her son and daughter are competing in a scholarship competition, she hopes the son will win because "he is a boy and a boy is a man and a man have the burden of the world on his shoulders in a way that a woman don't" (11). Eva is, throughout her narrative, quite sympathetic to the burdens borne by men and to the attempts by the various men in the book to assert their masculinity. She sees Bee as the head of their family and regards it as her duty to offer him whatever solace she can as a counter to what she sees as the humiliating feminization of her husband as a result of being forced to submit to the suppression of his church. The text as a whole shows the same sympathy, presenting the struggles of the various characters to establish a viable sense of their own identities as a principally masculine struggle.

There is a certain irony in Eva's comparison of Bolo's challenging Prince, to a fight between two male dogs struggling for sexual superiority (67). In general, however, Eva is uncritical in her presentation of the attempts of characters such as Bee, Bolo, and Morton to assert their masculinity. She thus relays, without irony, Buntin's description of the stickfight as important because the participants are men and men "must test theyself against each other in this dangerous battle, so as to keep alive the warrior in them, in us, to show us again that we have champions, that we have men" (92). This description provides a crucial key to the behavior of the champion stickfighter, Bolo, who otherwise describes his defiance of authority as an attempt to demonstrate that he is still a "man" (119). One can, of course, read "man" here to mean "human," but the gendering of Bolo's quest to define his manhood through violence is obvious. In this sense, Bolo's lifelong conflict with Morton is a version of the same attempt to demonstrate manliness that informs the stickfight. Thus, the generous Eva describes Morton's selfish, grasping quest for success as understandable given his need to demonstrate his "manness" through gaining a power that is unavailable to him within the subjugated context of Bonasse (135). Maybe, she concludes, Morton has turned his back on his people because "he couldn't be black like one of us ordinary Bonasse people and be a man too" (134). Further, she suggests that Morton's failure is at least partly attributable to the failure of his constituents to define their common goals, that Morton "couldn't be a leader because we wasn't a people" (136).

Eva seems only partly aware of the extent to which Morton, in his position of seeming power, must still submit to a variety of limitations and humiliations. After all, he succeeds primarily by bowing to his white supe-riors, serving as much as an agent for the British and American interests that continue to dominate Trinidad as do uniformed colonial servants such as Colonel Prince, of whom Eva notes: "The whiteman send him to do a job, and he do it" (36). After all, Morton's declared attempt to act white even if he can't be white implies a deep-seated acknowledgement of his own inferiority, as well as a belief that the best he can possibly hope to do is mimic his white masters. He is thus consigned, by his own attitudes, to a perpetually second-rate status.

In this sense, Morton is a recognizable postcolonial figure recalling such predecessors in Caribbean literature as Mr. Slime in George Lamming's *In the Castle of My Skin* (1953). Indeed, Lovelace's depiction of Morton, like Lamming's depiction of Slime, directly recalls the arguments of Frantz Fanon in his classic essay, "The Pitfalls of National Consciousness" (in *The Wretched of the Earth*), whose relevance to Lovelace's work has been noted by Gikandi (Gikandi 1992, 198). For Fanon, the colonial bourgeoisie tend to be mere imitators of their white masters. There is little chance that mimic men such as Morton, can ever provide the radical and energetic leadership required to transform dependent colonial societies such as Trinidad into genuinely vi-able independent states. For Fanon, the postcolonial bourgeoisie thus must be displaced from positions of power at all costs, including violent revolu-tion. In the Trinidad of *The Wine of Astonishment*, however, the time does not appear to be ripe for revolution. Bolo's attempt at violent resistance is a total failure. Meanwhile, the forces of anticolonial resistance on the island had gained important energies from the militant labor activism, centered among oil field workers, of the 1930s (Rennie 1973). But this former activ-ism (which forms the central material of Ralph de Boissière's novel *Crown Jewel* [1952]) lost its momentum with the onset of the world war. By the time *The Wine of Astonishment* ends, effective labor activism in Trinidad seems a thing of the past. When the workers on the Bonasse coconut plan-tation decide to strike to protest their exploitation under the management of the plantation's new American owner, police arrive with guns, batons, and steel helmets to attack the strikers, who are forced to return to work having gained essentially nothing from their effort (136–37).

Much of the sense of defeat that pervades Bonasse late in the text has to do with disillusionment with leaders such as Morton, who seem to regard the common people of Trinidad merely as "clowns digging the ground to grow food for them to eat" (132). In Morton's case, mean-while, it is important to note that he is not merely a failed leader, but a failed intellectual. As Thorpe notes, failed intellectuals, especially school-masters, are recurring figures of the false hero in Lovelace's fiction (Thorpe

1984, 93), but Morton's status as an intellectual also recalls Fanon's comments on the crucial role that needs to be played by intellectuals in the process of decolonization and the building of new postcolonial societies. However, Morton's retreat from his family home in the village into the mansion formerly occupied by the white man, Richardson, bespeaks the extent to which he has abandoned his origins in his attempt to follow in the footsteps of his white models. In particular, Morton's withdrawal from the world of his people is precisely the opposite of the intense engagement with the everyday life of the people that Fanon sees as crucial to the function of intellectuals in postcolonial societies. For Fanon, the "native intellectual" must "return to the people" and through his contact with popular life learn to provide intellectual leadership in the ongoing struggle against cultural imperialism in the postcolonial era (Fanon 1968, 47). Thus, Fanon approvingly quotes an address delivered by Sékou Touré at the 1959 Congress of Black Writers and Artists in Rome in which Touré notes that the intellectual

> must be an element of that popular energy which is entirely called forth for the freeing, the progress, and the happiness of Africa. There is no place outside the fight for the artist or for the intellectual who is not himself concerned with and completely at one with the people in the great battle of Africa and of suffering humanity. (qtd. in Fanon 1968, 206)

While Touré's comments, and most of Fanon's, refer specifically to Africa, they are clearly relevant to the Caribbean as well (Fanon himself was a native of Martinique). They are especially relevant to *The Wine of Astonishment*, in which the people of Bonasse look so hopefully to intellectuals such as Morton for leadership, only to be disappointed again and again.

This disappointment, in a sense, reaches its peak in the years immediately after World War II, when Eva, Bolo, Bee, and the other people of Bonasse discover that the cultural impact of the intrusive American preserve during the war is not so easy to undo. Eva has long assumed that the end of the war would also bring an end to the alienation and commodification that dominate Trinidadian life during the war. But these phenomena, once in place, are almost impossible to reverse as modernity marches forward. When the carnival is restored, Bolo and others find that the stickfight can no longer provide the sense of cultural identity that it once did. Even worse, from the point of view of Eva, the Spiritual Baptist Church no longer functions either. The book ends in 1951, when the ban on the church has finally been lifted, apparently largely through the efforts of Morton, hoping to win local support for his reelection campaign. Excited, Bee goes before his congregation to preach, but finds that both he and they have lost the spirit. Allowed to give free reign to their religious impulses, they find that those impulses are no longer available. Bee, despite his best efforts, leads a lifeless service virtually indistinguishable in spirit from those in Catholic or Anglican churches.

Bee and Eva leave the church, walking home feeling downtrodden and defeated. Then, however, they turn a corner and come upon some young men playing on the steel band and young women dancing to the music. Eva immediately recognizes that the spirit of Africa, which once animated the Spiritual Baptist Church, also resides in this music. The text thus ends on an optimistic note; Eva reassures Bee that the Spirit still lives and that Trinidad still has important cultural resources in its quest to define its own identity. The people of Bonasse, who have struggled in their various, often subtle ways to resist colonial domination throughout the text, will continue the fight.

Notes

See chapter 4 for historical background.

1. This motif is further developed in *The Dragon Can't Dance* (Lovelace 1979) in relation to the carnival and traditional Trinidadian music.

Chapter 9

Michelle Cliff:
Abeng

Abeng (1984) is a partly autobiographical work that focuses on the childhood of its protagonist, Clare Savage, as she attempts to negotiate a stable
and viable sense of her own identity amid the confusions not only of her
impending adolescence, but of the multifaceted and powerful social forces
that surround her in a colonial Jamaica that is moving toward independence. Clare, as she grows older, gradually becomes aware of the ways in
which class, race, and gender contribute to the definition of individual identities. Meanwhile, she finds herself in a particularly complex and precarious
position in relation to all of these social categories, complicating her own
identity all the more. Cliff, perhaps because she has experienced some of
Clare's difficulties firsthand, explores them in a sensitive and insightful way
that makes clear the intricate relationship between personal and private experience that goes into making Clare the person she is, a distinct individual
who nevertheless can take on her individuality only within the specific context of her Jamaican background.

Clare's story, like so many Caribbean novels, thus participates in the
genre of the bildungsroman, though it is also the case that *Abeng*, by
ending as Clare enters adolescence (on the night of her first menstrua-
tion), is something of a truncated bildungsroman. The novel is, in a
sense, only the first half of a bildungsroman relating Clare's growth and
maturation; the second half of this story is told in a sequel, *No Telephone to Heaven* (1987), which follows Clare through adolescence and
into early adulthood.[1] But *Abeng* is a self-contained story that provides
important insights into the issues it treats even without recourse to the
second novel.

That *Abeng* will be a political novel and not just a personal story of childhood is signaled by the title of the book, which, we are told in a note at the beginning of the text, is "an African word meaning conch shell." In particular, it refers to the conch shells that were used as signaling devices during the slave period in Jamaica, blown into to call the slaves to work in the cane fields. But, the note tells us, these same conch shells were also used by the rebel armies of Maroons (escaped slaves) to communicate among themselves and thus further their battle against their former white masters. In short, the abeng is an image of both subjugation and resistance; in particular, it is an image of the ways in which the tools of oppression might sometimes be turned against the oppressors. The relevance of this image within the context of Cliff's book is clear: though the novel as a genre has long been used as a cultural expression of the white European bourgeoisie to narrate and justify their domination not only of Europe but most of the world, the novel has also been a crucial mode of expression for anticapitalist and anticolonial writers who have sought to challenge the cultural hegemony of the European bourgeoisie. Cliff's novel clearly falls in this second category.[2] By telling the story of Clare, it also tells its own story and the story of Cliff's attempt to use the genre of the novel for her own potentially subversive purposes.[3]

Abeng begins in the summer of 1958 at the height of mango season, thus presenting an initial scene of Edenic subtropical abundance, especially as mango is a wild fruit that requires little or no cultivation. Indeed, the mango crop this year is the richest in recent memory. However, this initial idyllic scene is immediately interrupted by the reminder that, in 1958, Jamaica had "two rulers: a white queen and a white governor. Independence-in-practically-name-only was four years away" (5). Cliff then follows with a list of details that emphasize the cultural and economic domination of Jamaica by England. She then supplies some ethnographic information about the island's population, noting that it is "primarily Black . . . with gradations of shading reaching into the top strata of the society. Africans were mixed with Sephardic Jews, Chinese, Syrians, Lebanese, East Indians—but the large working class, and class of poor people was Black" (5).

In short, the situation in colonial Jamaica is not quite so Edenic. The island is strictly controlled by its British colonial masters, personified by Queen Elizabeth II, "the whitest woman in the world" (5). Moreover, Jamaican society itself is highly stratified, with a small white elite enjoying wealth, privilege, and power vastly beyond those of the black majority, with those of mixed race generally ranged somewhere in between on the social and economic scale. The novel then proceeds to detail a typical Sunday visit to the local Presbyterian Church by the Savage family, which consists of Clare, her younger sister, and their parents. But even this nuclear family, we learn, is riven by complex divisions. Mr. James Savage (generally called by his nickname, "Boy") is white, the descendent of wealthy planters, though he himself has inherited relatively little wealth. Mrs. Kitty Savage (née Freeman), on the other hand, is "red," that is, of mixed black and white descent. Of the two daughters, Clare resembles her father, appearing almost entirely white, with green eyes and wavy chestnut hair. Her sister, Jennie, five years younger, is much darker, with curlier hair. As a result, the family is essentially structured along racial lines. Clare is the favorite of her father, who treats her like the son her never had, sharing with her various interests, such as amateur paleontology (8). Kitty, meanwhile, seems to prefer Jennie, whose racial makeup appears more similar to her own.

Boy Savage is depicted as a racist who is somewhat contemptuous of black people. For example, he urges Clare to think of herself as white and to ignore the fact that her mother is, unfortunately, "colored" (73). Kitty, on the other hand, is intensely aware of the African element in her heritage. She is, we are told, deeply fond of the "country people of Jamaica" (52). Indeed, given her own rural background, she regards the poor, black population of the Jamaican countryside as her own people, and she is frequently engaged in charitable projects to help black Jamaicans who are less fortunate than herself. Her sense of connection to her African roots is also demonstrated by the fact that, despite Boy's Presbyterianism, she still prefers to worship at the "Tabernacle," a much less dignified church in which the congregation, consisting mostly of black women, partakes of an evangelical Christianity that is strongly influenced by African cultural traditions.[4]

To an extent, Kitty feels much more at home in this church than in the John Knox Memorial Church favored by her husband. On the other hand, separated from the other worshippers at the Tabernacle by her different class status, she is never fully able to participate in the rollicking, emotional services that are conducted there. Indeed, Kitty, perhaps because of her estrangement from the class into which she was born, is highly repressed and finds it very difficult to express any sort of emotion, even to her own daughters. It is only Boy, in fact, toward whom she seems able to express strong feelings, and many of those are angry reactions to his drinking and womanizing.

Much of Part One of *Abeng* is devoted to establishing the basic dynamics of the Savage family, with its complex mix of race and class backgrounds. It is highly indicative of Cliff's vision, however, that she establishes these dynamics not merely through a description of the current situation, but through an elaboration of historical background. Much of this initial part of the book consists of details of the family heritage of the Savages. We learn, for example, that Boy is descended from a family that was once renowned all over Jamaica for its great wealth. His great-grandfather, James Edward Constable Savage, had originally come to Jamaica in 1829, sent by the British Crown to serve as justice in the parish of St. Ann on the North Coast of the island. Once in Jamaica, he was able to establish a series of plantations and to amass a great fortune, largely based on the exploitation of slave labor. Leaving his wife and daughter behind in England, the justice took his son to Jamaica with him, establishing the strongly patriarchal orientation of the family. The justice seems to have taken great pleasure in the brutal punishment of wayward slaves. Meanwhile, though the family proudly claims that he had been one of the few white Jamaican planters never to impregnate any of their female slaves, the text also makes it clear that the justice, with his wife back in England, depended largely on the use of his women slaves for sexual release, setting the precedent for the interracial liaison between Boy and Kitty (29–30).[5]

Infuriated when slavery is abolished by the Crown in 1834, the justice retaliates by burning alive the more than one hundred slaves who still work on his plantation, arguing that they are his property and that he should be able to dispose of them as he wishes. Moreover, he declares his concern that, once free, his former slaves might begin to breed with white partners, contaminating the white race. The legacy of this horrifying event still haunts Clare, as does the legacy of slavery as a whole, though the family is careful never to discuss this heritage.[6] Nor do they discuss the fact that the family fortunes declined rapidly in the mid-nineteenth century, as the justice began selling off his plantations, diminishing the inheritance left for his Cambridge-educated son, who virtually finished off the family fortune with his heavy propensity for drink and heavy losses on horseracing.

In short, even the "white" side of Clare's family heritage is mixed. Her old and proud family is well stocked with lore about prominent ancestors and maintains a well-developed collection of family legends: "The definition of what a Savage was like was fixed by color, class, and religion, and over the years a carefully contrived mythology was constructed, which they used to protect their identities" (29). Unfortunately, this mythology is of relatively little use to Clare in her own attempt to construct an identity. For one thing, she is intensely aware that her own background includes elements of color, class, and religion that are outside the Savage mythology. For another, she is not all that comfortable with the mythology itself, given the legacy of brutality, rape, and murder of blacks that underlies it.

Among other things, Clare is vaguely aware that this mythology is based largely on fiction and that the official version of family history represses a great deal of the darker side of the family past. Thus, the family not only refuses to discuss the mass murder of the justice's slaves, but they also efface the real circumstances of their decline from prominence. In particular, family lore blames the decline on Mr. Levi, a Jewish estate manager hired in 1845, seeking to attribute their downfall to his mismanagement, or perhaps dishonesty, rather than to the shortcomings of their own ancestors.

Clare's uneasy relation to the Savage past (and the pun, on Cliff's part, is clearly intentional)[7] is dramatized in a number of ways in the text. Among other things, Clare's whiteness, though a form of empowerment, is also a form of marginalization in a mostly black society that is moving toward independence from white rule. In this sense, as in others, Clare's situation mirrors that of her author, whose own whiteness places her in the company of white creole writers such as Jean Rhys and Phyllis Shand Allfrey, all of whom have had difficulty gaining acceptance from critics who have felt that their works are not authentically Caribbean because of the authors' racial backgrounds.[8]

Among other things, Clare's sense of her own marginality leads her to become fascinated with Jews and the tribulations they have experienced throughout history, especially during the Holocaust, when so many Jews burned in the ovens of European concentration camps, thus echoing the experience of the justice's burned slaves. Clare's estrangement from her Savage ancestry can also be detected in the early scene in which she and her father visit the old family plantation house, now an abandoned relic, preserved simply to create atmosphere that might draw customers to the surrounding subdivisions that cover the land once belonging to the family. Somehow the decaying house seems smaller and less grand than Clare had expected, and she has difficulty connecting to the stories of past glories that her father tells her as they tour the building. Meanwhile, out back, they come upon vague traces of the outbuildings where the family's slaves once lived and worked, faint but powerful reminders of the source of the wealth that made the plantation house and its once-elaborate furnishings possible.

Clare does not really understand the meaning of the traces she finds in the backyard of the plantation house, but she is certainly aware that the Savages owned slaves and that she herself is descended not only from the white Savage family, but from the Freemans, descendents of slaves such as those who once worked—and were horribly murdered—on the Savage plantation. In later sections of the book, we learn a great deal about the family history of the Freemans, a long-established family of "red" farmers. Clare maintains her connection to this side of the family largely through summer vacation stays at the farm of her maternal grandmother, Miss Mattie. These vacations in the country allow Clare not only to experience rural life, but to meet Zoe, a black girl who is the daughter of a poor market woman who rents a small shack on a plot loaned to her by Miss Mattie. Zoe becomes Clare's best friend and shares her most intimate thoughts, many of which have to do with their merging sexuality as they near adolescence.

Cliff's account of the relationship between Clare and Zoe indicates the extent to which gender joins class and race as a complicating factor in the evolution of Clare's identity. Clare's subject position is precarious enough given her mixed participation in different classes and races, but she is further confused by a complex sexual identity. Not only does her father treat her like a son, but her only experience with adolescent sexual experimentation is with Zoe, though this experimentation certainly does not reach the level of demonstrating unequivocally that either Clare or Zoe is a lesbian. Still, Clare herself begins to suspect that she may be homosexual, wondering if she is thus following in the footsteps of her distant cousin, Robert, long described within the family as "funny" (124–26).

In a crucial scene late in the text, Clare, over Zoe's objections, steals a gun stored in her grandmother's house and decides to go hunting for Massa Cudjoe, a near-legendary wild boar who has long roamed the woods around Miss Mattie's house. Clare thus usurps a traditionally masculine role. Indeed, we have been informed in the text that the hunting of wild boars, as an exclusively masculine activity, once played an important, even sacred, role in the culture of Jamaica's Maroons (112).[9] There are thus special, if largely unconscious, reasons why her parents and grandmother are so horrified by Clare's behavior in this incident, reasons that go well beyond her accidental shooting of Miss Mattie's bull. The Savages, in fact, react to this situation as an emergency, sending Clare off to live with Mrs. Beatrice Phillips, an old white widow who is a bitter racist, but who will presumably teach Clare "proper" behavior—that is, teach her to behave as if she is white, middle-class, and conventionally feminine, removing all vestiges of her black, working-class, and lesbian inclinations.

Among other things, Clare's emerging sexuality is complicated by an overarching fear of rape that seems to pervade all she has heard about sex. Partly, this experience simply partakes of warnings issued to adolescent girls the world over, and the story, however unlikely, of a five-year-old girl who becomes pregnant, apparently by rape, provides a reminder that young girls are quite often subjected to rape. But, in the context of late colonial Jamaica, the pervasive fear of rape is also related to the legacy of the slave past, in which black women were so often raped by their white masters.

Thus, in *Abeng*, even ostensibly private experiences such as sex are related to public historical experience.[10] In the same way, it is clear that Clare's identity draws not just upon her family history, but on the larger history of Jamaica and even the world. After all, the Savages and the Freemans were who they were and lived the lives they did within a specific context that made those lives possible. We are reminded, for example, of the fact that Christopher Columbus "discovered" Jamaica in 1494, leading to the virtual extermination of the Carib Indians who already inhabited the island (66–67). But Cliff's sardonic presentation of the discovery of Jamaica, complete with an account of rumors that Columbus had in fact been Jewish, is indicative of the fact that her description of historical events often challenges official accounts. Probably the most important example here is Cliff's account of the history of slavery, which emphasizes the brutal punishments meted out to slaves who angered their masters, while also calling particular attention to the repeated rape of women slaves, who were commonly used by their white masters as sexual objects.[11]

Cliff, in her delineation of the economic aspects of slavery, places that phenomenon within the larger context of capitalist exploitation of labor throughout the modern era, in this sense recalling Eric Williams's characterization of slavery as an extreme version of capitalism (Williams 1944). Indeed, Cliff's narrator specifically states that "slavery was not an aberration— it was an extreme" (28). In this same vein, Cliff notes that slavery was abolished in the British Empire not out of humanitarian concern, but because it had become unprofitable. In addition, she points out that the ostensible end of slavery did not bring an end to the exploitation of the former slaves in colonial Jamaica and that "all the forces which had worked to keep these people slaves now worked to keep them poor" (28).

Importantly, a great deal of the historical information presented by Cliff in *Abeng* seeks not to recount the exploits of the Caribbean's European conquerors and colonial rulers, but to recover the counterhistory of the area's subjugated populations. This history of resistance extends from a description of the culture of the Caribs to a brief mention of the Castro-led revolt underway in Cuba in 1958 in the present time of the book, thus encompassing the history of the Caribbean somewhat in the mode of Eric Williams's history, *From Columbus to Castro* (1984).[12] But Cliff's principal emphasis is on the history of slave rebellions that informed the history of Jamaica and many other Caribbean islands during the slave period. In the case of Jamaica, with a large and essentially unsettled interior, these rebellions centered on the activities of the so-called Maroons, escaped slaves who established fugitive communities in the interior and carried on guerrilla campaigns against the island's white rulers.

Cliff's history of Maroon rebellions centers on the semilegendary figure of Nanny, a woman Maroon with reputedly magical powers, who "used her skill to unite her people and to consecrate their battles" as the Maroons waged war against the British from 1655 to 1740, though Nanny herself was killed in 1733. Nanny, meanwhile is presented as a predecessor of Mma Alli, a lesbian obeah woman and a slave of Justice Savage. As Belinda Edmondson notes, Cliff "casts Kitty—and indeed all black women in the novel—as having a direct and unmediated linkage to a positive black history and consciousness" through their relationship to such black women predecessors (Edmondson 1993, 188).

The importance of Cliff's account of this black, female Jamaican counterhistory is emphasized in the text by reminders that the colonial educational system of the island has long suppressed such accounts, making many Jamaicans largely unaware of the true nature of their history. Clare, in her Catholic school, learns bits and pieces of Jamaican history, but always with a Eurocentric bias. For example, she and her fellow students are assured that the Morant Bay uprising of 1865 had been "unwarranted and of little consequence" (30).[13] Similarly, we are told that the congregation of the Tabernacle, despite their seeming connection to the African past of their ancestors, in fact know very little about that past. They are aware of the story of Nanny, but seem to know few details about the Nanny Rebellion or about Maroon rebellions in general. They know even less about their more distant African predecessors:

> They did not know about the Kingdom of the Ashanti or the King-
> dom of Dahomey, where most of their ancestors had come from.
> They did not imagine that Black Africans had commanded thou-
> sands of warriors. Built universities. Created systems of law. De-
> vised language. Wrote history. Poetry. Were traders. Artists. Diplo-
> mats. (20)

In her description of the curriculum of the colonial school attended by Zoe (the same school earlier attended by Kitty Freeman), Cliff notes that the teacher, Mr. Lewis Powell, is instructed to teach straight out of manuals supplied by the British governments. Not surprisingly, these manuals emphasize the teaching of British culture and history, detailing Jamaican history only "as it pertained to England" (84). Meanwhile, the children are encouraged to read the works of British writers such as Tennyson, Keats, Coleridge, and Wordsworth. Mr. Powell, however, knows that a great deal is missing in this official curriculum. Having spent time in New York during the Harlem Renaissance, he is aware of the rich cultural heritage of black people in the Western hemisphere. And, having been heavily influenced by the black nationalism of the Jamaican-born Marcus Garvey during this same period, he is also aware of the long history of oppression of blacks by whites in America and of the heroic tradition of resistance to this oppression.

As a result of this experience, Powell attempts to supplement the official British-supplied curriculum of his school (a curriculum, the text notes, that was essentially the same throughout the British Empire, without reference to local traditions or cultures) with examples of black culture. He thus teaches the works of Langston Hughes, Countee Cullen, Jean Toomer, and Claude McKay alongside the works of the officially sanctioned white British writers, demonstrating that these black writers can easily hold their own in such lofty company: "He gave them McKay's poetry and Hughes's poetry and Toomer's poetry because he wanted them to know that there had been songs by Black men which were equal to any songs by Englishmen" (90).[14]

Powell, however, knows that he can only get away with so much, so "he carefully concealed the sources of many of the songs" in black historical experience (90). In short, he is reluctant to undertake the more radical project of providing a link to black history, a link that might potentially prove empowering to his students, inspiring them to mount their own resistance to oppression. It is, of course, precisely this link that Cliff seeks to establish in *Abeng*, and it is a link that is largely successful, though it is certainly possible to argue, as has Maria Helena Lima, that the language and style of Cliff's writing suggest that it is aimed primarily at a Western, middle-class audience rather than black Jamaicans (Lima 1993). On the other hand, perhaps because of the focus on a preadolescent protagonist whose own political consciousness remains undeveloped, the book is unable to present any sort of clear political vision that might provide actual guidance for specific political action.

Notes

See chapter 6 for historical background.

1. Even in this later book, however, Clare remains a "crossroads" character who is unable to find a comfortable place in Jamaican society, ending her life

by participation in an ill-fated guerrilla rebellion, in which she is killed, "burned into the landscape of Jamaica, by gunfire" (Cliff 1990b, 265).

2. The doubleness of the abeng is also contained in the name of the protagonist. Though Clare's mother allows Mr. Savage to think that the girl has been named for the Cambridge University college attended by his grandfather, in her mind the girl is named for Clary, a poor black girl who took the young Kitty (later to become Clare's mother) to a hospital and stayed with her when it was determined that she needed a tonsillectomy (141). See Lionnet (1995) for a discussion of Clare's naming as "a stunning act of 'signifying'" (46).

3. See Lima (1993), however, for an argument that the revolutionary potential of Cliff's writing is limited by its relatively traditional, Western style, which tends to contain it within a middle-class European novelistic tradition. Gikandi, on the other hand, finds Cliff's style and language richly evocative of important postcolonial dialogues (Gikandi 1992, 234–51).

4. It is indicative of the social structure of modern Jamaica that Kitty, who has herself married a white man, much to her family's horror, hopes that Clare will also marry a white man and be able to live as a white woman. See Edmondson for a discussion of this problematic motif in the book (Edmondson 1993, 188).

5. Actually, the justice's favorite sexual partner seems to have been Inez, an eighteen-year-old half-black, half-Miskito Indian woman who was not a slave, but who was brought before his court on false charges of theft. Rather than issue the usual punishment (to have her hands cut off, followed by a hundred lashes of the whip), the justice simply takes her home with him and makes her his sexual captive, repeatedly raping her (34).

6. The narrator, incidentally, points out that the justice's action was hardly unique and that similar acts occurred all over Jamaica on the eve of abolition (40).

7. See Cliff's own discussion of the significance of this name (1990b, 265).

8. See, for example, Kenneth Ramchand's analysis of what he sees as the "terrified consciousness" of white West Indian writers of the emergence of black political and cultural power in the Caribbean (Ramchand 1983, 223–36). See Edmondson for a discussion of the critical suspicion that Cliff's novels are "not truly part of an Afrocentric Caribbean discourse," but instead draw upon American feminism, discovering black identity only as a "fashion" (Edmondson 1993, 181–82).

9. Vestiges of this practice still reside in the continuing ritual importance of hog killing in the contemporary Jamaica of the novel. Significantly, Clare's experience with this practice, involving an encounter with some boys who exclude her from their ritual processing of the genitals of a slaughtered hog, itself has implications for her emerging sexuality (56–58).

10. Lemuel Johnson thus notes that Cliff, while focusing on feminine experience, avoids essentialism by demonstrating that: "woman does not, indeed cannot, exist outside so dynamic a conception of history" (Johnson 1990, 123).

11. In this sense, Cliff's book anticipates Toni Morrison's *Beloved* (1987), a book often credited with breaking new ground by calling attention to the sexual dimension of slavery in the American South. For more on this aspect of the slave experience, see Carby 1987 and Omolade 1983.

12. Castro's guerrillas toppled the regime of the U.S.-backed dictator, Batista, on January 1, 1959.

13. See chapter 11 for a discussion of Vic Reid's historical novel, *New Day* (1949), in which the Morant Bay uprising plays a central role.

14. One can note a masculine bias in the black cultural tradition taught by Powell. Indeed, the text specifically informs us that Powell was highly skeptical of the work of Zora Neale Hurston, the most important woman writer of the Harlem Renaissance, especially in relation to her work on Jamaican folk culture (87).

Chapter 10

C.L.R. James:
Minty Alley

As a central figure in the "Trinidadian Renaissance" that formed around such Trinidadian journals as *The Beacon* in the 1930s, C.L.R. James made crucial contributions to the birth of the Caribbean novel as an important phenomenon in the cultural history of the Caribbean and in the literature of the world in the twentieth century. With the publication of his own novel, *Minty Alley*, in 1936, James, himself, made a major contribution to the growth of the Caribbean novel as a cultural and political force. Indeed, Cynthia Hamilton has argued that James's only novel points toward his later critical and theoretical work in important ways, already showing "the sensitive social observation that forms the basis for much of his political and historical analysis" (Hamilton 1992, 432).

Minty Alley is one of the founding examples of the Caribbean "yard" novel. It focuses on the poor dwellers of No. 2 Minty Alley, which features a front house inhabited by the landlady, Mrs. Rouse, and several tenants; it also includes a backyard containing a number of outbuildings that she rents to other tenants. James makes clear the harsh conditions under which these tenants—and even Mrs. Rouse herself—must exist. However, he concentrates less on naturalistic descriptions of their impoverished living conditions than on human relationships, showing the element of communal cooperation that marks the lives of the alley's inhabitants, while at the same time indicating the ways in which the impact of colonialism has made this cooperation more difficult.

Conditions in the alley (and all of the events of the novel) are described entirely from the point of view of the protagonist, Haynes. In fact, James's use of point of view in the book is extremely interesting and significant. Though the book is narrated in third person, the narrator is not omniscient, but sees and knows only what Haynes sees and knows. As H. Adlai Murdoch suggests, this limited point of view can be read as a discursive enactment of the colonial condition. There is no authoritative and all-knowing position from which colonial experience, dominated from the distant metropolitan center of Europe, can be enunciated. Further, by choosing the middle-class Haynes rather than the poorer inhabitants of the household as the focal point for the narrative, James is able to suggest Haynes's privileged position in the colonial society of Trinidad. Thus,

> the fact that the re-presentation of the larger totality of colonized subjects can occur only through the sentence of one of their number, indeed the one who appears to approximate most closely the model of colonial assimilation, only serves to confirm the impression that the ultimate product of colonialism is the inability of the colonized to speak their own subjectivity. (Murdoch 1995, 66)

As the book begins, Haynes is forced, for financial reasons, to leave his middle-class home after the death of his mother. But it is also as a sort of declaration of his coming of age that he goes, accompanied by Ella, his faithful servant, to live in the far less commodious surroundings of Minty Alley. Initially, his middle-class background and perspective set him radically apart from the household's other inhabitants, and he is rather appalled not only by the material conditions in the household, but by the behavior of the tenants. He first views the household very much as an outsider, peering through a crack in the wall of his room so that he can observe the other inhabitants without being seen. In fact, he literally becomes a sort of peeping Tom. Having resolved to vacate the premises almost immediately after his arrival, he then decides to stay, after he is titillated by the sight of Mr. Benoit, Mrs. Rouses's common-law husband, making passes both at the maid, Wilhelmine, and another tenant, Nurse Jackson.

Haynes thus initially interacts with the other denizens of No. 2 Minty Alley not in a mode of communal fellowship, but by keeping them under surveillance. As the book proceeds, however, he becomes more and more involved in the life of the yard. Merle Hodge, in a review of the 1971 republication of the book, has argued, in fact, that the book's central project is a demonstration that cooperation between the Caribbean working class and the educated middle class is of value to both classes (Hodge 1972, 11). On the other hand, as Reinhard Sander points out, Haynes remains somewhat alienated from the other inhabitants of No. 2 Minty Alley during his stay there, even in the midst of the sexual relationship he establishes with one of them, Maisie (Sander 1988, 101). Even Maisie continues to address him as "Mr. Haynes," and she is aware from the beginning of their relationship that their class difference will preclude anything more serious between them than a brief fling. Meanwhile, the other inhabitants continue to treat Haynes, because of his superior education and class position, with a respect that borders on reverence. And there is an element of power and control that resides even in his attempts to be helpful, as when he comes to the aid of Mrs. Rouse by assuming control of her business affairs (173).

Maisie, barely seventeen years old, is the only one of the inhabitants of No. 2 who overcomes the general reverence for Haynes. Her attitude arises partly, of course, from the intimate nature of their relationship, but it also arises from the strength, independence, and determination that Maisie demonstrates in all of her activities. Maisie realizes early on that the inexperienced Haynes, himself only twenty, is hopelessly naïve, not only about sex, but about human relationships in general. Maisie, on the other hand, has had to fend for herself from childhood and is thus much wiser, despite her young age, in the ways of the world. Haynes, in fact, learns a great deal from Maisie, including a final lesson in determination and fortitude when Maisie decides to travel to America to seek higher wages than she could possibly obtain in Trinidad. Lacking funds to pay her passage, she decides to work her way over on a ship, the white officers of which have a fondness for "young coloured girls." Realizing the implications of this arrangement, the still-squeamish Haynes is horrified, but Maisie quickly sets him straight: "Mr. Haynes, I want a job and I am going to get it. The captain and the whole crew can't get anything from me unless I want to give them" (226).

Victimized throughout her life, Maisie refuses to remain merely a victim and is determined to use whatever resources she has to improve her situation. Thus, as Barbara Paul-Emile notes, Maisie is a strong figure who can be seen as an "embodiment of the female/warrior archetype" (Paul-Emile 1995, 77). Not surprisingly, Maisie's strength and determination lead to conflicts with Mrs. Rouse, the presumed ruler of the household. Indeed, these disagreements are one of the major reasons Maisie decides to leave the household, which is marked by a number of other battles as well, especially between Mrs. Rouse and the nurse, after the former discovers the latter's sexual liaison with Benoit. Many of these conflicts are related to race, and a consciousness of racial difference, a legacy of colonialism, underlies all of the relationships among the inhabitants of No. 2 Minty Alley, disrupting their sense of community. Haynes, as the figure who has most thoroughly assimilated British colonial attitudes, is also the most thoroughly conscious of race. Thus, when he arrives at his new abode and begins to observe his fellow tenants, he immediately begins to rank and categorize them according to race. In such moments, his consciousness of race becomes clear. His initial shock at finding the nurse's almost white son among the inhabitants is particularly telling (29).

The nurse, it turns out, is nearly white as well, and it is clear that her white skin is crucial to both Benoit's attraction to her and Mrs. Rouse's animosity. Mrs. Rouse's race consciousness leads to particularly ugly consequences late in the book when a local obeah man, on whom the religious-superstitious landlady often relies for spiritual advice, warns her that she will have bad fortune as long as "coolies" are around her (240). As a result, Mrs. Rouse drives her faithful and hard-working Indian servant, Philomen, out of the household. By this time, Nurse Jackson and her son have been driven out as well, and Benoit has moved out in order to marry the nurse. In the end, Mrs. Rouse decides to sell the house, and Haynes moves out as well, completing the disintegration of the household.

Haynes continues to have certain nostalgic memories of Minty Alley, where he experienced a sense of human authenticity he had never known before. Nevertheless, he gradually begins to forget his former neighbors, again emphasizing the alienation between his middle-class perspective and the working-class perspectives of the other characters. Though James leaves this important problem of alienation between the classes in Trinidadian society unsolved in *Minty Alley*, the book at least begins to address it and to suggest its importance. Indeed, Kenneth Ramchand, in his introduction to the book, sees the delineation of this crucial problem as the most important project of James's novel (Ramchand 1997, 13).

In addition, as Sander notes, James's "presentation of lower-class life itself " is also a "pioneering achievement" (Sander 1988, 102). This focus on the lower classes would go on to become crucial to the development of the Caribbean novel as a whole, though, as Hazel Carby has emphasized, James's early work, like the rest of the Trinidadian Renaissance, should be read within the context of global developments in proletarian culture in the 1930s (Carby 1988, 39). *Minty Alley* makes clear the difficulties faced by its working-class characters and shows a genuine sympathy for their plight without sensationalizing or romanticizing their hardship. In its sympathetic understanding that its working-class characters, of both genders, are not merely victims of economic oppression, but genuine human beings with rich interior lives and considerable personal resources, *Minty Alley* broke new ground in the literary representation of Britain's colonial subjects and of Britain's working class in general. Though James would concentrate, after *Minty Alley*, on the writing of history and political commentary, his one book-length work of fiction is a successful and important contribution to both Caribbean literature and international working-class literature.

Note

See chapter 4 for historical background.

Chapter 11

V. S. Reid:
New Day

New Day is a sweeping historical novel that begins with the anticolonial violence of the Morant Bay uprising in 1865 and culminates on Constitution Day in November 1944. As Louis James notes, the book, appearing in 1949, made a major contribution to the development of Caribbean literature, providing a "pioneering claim that a West Indian island could have its own national history and culture" (James 1968, 64). The book thus counters the attempts of colonialist historiography to dismiss the history of Jamaica and other colonial possessions as a simple footnote to British history. Reid's book is also important for its focus on the contributions of the common people of Jamaica to the island's national history and for its vivid evocation of the Jamaican landscape and the texture of everyday Jamaican life and culture. This latter aspect of the book is supplemented by the effective use of Jamaican dialect in the narration, thus enhancing the feel of the text as a genuinely Jamaican cultural production.[1]

New Day was, in fact, the first Caribbean novel in English to be narrated in dialect throughout, and the novel has been much praised for its effective and ground-breaking use of dialect. The narration captures much of the character and rhythm of Jamaican speech, while remaining easily accessible to non-Jamaican readers. Thus, Edward Kamau Brathwaite applauds the book for its "feeling for the poetry of the spoken word, and an imagination capable of giving those spoken words life" (Brathwaite 1960, 207). And later, in a discussion of the use of jazz music as a structural model for Caribbean literature, Brathwaite praises Reid's novel for its ability to establish links between jazz rhythms and oral narrative traditions, thus providing an effective "expression of a West Indian 'creole' experience" (Brathwaite 1967b, 51).

Ultimately, however, *New Day*'s most important contribution to the development of the Caribbean novel is probably its effective use of Caribbean history as narrative material. In particular, the novel draws not on official historical accounts, but on the rich history of resistance to colonial domination in Jamaica. In so doing, Reid reminds his readers that the colonial history of Jamaica was not merely one of colonial dependency and passive submission to British domination, but of active and continual resistance to this domination, beginning with numerous slave rebellions and extending into labor activism in the twentieth century.[2] At the same time, while identifying working-class activism as the most important locus of this resistance, Reid also identifies the sources of the official authority (the colonial state, the Anglican Church, and rich planters) that has attempted to smash this resistance and subjugate the Jamaican people. Reid thus provides important historical background for the movement of Jamaica toward independence, while at the same time pointing the way for numerous postcolonial novelists who would subsequently pursue similar projects.[3]

New Day is narrated by John Campbell, nearly ninety years old, as he sits alone on the eve of Constitution Day and ponders the historical changes he has observed in Jamaica during his long life. His personal memories of the events described are, in the course of the novel, transformed into public history, making his individual life an emblem of the history of Jamaica, much in the mode discussed by Fredric Jameson in his delineation of the notion of "national allegory" (Jameson 1986).[4] The story begins with the Morant Bay uprising of 1865. John, then eight years old, has only a vague understanding of the issues at stake in the rebellion as it occurs, but he supplements this understanding with knowledge gained through the years, describing the rebellion in a way that authentically represents his eight-year-old perspective, while at the same time making clear the political and economic foundations of the uprising. Indeed, many of John's early experiences prepare the way for his later narration, as when he gradually becomes aware (partly through the commentary of his brother, Davie) that the colonialist version of history being conveyed in his government school is a distortion designed to "fool poor people's children" (81). John will later pass on a similar wisdom to Davie's grandson, Garth, correcting through his personal recollections the accounts in Garth's history class of the Morant Bay uprising as an insurrection of demonic rebels against a saintly colonial administration (277).

Davie, in fact, is an important mentor and role model for the young John. When the Morant Bay uprising actually begins, Davie is, not surprisingly, among the rebels, who are led by Deacon Paul Bogle and supported by prominent planter and assemblyman George Gordon. Governor Edward John Eyre brutally suppresses the uprising. Many of the rebels are killed in clashes with government troops, and both Bogle and Gordon are hanged. Davie is forced to flee Jamaica and take refuge, along with John and a young woman, Lucille Dubois, on an uninhabited cay off the coast of the main island.

In the aftermath of the uprising, Eyre is recalled as governor, and Jamaica's semiautonomous representative government is deposed by Great Britain in favor of direct colonial rule. Davie receives a pardon for his involvement in the uprising after testifying in the Crown's investigations of the event. He remains on the cay, founding a utopian community there based initially on essentially socialist principles. As time goes by, however, the responsibility of heading the community, called Zion, begins to wear on Davie. He becomes more and more somber and humorless, gradually descending into religious fanaticism. Nevertheless, the community prospers until a hurricane destroys much of the cay, killing Davie and leaving Lucille shipwrecked in Cuba, where she is forced into prostitution. In 1882, the survivors on the cay, now led by a twenty-five-year-old John, petition Great Britain to take possession of their small island in order to protect them from the increasing danger of domination by American companies that are beginning more and more to seek economic control of the Caribbean.

John moves to the main island and begins, with the help of James Creary Campbell, the son of Davie and Lucille, to build a prosperous family business, producing bananas, sugar, and rum. In 1920, both James Creary and his English wife die of smallpox, and John assumes the care of seven-year-old Garth Campbell, who will become the real protagonist of the second half of the book. Garth, loosely based on Jamaican political leader Norman Manley, has inherited both Davie's fervent desire for justice and John's cautious wisdom. A promising student, he is educated in England and becomes a successful solicitor and advocate for the poor and downtrodden of Jamaica. Though the violence of 1938 represents a substantial setback, Garth eventually leads the way to the new constitution, with the aid of his cousin, the trade union leader Carlos Fernandez, who is loosely based on Jamaican labor leader Alexander Bustamante (in reality, a distant cousin of Manley). Indeed, *New Day* emphasizes the importance of trade union activity, in which Garth has also been involved, as a key element in Jamaica's quest for a more democratic society. As the book closes, Garth is expected to become the head of the new Jamaican government, as Manley would, in fact, become.

In the meantime, Garth, because of his education and sophistication, is the novel's principal political spokesman, noting in numerous speeches and conversations the legacy of social and economic injustice that has triggered Jamaica's tradition of militant resistance. His central project is self-government for Jamaica, on the basis of the fact that the island's distant colonial readers are in no position to understand the plight of the poor working people of Jamaica, even if they wanted to do so. On the other hand, as Selwyn Cudjoe points out in a rather critical reading of the novel, Garth's attitude is rather moderate and seems based on the desire for some degree of self-determination rather than complete independence. Thus, Cudjoe points out that Garth not only sees England as the appropriate model for Jamaican nationhood, but envisions the future Jamaica as remaining to some degree linked to England, almost in the mode of a child remaining loyal to its parent (Cudjoe 1980).

If Reid's historical vision is thus to some extent limited, his engagement with history from an anticolonial perspective and his strong sense of fiction as a potential weapon in the fight for social and economic justice nevertheless represented an important step forward for the Caribbean novel, pointing the way for Jamaican novelists such as John Hearne, Roger Mais, and Michael Thelwell to pursue a similar project. His sense of connection to the lives of the common people of Jamaica is particularly important, and *New Day* succeeds well in fulfilling Reid's own description of the book's goal in his introduction:

> What I have attempted is to transfer to paper some of the beauty, kindliness, and humor of my people, weaving characters into the wider framework of these eighty years and creating a tale that will offer as true an impression as fiction can of the way by which Jamaica and its people came to today. (viii)

Notes

See chapter 6 for historical background.

1. George Lamming thus notes that Reid, like Sam Selvon, is a "peasant" writer who maintains his roots in the common people of Jamaica, thus invigorating his writing (Lamming 1992a, 45).

2. For scholarly discussions of this history of resistance, see Bakan 1990, Hart 1989, and Holt 1992.

3. In this sense, Reid's novel anticipates the work of the Kenyan novelist Ngugi wa Thiong'o in a particularly direct way. The emphasis on labor activism as a key mode of resistance also anticipates such African novels as Ousmane Sembène's *Gods Bits of Wood* (1962), as well as Caribbean novels by writers such as Ralph de Boissière.

4. For a fuller discussion of this motif, see chapter 3.

Chapter 12

Ralph de Boissière:
Crown Jewel

Written in a mode of critical realism, *Crown Jewel* (1952) is an important historical novel that indicates, in the manner praised by Georg Lukács (1983) in relation to the great European historical novels of the early nineteenth century, the interconnectedness of all aspects of Trinidad's society during the period 1935–39. The sequel, *Rum and Coca-Cola* (1956), then extends this historical coverage through World War II, to 1945. The decade 1935–45 is well chosen for de Boissière's project. The last half of the 1930s represented a time of sweeping change in Trinidadian society, when militant labor activists began to organize Trinidad's workers in a demand for social, political, and economic justice. In the process, the workers gained self-respect and a sense of the potential collective power of workers not only in Trinidad, but worldwide, as workers in other countries similarly began to organize. World War II further extended Trinidadians' sense of participation in a global community. The war also marked the end of Great Britain as a dominant world power, followed by the relatively rapid dismantling of the British Empire.[1] De Boissière's two historical novels do an excellent job of capturing this process of intense and dramatic historical change; at the same time, as the author points out in a brief prologue to *Crown Jewel*, the events of these years should be viewed as the culmination of more than four hundred years of colonial history in the Caribbean. Together, then, de Boissière's historical novels demonstrate a genuine historical sense, again recalling Lukács's comments on the historical novel.

Lukács's work is also particularly relevant to the way in which de Boissière carefully connects the large public events of his narrative with the private experience of specific individuals by interweaving the life histories of individual characters from a variety of backgrounds with one another and with the history of Trinidad. *Crown Jewel*, which focuses on the years leading up to and following the tumultuous labor disputes of 1937, features André de Coudray, partly based on the author, a member of the mixed-race middle class who begins to feel guilty about his relatively privileged position as the near-white son of a well-to-do family. André engages in personal relationships with two different poor black women, but these relationships are not merely private experiences. They contribute to the gradual development of his political consciousness, as he ends up an active participant in the movement for working-class liberation. De Coudray is, however, far from a dominant figure in the text, which avoids the typical Western focus on an individual protagonist in favor of an ensemble cast of different characters from different backgrounds. André, in fact, makes relatively little contribution to the events that occur in the book. He is more an observer than a maker of history, thus recalling Lukács's comments that in the great historical novels of Walter Scott, the "hero" is "always a more or less mediocre, average English gentleman," which for Lukács is "the clearest proof of Scott's exceptional and revolutionary epic gifts" (Lukács 1983, 33).

Lukács's point is that Scott does not need a strong, heroic protagonist because the narrative of his novels is carried by the momentum of history itself. The same might be said for *Crown Jewel*. Indeed, the true protagonist of the novel is the Trinidadian working class as a whole, shown in the early process of the development of a genuine class consciousness. *Crown Jewel* can, in fact, be regarded as a sort of collective bildungsroman; rather than trace the growth of a mature, adult consciousness in the life of an individual, as in the conventional bildungsroman, it traces the development of a mature historical consciousness in a class. This development, however, is incomplete. The events depicted in the novel are merely a first step toward a longer historical process that de Boissière envisions as eventually leading to genuine liberation.

Because of this collective emphasis, there are a number of other characters in the book who are almost as important as de Coudray. One of these is Cassie Walcott, who evolves in the course of the book from a timid servant into a confident, self-assertive, and effective member of the working-class movement. Both Cassie and André, in their move toward a sense of solidarity with the working class, are counterpointed by Joe Elias, son of a rich merchant, who becomes involved in working-class politics as an opportunistic way of achieving fame and power, then moves in the other direction, away from a commitment to the working class. Another important character is Popito Luna, a poor worker, who finally learns to fight for justice, but is then murdered by the police. Also important is Luna's sister, the poor seamstress, Aurelia Enriques, and Aurelia's daughter, Elena, with whom both Elias and de Coudray are for a time in love. Labor leaders such as Percy French and Clem Payne are also crucial characters.

Probably the book's most admirable figure is the oil field labor leader, Ben Le Maître, who is loosely based on a combination of the historical Trinidadian working-class leaders Jim Barrette, leader of the Negro Welfare Association, and Uriah Butler, leader of the British Empire Workers and Citizens Home Rule Party. Le Maître, who is thus the closest thing in the book to the "world-historical" figures described by Lukács, serves as something of a mentor for both André and Cassie. Le Maître eventually marries Cassie, whom he treats as an intellectual equal and an important ally in the struggle for justice. Indeed, her role in the book as a whole (which is enhanced in the 1981 edition) helps to make her a symbol of equality of the genders, so that gender joins race as a principal focus of the book's critique of social inequalities; at the same time, de Boissière maintains a consistent emphasis on class as the most important social category of all.[2]

In this and in other ways, *Crown Jewel* participates in a long tradition of leftist novels, a tradition that experienced a particular flowering in the United States and Britain during the Depression decade of the 1930s.[3] Indeed, *Crown Jewel* is not only set in the 1930s, but de Boissière in fact began writing it during that decade, immediately after the historical events on which it is based. The book should, in fact, be regarded as a product of the Trinidadian Renaissance of the 1920s and 1930s, a phenomenon that, as Hazel Carby has argued, needs to be read within the context of global leftist culture during that same period (Carby 1988).

De Boissière's vivid depictions of the poverty and hardship endured by poor characters such as Aurelia and Elena are powerful and effective, reminiscent of the work of writers such as the Russian writer Maxim Gorky, who was an important influence on British and American proletarian writers of the 1930s. Indeed, *Crown Jewel* made an important contribution to the tendency of Caribbean novels to focus on the experiences of the poor and disenfranchised, as opposed to the best-known American and British novels, which tend to focus on middle-class characters. De Boissière's impoverished characters maintain their human dignity and are not merely passive victims. Nor is their suffering romanticized; it is presented, in fact, as something to be overcome by collective action. De Boissière, however, realizes that such action is difficult, especially in the colonial context of Trinidad, where powerful forces work to disrupt class consciousness and to discourage collective action.

Of these forces, race is particularly important, and de Boissière carefully delineates the racial prejudices that prevent Trinidadian workers from developing a common identity. De Coudray, for example, is forced by pressure from his family to break off his courtship with Elena Enriques early in the book simply because she is black, though, having learned important lessons, he resumes the courtship at the end of the book. These racial prejudices are largely a result of the special history of Trinidad and other Caribbean colonies, in which the economy was dependent, for hundreds of years, on the labor of African slaves. The end of slavery in the 1830s then led to the importation of large numbers of Indian and Chinese indentured servants, resulting in a situation in which different groups of workers with different ethnic and cultural identities were encouraged to compete for jobs, thus keeping wages low. De Boissière demonstrates in *Crown Jewel* the continuing importance of this divide-and-conquer strategy. In addition to reminders that the legacy of slavery contributes to prejudices against black Trinidadians, he also indicates the ways in which centuries of slavery separated Trinidadian blacks from their African heritage, thus hampering their ability to develop a positive sense of their own cultural identity: "Behind every Chinese, every Indian, lay timeless accretions of wisdom and culture their hands could fondle and the spirit relish; but behind every Negro lay the barren windswept earth and the ghosts of a time too long vanished, too long forgotten to nourish the soul" (310).

De Boissière is highly sympathetic to the cultural impoverishment of Trinidad's black workers. However, he emphasizes that they are, first and foremost, workers. For de Boissière, the continuing racial oppression of blacks occurs largely because they still represent the majority of Trinidad's workers, so that it is in the interest of the capitalist economy to prevent them from establishing a sense of their own worth and power. But de Boissière, like Le Maître, understands the need for all workers of whatever race, gender, or cultural background, to stand together to resist oppression. Thus, Le Maître's efforts initially focus on organizing black workers under the banner of his political party, the Negro Welfare Party, but the name of the party is later changed to Workers' Welfare to indicate the extension of their efforts to workers of other races.

This effort eventually leads to a series of strikes that police attempt to suppress through the use of official violence, leading to a wave of rioting that spreads across the island. This phenomenon, based on actual historical events, calls attention to the plight of the poor in Trinidad, a plight to which the upper classes seem to have previously been remarkably oblivious.[4] This new awareness, however, leads to little direct reform. Indeed, the British governor is recalled after he suggests that perhaps something should be done to alleviate the suffering of the poor. Meanwhile, the strike is broken, and Le Maître is imprisoned, but it is clear that the events described in the book have unleashed historical forces that will eventually lead to the end of British colonial rule in Trinidad. De Boissière's emphasis on the role played by workers in this process provides an important reminder of aspects of history that are often ignored in official accounts. As Reinhard Sander notes, "*Crown Jewel* does not merely reconstruct Trinidad history during the late 1930s: It interprets this history from a militant, working-class perspective" (Sander 1988, 131). This historical vision combines with the book's critical presentation of social injustice and positive focus on the potential of working-class action to make *Crown Jewel* a highly effective novel. Indeed, Trinidadian critic Clifford Sealy has described the book as Trinidad's "most important political novel" and as "the fundamental work of fiction in our society" (Sealy 1973, 1–3).

Biographical Background

Born in Trinidad in 1907, Ralph de Boissière developed an interest in writing in the 1920s under the encouragement of C.L.R. James and Alfred Mendes. In 1937, he observed the major social upheavals that engulfed Trinidad at the time in the wake of a bitterly fought strike by the island's oil field workers. As a result, he became involved in radical trade union activism, a commitment that would greatly inform his subsequent writing. In 1947, after a brief stay in the United States, he immigrated to Australia, where he worked in a General Motors plant in Melbourne, thus enriching his understanding of and sympathy for the urban proletariat. Among other things, this experience led him substantially to revise his first novel, which was already in manuscript when he came to Australia. De Boissière's interactions with militant Australian workers influenced him to move more and more to the Left. He studied Marxism extensively and then joined the Communist Party in 1951; his three novels were all initially published by a left-wing publishing house in Australia. One novel, *No Saddles for Kangaroos* (1964), is based directly on his Australian experience, though the two earlier novels, *Crown Jewel* and its sequel *Rum and Coca-Cola* (1956), are firmly rooted in the history of the Caribbean. These remain his best-known works, especially as they were reissued, in well-received and substantially revised versions, by the British publishing house Allison and Busby in the 1980s.

Notes

See chapter 2 for historical background.

1. See Rennie 1973 for a scholarly discussion of these historical events.

2. For a discussion of the importance of race in the movement toward Trinidadian independence, see Ryan 1972.

3. See Booker 1998b for discussions of a large number of modern British novels of the Left.

4. In one telling satirical scene, an official commission investigates the living conditions of the poor in an attempt to determine the minimum possible amount on which a poor family can live. In the process, the members of the commission demonstrate a complete ignorance of the lives of poor people, while regarding them as objects of study rather than living human beings (261–68).

Chapter 13

Roger Mais:
The Hills Were Joyful Together

The Hills Were Joyful Together, initially published in 1953, was one of the first Caribbean novels to focus on the lives of the urban poor. It thus helped to set important trends for future Caribbean novelists. On the other hand, while Mais provides extensive material descriptions of conditions in the urban yard where his characters live, his book is less graphic in its representation of physical urban poverty than Orlando Patterson's later *The Children of Sisyphus* (1964). Instead, Mais focuses on the spiritual impoverishment associated with life in an urban colonial slum, where the inhabitants have to deal not merely with material hardship, but with the psychic situation of being considered outcasts from mainstream society. There is a certain sense of outrage in Mais's portrayal of the impoverished lives of his characters, and Kenneth Ramchand rightly notes that the book can be read as a work of social protest, even though it is not explicitly political in the sense of recommending specific action to overcome the objectionable conditions being described (Ramchand 1976, 13).

While *The Hills Were Joyful Together* does have a plot (several, in fact), it is an essentially episodic work designed to present readers with a view of life in an impoverished urban yard in Kingston at the beginning of the 1950s. As such, the book centers on the description of various characters, and its main strength is Mais's success in presenting the various inhabitants of the yard as distinct individuals with their own histories, needs, and desires, while at the same time making it clear that all of them are members of a single community and that they are all the products of their experience in that community. So many characters are introduced that the book begins by listing them, accompanied by descriptions of each. This list is quite helpful in the early going, though the reader gradually comes to know most of the characters well and to understand the relationships among them without additional aid.

Relationships are, in fact, crucial in *The Hills Were Joyful Together*, and the individual characters are largely defined in terms of their relationships with the others. Even characters who essentially stand alone in the text, such as the gentle Rastafarian, Ras, and the kind-hearted prostitute, Zephyr, are defined largely through the kindness and support they provide to others in times of need.[1] Other characters, however, are best understood as members of subgroups within the yard. One complex of images and events, for example, surrounds the sometimes criminal Surjue and his woman, Rema, whose passionate love is contrasted with the failing relationship between another couple in the yard, Shag and Euphemia. A third grouping involves several teenagers who live in the yard, including Manny and Wilfie, both about seventeen and both vying for the affections of Ditty, a teenage tart who constantly flaunts her emerging sexuality.

The events surrounding Shag and Euphemia revolve around her growing revulsion toward him, even though he treats her well and works hard to supply her with money, much of which she gives to the shiftless Bajun Man, her lover. Despite Zephyr's efforts to comfort her, Euphemia grows increasingly terrified of Shag, convinced that he is dangerous, especially after he begins dreaming about a man he once knew who brutally murdered his woman for being unfaithful. And Euphemia's fears turn out to be well founded. When the usually mild-mannered Shag discovers her with Bajun Man, he explodes into a rage and brutally murders her.

Even the lives of the teenage characters are already filled with tragedy and violence. The sexually precocious Manny is proud to have contracted gonorrhea, which he feels makes him a man and which he does not hesitate to spread to others. During the book, Manny's father, Bedosa, is run over by a train and killed. Manny himself is nearly killed when he torments Pattoo, the idiot son of Cassie, a woman who lives with Ras, causing Pattoo to fly into a rage and attack him with a knife. Manny, meanwhile, turns to violence when he rapes Nanine, seemingly the only girl in the yard who resists his sexual advances. Ditty is seduced by her own father, Puss-Jook, then badly beaten by her mother, Goodie, when Goodie finds Ditty and Puss-Jook together. The sensitive Wilfie does not become involved in violence, but looks on as all of these other events occur.

Probably the most important strand of the plot is that which involves Surjue, who, desperate for cash, is convinced by his associate, Flitters, to participate in a robbery. Surjue is captured by the police due to the treachery of Flitters, a fact that leads to the murder of Flitters by two of Surjue's friends. Meanwhile, Surjue is taken to jail and then to prison in a motif that allows Mais to make his strongest protests against the social and political system of colonial Jamaica.[2] The police are depicted as vicious tormentors who take sadistic pleasure in torturing their prisoners. The prisoners, in turn, receive virtually no protection from the legal system and are very much at the mercy of their tormentors.

Surjue is treated brutally, beaten so badly by the police that he has to be hospitalized. And such beatings, we learn, are commonplace, either as unofficial methods of interrogation or as official methods of corporal punishment. Mais includes, for example, a viscerally powerful description of a prison flogging (259–61). Conditions in the squalid, rat-infested prison are graphically described, while Surjue's suffering there is made even worse when he learns that Rema has gone mad and is about to be committed to an insane asylum. Aided by his friend, Cubano, he resolves to try to escape to go to her. In the process, Surjue kills a prison guard who tries to stop them, then is himself shot to death during the escape, falling to the ground with arms outspread in an obviously Christlike pose. Rema also perishes, having set a fire in her room to ward off some hallucinated creatures she believes are tormenting her, then dying in the flames.

Ramchand notes that *The Hills Were Joyful Together*, in its treatment of Surjue's experience with the legal system,

> makes a systematic attack upon a set of laws that can permit the wholesale banditry of business places yet is severe upon the petty thefts of the small unemployed man; a prison system that knows only punishment, with conditions (beatings, lack of sanitation, unwholesome food, the crudest form of medical attention) that reduce men to the level of animals in a pen. (Ramchand 1976, 13)

In addition, through the evocation of the insane asylum, Mais suggests an even broader failure of colonial social institutions to meet the needs of the people of Jamaica. It is clear that, if institutionalized, Rema would not receive proper treatment, but would simply be locked away in squalor, treated like an animal, essentially punished for her illness.

But Mais's indictment of the social system of colonial Jamaica goes beyond specific carceral institutions such as prisons and mental asylums. In one key passage, Euphemia complains to Zephyr that her life in the yard feels "just like I was in prison" (143). Indeed, Mais carefully parallels Surjue's experiences in the prison to the experience of life in the yard to suggest that the latter is informed by a similar atmosphere of confinement, fear, and violence. To an extent, Mais's project in this sense anticipates the work of Michel Foucault, who, in *Discipline and Punish*, his important history of the prison as an institution, argues that modern "prisons resemble factories, schools, barracks, hospitals, which all resemble prisons" (Foucault 1978, 228). For Foucault, modern society itself is carceral in nature, designed to provide an almost total control of the thoughts and actions of individuals. Thus, the difference between life inside a prison and that outside is not so large as might first appear, and indeed the obvious lack of freedom in a prison is designed primarily as a strategy to disguise the less visible lack of freedom in the world at large.

On the other hand, Foucault's analysis, which applies primarily to Europe, differs from that of Mais in important ways. In particular, Foucault argues that the carceral social systems of modern Europe are based on subtle and sophisticated techniques of psychological control that make violence largely unnecessary, thus helping to keep the workings of power largely invisible and to further the illusion that individuals in the West are free of social control. In Mais's Jamaica, however, the workings of power are far more obvious, and there is no attempt to disguise the brutal force with which the colonial legal system operates. Even before the work of Foucault, Frantz Fanon noted this difference between the subtle workings of power in the metropolitan center and the more overt exercise of power in the colonial world:

> In the capitalist countries a multitude of moral teachers, counselors and "bewilderers" separate the exploited from those in power. In the colonial countries, on the contrary, the policeman and the soldier, by their immediate presence and their frequent and direct action maintain contact with the native and advise him by means of rifle butts and napalm not to budge. It is obvious here that the agents of government speak the language of pure force. (Fanon 1968, 38)[3]

Fanon argues that, in order to overcome this legacy of colonial violence, colonial subjects must rise up in violent rebellions of their own. Mais makes no such suggestion and indicates no means by which the conditions he describes might be overcome. On the other hand, *The Hills Were Joyful Together* is not entirely bleak and does suggest a few rays of hope. One of the book's most powerful descriptions of conditions in Surjue's prison occurs in one of the lyrical passages that begin many of the chapters, suggesting a broad relevance of the conditions being described that goes beyond the experience of individual characters:

> Walls, walls, and all that passed between them ... enclosed within
> these walls a man was shut from light, like a seed struggling toward
> the sunlight from between damp stones ... shut away a man like
> this and all you had was his skin—stretched tightly against his body
> that knew the pang and torture and bitterness and degradation of
> the whip and bludgeon and ankle-chain, and his shame, and the
> shame of others with him ... their manhood slowly squeezed from
> them, to be drunk up at last by the screaming murderous walls.
> (209–10)

The image of the struggling seed in this otherwise unremittingly bleak
passage is somewhat reminiscent of the title image from Émile Zola's *Germinal* (1895), in which a failed coal miners' strike is envisioned as the plant-
ing of a seed that might eventually grow and blossom into a new world of
social and economic justice for workers everywhere.[4] Similarly, Ramchand
notes that this image, in Mais's passage, "gives expression to the frail testimony of human spirit that can turn pathos into the dignity of tragedy"
(15). Surjue triumphs in the sense that he is able to retain his humanity,
and his ability to feel compassion for others, in spite of all that has hap-
pened to him. Similarly, the inhabitants of the yard are able to maintain a
certain humanity, and even dignity, despite the squalor and violence that
surround them. Zephyr remains kind; Ras remains gentle; Cassie remains
patient. And, beyond the continuing human qualities of individual characters, the various "inmates" of the yard, despite the often violent squabbles
that sometimes spring up among them, retain the ability to come together
as a community at special moments.

Some of the most striking scenes in the book involve these special
moments of community. Near the beginning of the book, an unusual
water condition causes the death of numerous fish, who wash ashore near
the yard. The inhabitants take advantage of this unexpected windfall by
gathering up the fish and holding a fish-fry in which they all not only
share this unusually abundant supply of food, but also sing, dance, and
tell stories, making of the event an important moment of mutual cultural
expression. This event, with its clear resonance of rural communal life,
clearly indicates the way in which the inhabitants of the yard retain roots
in their peasant past. Meanwhile, near the end of the book, a second,
less joyous communal festival is held, the "nine-night" organized by the
Sisters of Charity to mourn the death of Euphemia. The inhabitants of
the yard all know what it means to experience suffering and loss, and
they come together at this moment in a show of solidarity in which they
put aside their individual differences.

That these differences soon again erupt is testimony to the difficulty of life in the yard, and the book ends in a cascade of violence and death. As Williamson and Dabydeen put it, such communal scenes "occasionally override pettier rivalries and conflicts. But both as symbol and, later, as a presence, the prison overshadows these brave and pathetic attempts to transcend the miseries of the common lot" (Williamson and Dabydeen 1988, 64). Nevertheless, *The Hills Were Joyful Together* shows its characters in a heroic struggle to maintain their humanity despite the dehumanizing conditions that surround them and treats its characters not simply as passive victims, but as genuine human beings. In so doing, Mais treats them with sympathy, but not pity; he shows admiration for their strength without minimizing their difficulties or romanticizing their plight.

Notes

See chapter 6 for historical background.

1. Mais's characterization of Ras is one of the first positive representations of Rastafarians in Caribbean literature, a motif he extends with his next novel, *Brother Man* (1954), in which the main protagonist is a Rastafarian.

2. Mais himself spent six months in a British colonial prison as punishment for anticolonial newspaper articles he wrote in 1944.

3. For a detailed discussion of the more overt exercise of power in the colonial world as opposed to the Western world, see Booker 1997.

4. The title of Mais's novel, derived from a revival song that is based on Psalm 98 and that celebrates the coming of the Lord to earth to restore justice, similarly suggests a coming better future.

Chapter 14

V. S. Naipaul:
Miguel Street

Miguel Street (1959) consists of a series of seventeen sketches, each of which characterizes one of the inhabitants of Miguel Street, an urban neighborhood in Port of Spain in colonial Trinidad in the years just before and during World War II. The sketches are interconnected by their common focus on a single neighborhood, with characters from one sketch often reappearing in others. In addition, the sketches are linked through the presiding consciousness of a single unnamed narrator, a boy who lives on Miguel Street, gradually growing to the age of eighteen, when he leaves Trinidad to study in England. Because of these interconnections, it is appropriate to view *Miguel Street* as a novel rather than a series of short stories, as Laban Erapu suggests in his introduction to the book (Erapu 1974, ix).

Erapu notes that the different sketches in *Miguel Street* are also linked by a common theme, the repeated demonstration that "in a society like this which has not yet defined its goals, the individual is limited to the extent of never being able to achieve fulfillment in life" (Erapu 1974, xvi). "A society like this" is, of course, a colonial society, and Naipaul's depiction of colonial Trinidad as a land of backwardness and futility lays the foundation for a negative depiction of the Third World for which Naipaul's writing would eventually become infamous. Indeed, most of the sketches in *Miguel Street* follow a similar structural model: One of the inhabitants of the street conceives a dream to make his or her life better, only to fail dismally in the attempt to fulfill that dream.

The protagonist of the first sketch is known to the locals as "Bogart," after the star of the 1942 American film, *Casablanca*, which, the narrator tells us, was hugely popular in Trinidad (1). Bogart is a rather mysterious

figure, popular on the street, but not well known to any of the other inhabitants. In fact, he periodically disappears from the street for months at a
time without explanation. Finally, a policeman appears to arrest Bogart for
bigamy: It turns out that he had deserted his first wife in the town of
Tunapuna because she couldn't have children, fleeing to Miguel Street. Then,
without divorcing his first wife, he married his subsequent girlfriend in the
town of Caroni after she became pregnant. He then deserted the second
wife in order to return to Miguel Street "to be a man, among we men" (7).
Bogart's failure to find happiness in his personal relationships sets the tone
for much of the rest of the book, as does the fact that he takes his name
(and much of his personal style) from an American movie star, suggesting
the lack of indigenous role models in Trinidad.

The narrator himself is an obvious fan of American films and often interprets his experiences in terms of films he has seen. Indeed, Americans
and American culture constitute a major presence throughout the book,
which is largely set during World War II, when American troops established
bases on Trinidad and other islands to guard against a German invasion of
the Caribbean. Port of Spain, in particular, is swarming with Americans,
and many of the projects undertaken by the inhabitants of Miguel Street
involve attempts to profit from the presence of the affluent invaders. Thus,
the narrator himself works for a time begging American soldiers for handouts of gum and chocolate, which he then resells to Hat, one of the most
prominent inhabitants of the street (49–50). In "The Mechanical Genius,"
Mr. and Mrs. Bhakcu try running a trucking service, then a taxi, hoping to
get American customers. And, in "Until the Soldiers Came," Hat's brother,
Edward, goes to work on the American base at Chaguaramas and becomes
an avid devotee of all things American, alienating him from his former
friends in Trinidad. Predictably, none of these activities work out well. The
narrator gives up begging after he is almost beaten up by a hostile American
soldier; both Bhakcu businesses go bust; and Edward, through his work at
the base, meets and marries a "white-skinned woman," who eventually breaks
his heart by running off with an American soldier (147).

The second sketch in *Miguel Street* features Popo the carpenter, who spends
all of his time hammering and sawing and planing, but never seems actually
to build anything. In fact, he is supported by his wife, who works as a cook,
leading the other men in the street to cast aspersions on Popo's manhood.
After Popo's wife leaves him, he manages to bring her back, then sets about
trying to provide a better home for her. It turns out, however, that he does
so by theft, eventually leading to his arrest and to a jail sentence that breaks
his spirit. Popo's unhappy personal life thus repeats that of Bogart, while
the ultimate jailing of both men suggests their powerlessness in the face of

larger forces of official authority. Indeed, the inhabitants of Miguel Street
have frequent run-ins with the law, and the protagonists of several sketches
wind up in jail.

The third story features George, whose main occupation seems to involve beating his wife, son, and daughter. Such beatings are central to many
of the stories and are a central fact of life in Miguel Street. Eventually,
George's wife dies, and neighborhood rumors have it that he beat her to
death. Meanwhile, George experiences a brief period of relative prosperity
after he turns his house into a brothel to service American soldiers. Eventually, however, he loses most of his clientele to more luxurious houses, then
declines and dies in failure. This failure motif carries over to the next generation, as well. His son, Elias, is touted as a promising student and sets his
sights on becoming a doctor. Titus Hoyt, a teacher who runs a private
school at the other end of Miguel Street, assures everyone that the boy is a
genius and will have no trouble winning a scholarship to go to study medicine in England. Unfortunately, Elias repeatedly fails his scholarship exams
and eventually even fails a local exam required of those who seek to become
sanitary inspectors. Ultimately, he becomes a cart-driver, essentially a garbage collector, though he claims to like the job, which in fact many of the
local boys think of as a choice occupation.

Elias's repeated examination failures are typical of the woeful experience
of the inhabitants of Miguel Street. For example, Elias's failures can also be
interpreted as failures for his teacher, Titus Hoyt, who dreams of fame
through intellectual achievement, but is obviously incompetent as a teacher.
In "The Pyrotechnicist," Morgan dreams of success as a designer and maker
of fireworks, but succeeds only in burning down his own house, though the
resultant fireworks explosions are indeed spectacular (66–67). In "B.
Wordsworth," the protagonist dreams of being a famous poet and writing
the greatest poem of all time. Though he is able to support himself in the
related occupation of singing calypsoes, he accomplishes nothing as a poet
and eventually dies, leaving his great poem unfinished. His house is soon
torn down, and it is as if this man who was to live forever in the annals of
poetry had never existed (46). In "The Coward," Big Foot, the neighborhood tough guy, turns to boxing as a career, eventually gaining a big match
with an Royal Air Force champion from Britain. Not only does Big Foot
lose the fight, but it is soon revealed that his opponent was an imposter, not
even a real champion. Big Foot leaves the neighborhood in defeat and dis-
grace, going away to become a common laborer.

The inhabitants of Miguel Street seem to have a way of failing even
when they succeed. Thus, Bolo the barber, after numerous failed attempts,
finally wins a newspaper sweepstakes, but refuses to believe he has won and

thus fails to collect his winnings (135–36). One of the few seemingly successful undertakings in *Miguel Street* involves an outing on which Hat takes
a number of the neighborhood boys to a big cricket match between Trinidad
and Jamaica. The boys, including the narrator, have a wonderful time, and
the Trinidad team plays an inspired match, winning an overwhelming victory. Given the importance of cricket in Trinidadian culture, the moment is
a golden one. [1] Hat, meanwhile, wins an unlikely bet that he places on the
game (156). Even this motif, however, has a dark side. For one thing, cricket
is the ultimate English sport and thus its popularity is a legacy of Trinidad's
long colonial domination by England. In addition, the star player on the
Trinidad team is white, leading Hat to acknowledge the secondary racial
status of the majority of Trinidad's inhabitants by declaring, "White people
is God, you hear!" (154).

In any case, the moment of triumph is short-lived. We are immediately
told that Hat typically loses his bets, then we are treated to a description of
his frequent troubles with the police, which culminate in his arrest from
watering the milk he sells from the cows that he keeps as a major source of
income. Finally, in a typical Miguel Street episode, Hat brings home a
woman, then violently beats her after he chases her down when she runs off
with another man. Hat is arrested for assault and subsequently serves three
years in prison, returning to Miguel Street a shell of his former exuberant
self.

Hat's final defeat is also a defeat for the narrator, who had much admired
him. Indeed, as the narrator grows older, he gradually comes to feel that the
neighborhood and its heroes are small and squalid, not nearly as exciting as
they had seemed in his childhood. Eddoes, the cart-driver, who had seemed
an impressive figure, now seems "weak and thin," while Hoyt, the neighborhood intellectual, seems "stupid and boring" (165). It comes as no surprise, then, that the narrator decides to leave Miguel Street and, indeed,
Trinidad. In a final comment on conditions in the colonial world, the narrator uses bribery to win a scholarship to study in England. As the book
ends, he departs, having bid farewell to his old neighborhood, though, of
course, his plane is delayed for several hours. He then goes out into the
larger world, in a move that is depicted very much as an escape from carceral
confinement. [2]

Despite the general theme of futility and failure that pervades the sketches
in *Miguel Street*, it should be emphasized that the book is not entirely negative. The inhabitants of Miguel Street are poor, but none of them starve.
And, while they have frequent conflicts, they also often help one another,
coming to the aid of those who are in special distress. They also have a
lively culture of their own, even if, as Michael Gorra notes, this culture is

presented in the text as an incoherent jumble of elements (Gorra 1997, 83). This culture is represented particularly by the frequent quotations from calypsoes that punctuate the text, commenting on the action from the point of view of a distinctively Trinidadian cultural form.[3] In addition, though the principal narration is in standard English, the text also derives important energies from the colorful, rhythmic speech of the inhabitants of Miguel Street.[4] As Renu Juneja notes, "the sparkle and wit of language is one of the means by which the denizens of this benighted corner of the world live with their failures and mock their impotence" (Juneja 1996, 151). Because of these positive elements, it is possible to read the book as a comment on the oppressive effects of colonialism, effects that the vitality of the people of Miguel Street might have some chance of overcoming if given the opportunity. Unfortunately, one cannot always say the same for Naipaul's later fiction, which tends to depict the inhabitants of the former colonial world as incapable of rising above a state of material and spiritual poverty.

Notes

See chapter 4 for historical background.

1. See C.L.R. James's *Beyond a Boundary* (1993b) for a discussion of the role of cricket in the culture of Trinidad.

2. See Williams 1986.

3. For a discussion of Naipaul's use of calypso in *Miguel Street*, see Thieme 1981, and Dabydeen and Wilson-Tagoe 1997 (75–77). Note, however, that, by *The Middle Passage* (1962), Naipaul is beginning to suggest that calypso has become a commodified tourist attraction, merely another marker of Trinidad's secondary status in world culture. The change in attitude between *Miguel Street* and *The Middle Passage* is partly in Naipaul. However, it can also be taken as a comment on the growing commodification of calypso as a tourist attraction between the 1940s and the 1960s.

4. See Mair 1989.

Chapter 15

Wilson Harris:
The Palace of the Peacock

The Palace of the Peacock (1960) is the first volume of Harris's "Guyana Quartet," which also includes *The Far Journey of Oudin* (1961), *The Whole Armour* (1962), and *The Secret Ladder* (1963). Together, these volumes interweave history and myth to present a surreal rendering of the Guyanese past through a series of fragmented but reoccurring and interconnected images. In this sense, Harris departs from the realist mode that is typical of most Caribbean novels. Instead, he draws upon the experimental forms of European modernism, which were, after all, originally intended as a protest against the numbing routinization of literature (and life) under modern capitalism.[1] Thus, while Harris's modernist writing strategies may be derived from European models, they can still be interpreted as a legitimate attempt to counter the European cultural domination of the Caribbean during hundreds of years of colonial rule. These strategies also make Harris's novels difficult for most readers, of course, but many have found them powerful in their evocation of the fractured history of the Caribbean, in some ways reminiscent of the magical realism associated with the work of writers such as Alejo Carpentier and Gabriel García Márquez. Indeed, Harris's numerous novels, combined with his extensive body of critical commentary, have made him one of the major figures of Caribbean literature.

The mood of *Palace of the Peacock* is set early on, as the nameless narrator describes a scene in which he observes a horseman being ambushed and shot off a horse. This horseman turns out to be the narrator's brother, Donne, who will be the central figure in the remainder of the text. Donne's mistress, Mariella, appears to be his killer. However, it quickly begins to appear that the scene is actually a dream, though dream and reality are intermixed in the scene in a complex way. Moreover, as the narration proceeds, it becomes increasingly unclear whether Donne and the narrator are really two distinct individual characters or whether they are merely two aspects of a single consciousness. Indeed, the boundaries between characters tend to fade and merge throughout the text, defeating the individualist mode of characterization that is typical of European realism.[2]

The violent, dangerous, and domineering Donne is clearly a figure of the colonial conqueror. He appears to be the owner of a coastal plantation from which the workers have all fled into the dense Guyanese wilderness. He thus decides to make the difficult journey upriver into this wilderness, seeking to find the "folk" (Amerindians) and to force them to work for him. In this sense, the basic plot structure of the novel resembles the Western quest myth, with the historical search for the legendary city of El Dorado (rumored to lie, among other places, in the interior of Guyana) serving as a particularly important model. Donne's intention to enslave the folk thus provides an important reminder that the real El Dorado discovered by Europeans in the New World was not a city of gold, but the forced labor of the native inhabitants and the African slaves and East Indian indentured laborers who were later brought in to supplement and replace them. Of course, Harris supplements his use of European myth with African and Caribbean myth. Thus, images of Anancy, the spiderlike trickster figure central to much of West African folklore, appear frequently in the text (Drake 1986, 58–59).[3]

Meanwhile, the quest structure of *The Palace of the Peacock* recalls a number of works of European literature and thus enters into a complex dialogue with those works. Joseph Conrad's *Heart of Darkness*, in which a European boat commanded by the narrator, Marlow, moves up the Congo River to probe the interior of Africa, is a particularly important predecessor.[4] Thus, if the name of Conrad's narrator suggests the English Renaissance poet and dramatist Christopher Marlowe (1564–1593), Harris's protagonist recalls the poet John Donne (1572–1631).[5] Indeed, Harris, by including a quotation from Donne as the epigraph of Book Three of the novel, makes this link explicit. Donne, of course, is not only a near contemporary of Marlowe, but also a contemporary of the major attempts to find El Dorado, some of the most famous of which were carried out by the English courtier, explorer, and poet Walter Raleigh, in 1595 and 1617.[6] Harris's evocation of Donne (and, indirectly, Raleigh) thus provides an important reminder that Renaissance England, often celebrated as a Golden Age of artistic and literary achievement, was also an age of

brutal and murderous colonial expansion, an expansion in which Renaissance culture is implicated, as can be seen overtly in works such as
Shakespeare's *The Tempest*.

The text proceeds, in the second chapter, to introduce the crew of the
boat that Donne commands, in what appears to be a more conventional
mode of narration. The crew includes: the wily old bowman, Schomburgh,
who steers the boat; Schomburgh's assistant, Wishrop; the Indian guide,
Vigilance; Vigilance's young black cousin, Carroll; the moody Cameron,
part Scot and part African; the mechanic, Jennings, who keeps the boat's
motor operating; and the da Silva twins, who again may actually be different parts of a single personage. It is, of course, anachronistic that the boat
has a motor, but this merging of the seventeenth and twentieth centuries is
typical of the book's depiction of Guyanese history as muddled and confused. It also suggests that the rapacious impulses of seventeenth-century
colonial expansion are still alive and well in the present day. Indeed, such
links between the present and the past run throughout the text, which often contains vague hints that all the events that occur have somehow hap-
pened before.

The crew reaches the Mission of Mariella without major incidents, and
it becomes clear that this mission and Donne's mistress are one and the
same, different aspects of a single image. They find, however, that the
mission is deserted, its Arawak inhabitants having fled into the jungle
upon the approach of the boat. The explorers do, however, manage to
capture one old woman, extracting from her the information that they
may be able to overtake the other Arawaks by continuing up the river.
They decide to do so, then proceed up the treacherous river. One after
another of the crew is killed, either through encounters with the violent
rapids, or through altercations among themselves. Cameron, for example,
is killed by da Silva after he maliciously pelts a parrot that seems to belong to da Silva's Arawak mistress. Meanwhile, the narration becomes increasingly strange and surreal, presumably mirroring the increasingly unusual and foreign surroundings of the semimythical landscape into which
the crew moves. This motif again recalls Conrad's use of impressionistic
techniques to suggest the strangeness of the African jungle to his European protagonist in *Heart of Darkness*. The mood (and basic plot) of this
journey also recalls the powerful 1972 German film, *Aguirre, Wrath of
God*, based on an ill-fated 1560 river journey led by one of the lieuten-
ants of the famous conquistador, Pizarro.

By the end of the journey, only Donne, Jennings, one da Silva, and the
narrator (who never seems quite present on the journey, though he is always
there to observe it) are left alive, though the "dead" crew members continue

to fade in and out of the text, which refuses to recognize conventional boundaries between the living and the dead. This strategy might be interpreted as a comment on the greater sense of connection to one's ancestors that informs African and Native American cultures relative to European cultures; alternatively, it might be taken as a suggestion that colonial conquerors such as those represented by Donne and his crew are already spiritually dead, so that their deaths represent relatively little change in their status. Indeed, both of these interpretations, though seemingly contradictory, are appropriate, and one of the distinctive features of *The Palace of the Peacock* is its ability simultaneously to support different, even opposing, interpretations. The text thus challenges the European tendency to see the world in dualistic "either-or" terms, a tendency that leads to a dynamic of self versus other that is central to the ideological underpinnings of colonialism, allowing Europeans to regard colonized peoples as foreign to themselves and thus not fully human.[7]

The remaining crew members then apparently plunge to their death as they attempt to climb the steep face of a waterfall. However, in the last chapter, on the eleventh day of the voyage beyond the mission, all of the crew members are reunited in the Palace of the Peacock. At this point, the crew seems to have achieved a sort of transcendent paradise in the form of a union with the cosmos, apparently free of the material concerns and the struggle for power that had informed their life on earth. In this sense, the movement of Harris's text recalls Dante's *Divine Comedy*, which is also an important structural model for Harris's later *Carnival Trilogy* (1993). As Webb notes, they are thus delivered from 'the alienating effects of the historical process," moving instead into the world of myth (Webb 1992, 81). The radical difference between conditions that obtain in the mythical Palace of the Peacock and those that can be found in the real historical world of Guyana thus calls attention to the crippling impact of colonialism on the psyches of colonial people, henceforth rendered divided not only from the world and their fellow colonial subjects, but even from themselves.

The Palace of the Peacock makes a number of potentially powerful points about the impact of colonialism on the history of Guyana and the rest of the Caribbean. On the other hand, the text might be criticized for its failure to provide a viable alternative—it is clear that the Palace of the Peacock is purely mythical and symbolic and does not represent a condition that the Guyanese people might attain by their own collective effort. These people, after all, must live in the material world of history, not in the imaginary world of myth. Thus, while the book's ending does provide a striking utopian image, it is not an image that is actually accessible. Finally, the book also fails to provide practical help to the people of Guyana in that it is so complex and difficult that few ordinary people can read or understand it. Nevertheless, *The Palace of the Peacock*, like most of Harris's work, represents an important literary experiment that has opened new possibilities to the Caribbean novel.

Historical Background

Formerly the colony of British Guiana, Guyana is an independent republic on the northern coast of South America. Because of its British colonial heritage and the rugged terrain that separates it from most of its South American neighbors, Guyana maintains strong cultural links to the West Indies. The country covers 83,000 sq. mi. (214,969 sq. km) and is thus by far the largest nation associated with the West Indies, nearly twenty times the size of Jamaica. It is, however, sparsely inhabited, with a total population of about 800,000 living mostly along the coast. More than half the population is of East Indian descent, about 40 percent are of African descent, and the remainder are of primarily Amerindian, European, or Chinese descent. The capital and largest city is Georgetown, with a population of about 200,000. Sugarcane and rice are the leading crops, while timber and minerals (including bauxite, manganese, gold, and diamonds) are among the leading exports. Education is compulsory to age fourteen, and the literacy rate is approximately 90 to 95 percent.

Most of what is now Guyana was controlled by the Warrau Indians under the arrival of Dutch settlers in the seventeenth century. Several other Amerindian groups, including the Arawaks, inhabited the area, as well. England and France soon followed the Dutch in establishing colonies in the area, though the Treaty of Breda (1667) ceded all of English colonies in the area to the Dutch. Various parts of the region repeatedly changed hands over the next century and a half, with the British finally gaining control of most of the region in 1815 after their victory in the Napoleonic Wars. The British territories in the region were united as British Guiana in 1831. The official abolition of slavery in the British Empire in 1834 meant that the plantations and mines of British Guiana had to be worked primarily by indentured laborers, most of whom were brought in from India—thus the large East Indian population of Guyana today. Meanwhile, as detailed by Walter Rodney (1982), the harsh treatment of these workers by their white masters led them to develop a strong sense of collective solidarity, a phenomenon reflected in the strongly proletarian orientation of the Guyanese government even today. The area remained relatively peripheral to the British Empire until the discovery of gold in the interior in 1879, leading to rapid British movement into the area and to a bitter boundary dispute with Venezuela, the colony's neighbor to the west. This dispute, with U.S. mediation, was finally settled in 1899, generally to the advantage of the British.

An important step toward Guyanese independence was taken with the adoption of a constitution in 1952 and the holding of popular elections in 1953. However, these elections were easily won by Cheddi Jagan and his People's Progressive Party (PPP), which was judged to be procommunist by the British, who subsequently suspended the constitution and voided the elections. Subsequent elections in 1957 and 1961 were again won by the PPP, complicating the movement toward independence as both Britain and the United States sought to prevent the Jagan government from taking power. Independence was finally granted in 1966 after the PPP was supplanted (with the help of British and American covert action) by the more moderate People's National Congress (PNC) as the leading Guyanese political party. The new parliamentary democracy became a republic in 1970. Since that time, the region has been troubled by additional boundary disputes with both Venezuela and Suriname (to the east) and by tensions between the East Indian and African populations. The area also gained notoriety in the United States as the site of mass suicide-execution of the members of the Jim Jones-led People's Temple cult in 1978. In most of the years since independence, the strongest political party has remained the PNC, but the extremely leftist PPP has remained powerful, as well. Indeed, Jagan, the longtime PPP leader, regained the presidency in 1992. After his death in 1997, his U.S.-born widow, Janet Jagan (a thirty-year member of the Guyanese parliament), was elected to replace him.

Notes

1. In his critical work, Harris is quite open about his debt to European modernism, which he describes in an essay as a "literary revolution" (Harris 1967, 46). In this same essay, incidentally, he notes the historical complicity between European capitalism and the realist novel (29).

2. Harris himself has described his characters as "agents of personality" rather than "sovereign" individuals (Munro and Sander 1972, 52). Perhaps the closest literary analog to Harris's characterization in *The Palace of the Peacock* occurs in James Joyce's *Finnegans Wake*, in which the characters represent not individual human beings so much as abstract textual forces. For a discussion of Joyce's scheme of characterization in *Finnegans Wake*, see McHugh 1976.

3. Images derived from European alchemy also circulate through the text. See Gilkes 1975 for an extended discussion of the importance of alchemical images in Harris's fiction.

4. See Webb 1992 (61-81) for a discussion of parallels between *The Palace of the Peacock* and Carpentier's *Los pasos perdidos*, which she also relates to the El Dorado legend.

5. For more on links between Harris and Conrad, see Ross 1992 and Huggan 1988.

6. For more on the search for El Dorado from a Caribbean perspective, see V. S. Naipaul's *The Loss of El Dorado* (1970).

7. Among other things, this ability to support multiple interpretations introduces a richness into the text that can be teased out only through detailed close reading. See Maes-Jelinek 1976 for an example of such readings.

Chapter 16

Orlando Patterson:
The Children of Sisyphus

The Children of Sisyphus (1964) is a powerful novel that vividly portrays life in the "Dungle," a squalid urban slum in Kingston, Jamaica. In this sense, the book has much in common with works of Western naturalism by such authors as Émile Zola, George Gissing, and Upton Sinclair. As Victor Chang notes in his introduction to the book, "Patterson's depiction of the deprived and destitute urban working class in the Kingston of the late fifties . . . was something of a landmark" (Chang 1986, x). However, as the title indicates, the book also employs mythical and symbolic connections to suggest that the Dungle, despite the extreme poverty of its inhabitants and the fact that this poverty has specific and identifiable social and historical causes, can be seen as representative of the meaninglessness and futility of human life as a whole. In this sense, the book is clearly influenced by European existentialism.[1] Indeed, the title of the book refers not just to the classical myth of Sisyphus, but to the work of French existentialist author Albert Camus, who employed the same myth as a central image in his own work, especially in *The Myth of Sisyphus*.

This myth, in which Sisyphus is doomed to the eternal torment of struggling to roll a giant boulder up a hill, only to have it come tumbling back down again, is an apt symbol for life in the Dungle as presented by Patterson. The book makes the intense poverty of the Dungle clear in an early scene in which garbage men cart refuse into the Dungle, then shovel it onto the ground, where the inhabitants frantically snatch at it, hoping to find morsels of edible food amid the poison and rot. Conditions in the slum, essentially a collection of makeshift shacks built atop a garbage heap, are so oppressive as to make the situation seem hopeless. Yet the inhabitants, like Sisyphus, do continue to struggle, hoping to find a better life.

The central example of this attempt to maintain hope involves the Rastafarian cult, members of which constitute an important element of the population of the Dungle. The Rastafarian religion, a sort of black Zionism, is based partly on a statement by black nationalist leader Marcus Garvey that appeared to prophesy the 1930 coronation of Ras (Prince) Tafari as Haile Selassie, Emperor of Ethiopia. The religion holds Haile Selassie to be the second incarnation of Christ. Rastafarians believe that black Africans are descended from the lost tribe of Israel, that they are God's chosen people, and that they are destined to establish a paradise on earth in Africa. The religion thus differs substantially from conventional Christianity in that its vision of a utopian future is set not in the afterlife, but in life on earth. Rastafarianism thus has strong political implications, because its members are counseled to work to improve life on earth rather than to wait for a better life in heaven.[2]

The most important Rastafarian figure in *The Children of Sisyphus* is Brother Solomon, a former Anglican priest, who has come to the Dungle to lead the Rastafarian brethren there.[3] Brother Solomon is in some ways a positive figure, who genuinely desires to help the people of the Dungle to a better life. However, he also serves as something of a spokesman for the book's existentialist viewpoint, and it is clear that he himself is not at all convinced that the Rastafarian paradise on earth can be achieved. In fact, his extreme skepticism that human endeavor can ever really accomplish anything eventually leads him to emphasize only the escapist aspects of Rastafarianism, as in the tendency to seek momentary relief from life's woes through the smoking of ganja (marijuana). It also leads him to fabricate news that Haile Selassie is sending ships from Ethiopia to transport the brethren from Jamaica to Africa to begin building their paradise: Even though he knows that the duplicity of this news will eventually be revealed, he feels that the anticipation will at least allow the brethren a few weeks of happiness.

In the final analysis, Brother Solomon adopts the profoundly un-Rastafarian notion that all human striving is pointless and even absurd. As he explains when his fabrication about the ships is revealed, life is a "long, comic repetition." It may offer a few fleeting moments of pleasure here and there, but ultimately the quest for human happiness is a "complete comedy, for when the mirage vanish you have not just the agony of your own thirst still unquenched but the added agony of knowing that the mirage was always unreal. Hear me, Brother, to seek after God, to seek for some meaning, some essence, is unreality twice times over" (186).

Brother Solomon, of course, can be interpreted simply as a bad Rastafarian, contaminated, perhaps, by his earlier Anglican training. On the other hand, his story is based on historical reality. Many Rastafarians literally did believe, in 1959, that ships were on the way to take them to the promised land of Africa, expecting them to arrive in Jamaica precisely on October 5 (McDonald 1989, 63). Thus, Patterson's depiction of Brother Solomon can be taken to suggest that Rastafarianism in general offers false hope to its believers. As Dabydeen and Wilson-Tagoe note, Patterson depicts Rastafarianism as "a sophisticated personal and spiritual escapism which is part of the general absurdity of man's condition in Jamaica" (Dabydeen and Wilson Tagoe 1997, 56). Still, Rastafarianism fares quite well in comparison to revivalist Christianity, another movement that was popular in Jamaica in the 1950s and that is represented in *The Children of Sisyphus*. However, unlike Brother Solomon, who at least means well, Shepherd John, the revivalist leader, is a complete charlatan who preys upon the poor for his own gain. Revivalism, Patterson seems to suggest, is essentially a con game that takes advantage of earthly despair by offering a promise of a better life in heaven.

Such promises, of course, make it even more unlikely that the poor inhabitants of the Dungle will ever be able to do anything to improve the horrible conditions under which they live. On the other hand, in Patterson's vision, there seems little likelihood that such improvement can be achieved in any case. The central character who attempts to make a better material life in the book is Dinah, the book's real protagonist. Though not herself a believer in Rastafarianism, Dinah lives in the Dungle with her man, Cyrus, a Rastafarian, and their child, Nicholas. Cyrus spends most of his time waiting for the promised Rastafarian salvation, but doing nothing to help achieve it. As a result, Dinah is forced to support the family by prostitution, the only real choice available to her in the world of the Dungle.

In the course of her work as a prostitute, Dinah meets Alphanso, a policeman, who is so taken with her that he offers to make her his mistress. Desperate to escape from the Dungle, Dinah accepts his offer and moves into his room in an urban yard. At first, Dinah is amazed at the relative luxury of her new surroundings, only gradually coming to understand that the yard is itself a slum only a notch above the Dungle on the social scale. In the meantime, she also becomes disillusioned with the insensitive Alphanso, who seems far more enamoured of his police uniform and the power it entails than of his new mistress.

Dinah is thus reluctant to depend entirely on Alphanso for her sustenance, perhaps realizing that her relationship with him is merely another form of prostitution. She therefore decides to seek other work, becoming a servant in a posh suburban home. In this world, she is completely out of place, and the vast gulf between the poverty of the Dungle and the luxury enjoyed by the rich Watkins family makes a powerful statement about the inequities of class society in colonial Jamaica. Patterson emphasizes, in fact, that the gulf is a matter of class rather than race. Though Mrs. Watkins and most of her friends are white or near-white, Dinah observes that at least one of the women who gather for tea in the Watkins parlor is black. Moreover, the black woman, Mrs. Brooks, perhaps because she has to prove that she belongs, seems "the very embodiment of the whole group, more like it and more of it than anyone else among them" (119).

Such class differences are emphasized in other ways, as well, as in Patterson's description of the factories that tower above the Dungle, outposts of a capitalist world that generates great wealth for the ruling class, but merely contributes to the poverty and misery of the Dungle (6). However, Patterson, in keeping with the philosophy of despair that permeates the book, does not suggest that anything might be done about these inequities. Dinah eventually abandons her attempt to make a better material life for herself and is lured into the revivalist sect headed by Shepherd John. There, she finds herself subject not to spiritual healing, but to the sexual advances of the shepherd, who then announces to the congregation that he has decided to leave for England with Dinah. A melee results, and Shepherd John is killed. Believing Dinah to be his murderer, the congregation becomes an enraged mob and sets upon her, literally tearing her apart. She crawls, bleeding, back to the Dungle and dies at the feet of Cyrus, just as Brother Solomon, finally overcome by the sense-lessness of it all, hangs himself.

This ultimate depiction of the futility of the efforts of the various characters to achieve salvation is all-encompassing, and Patterson presents absolutely no suggestion that other alternatives might be available. In *The Children of Sisyphus*, all efforts fail. Mary, the woman who works as a prostitute in order to try to obtain an education for her beloved daughter, Rossetta, is brutalized by police and loses the girl, who is taken away by authorities to be adopted by a wealthy family, who will probably use her as an unpaid servant. And even if education can be achieved, it may do little good. A university student, who comes to speak to the Rastafarian brethren, is depicted as a pompous and essentially ridiculous figure. Political action seems useless as well. A new party, supposedly representing the interests of the people, has just come to power, but the party leader, Seymore Nathaniel Montsaviour (apparently based on the labor leader and politician Alexander Bustamante), is thoroughly estranged from the people and has no real sympathy for them.

In short, *The Children of Sisyphus* is bitterly critical of existing conditions in colonial Jamaica at the end of the 1950s, but does nothing to suggest that better conditions might be possible. As Avis McDonald notes, the book never presents a "contrasting good, just, or great society for which the people of the Caribbean or of the world in general might aim" (McDonald 1989, 75). He goes on to note that the book "insistently equates the desperate condition of the prisoners of poverty in post-colonial [*sic*] Kingston, Jamaica, to the exilic crisis of alienation and powerlessness" (76). Patterson, in other words, seems to suggest that the suffering he describes in the book is endemic to the human condition and not merely to conditions in slums like the Dungle. This being the case, there can be no escape, a dangerous conclusion that tends to recommend inaction in the face of poverty and injustice. Indeed, *The Children of Sisyphus* ultimately ignores injustice altogether, essentially equating the existential predicament of Dinah and the inhabitants of the Dungle with that of Mrs. Watkins and her wealthy neighbors in the suburbs.

Notes

See chapter 6 for historical background.

1. On Patterson's debt to the existentialists, see Bridget Jones (1975).

2. On Rastafarianism and its political implications, see Barrett 1997, Chevannes 1994, Turner and Ferguson 1994, and Waters 1989.

3. Haile Selassie was believed to be directly descended from the biblical King Solomon, a notion indicated in the name of Brother Solomon.

Chapter 17

Jean Rhys:
Wide Sargasso Sea

Wide Sargasso Sea (1966) tells the story of Bertha Mason, the "mad" wife whom Edward Rochester keeps locked away in the attic of Thornfield Hall in Charlotte Brontë's *Jane Eyre* (1847). In so doing, Rhys's novel openly confronts one of the classic works of British literature, while giving voice to one of the most marginal characters of that literature.[1] In her novel, Rhys provides the background of Bertha Mason, reaching back to her childhood in Jamaica, as Antoinette Bertha Cosway, the daughter of the owners of a failing plantation that is virtually finished off by the abolition of slavery between 1834 and 1838. In so doing, *Wide Sargasso Sea* challenges many of the assumptions of Brontë's novel, which seems to efface Antoinette's humanity altogether. The book also challenges British representations of the Caribbean, opening a space for Caribbean writers, especially Caribbean women writers, to speak in their own voice. However, it is also the case that, aesthetically, Rhys's novel resides comfortably in the European literary tradition, while Rhys's own position within Caribbean culture remains firmly situated within the world of the Caribbean's white, upper-class minority.

The first segment of *Wide Sargasso Sea*, narrated by the young Antoinette, describes her childhood experience living with her mother, Annette, a white Creole from Martinique, on Coulibri Estate, near Spanish Town, Jamaica, in the years after the death of Antoinette's father and the abolition of slavery. It is clear that the estate, due to Mr. Cosway's philandering, was on the decline well before the end of slavery. However, the end of slavery has accelerated the decline of the estate, which is now essentially in ruins. Also living on the estate as the book begins are Pierre,

Antoinette's physically and mentally feeble brother, and a few loyal former slaves, now servants, including Christophine, a woman from Martinique who had been given to Annette by her husband as a wedding present. The Cosways, meanwhile, have few white friends, and Antoinette grows up in essential isolation, radically alienated from other people, to whom she prefers nature, even snakes (28).

Most of the former slaves seem, understandably, to regard the Cosways with contempt, referring to them as "white cockroaches," though Antoinette, in her childish innocence, finds this attitude difficult to understand. After all, some of the most important people in Antoinette's life are black. Christophine has practically raised her, and her only childhood playmate is a black girl, Tia, daughter of one of Christophine's friends. Rhys makes it clear, however, that Antoinette has nevertheless absorbed some of the racist attitudes of her class. Thus, when Tia angers her one day, she immediately labels her supposed friend a "cheating nigger." Tia, on the other hand, responds with her own show of racial contempt: "Old time white people nothing but white nigger now," she reminds Antoinette, "and black nigger better than white nigger" (24).

The decline of Coulibri Estate is momentarily arrested when Annette, amid much local gossip, marries Mr. Mason, a rich Englishman who hopes to revive the rotting plantation and make it profitable again. Mason is presented as a paragon of British virtues, and he approaches the project of rebuilding the estate with a confidence informed by imperial arrogance, even though Annette urges him to give up the project and flee the area. There are also hints that he is something of an opportunist, seeing Jamaica, with its economy in ruins, as ripe territory for exploitation by the wise businessman he believes himself to be. In this, he is not alone. Among other things, the local gossips suggest that he came to the West Indies purely "to make money as they all do. Some of the big estates are going cheap, and one unfortunate's loss is always a clever man's gain" (30).

Mason brings in additional servants and makes plans to import indentured East Indian laborers to get the plantation back into production. These plans would displace the former slaves altogether, leaving them unemployed and homeless. They thus become increasingly hostile and seemingly sinister, and Rhys's depiction of these former slaves as a dangerous and frightening force tends to verify Kenneth Ramchand's argument that the novels of white Caribbean writers such as Rhys tend to show a "terrified consciousness" of the growing power of blacks in the region (Ramchand 1983, 223–36).[2] The former slaves eventually respond to the threat posed by Mason by attacking the estate and setting fire to the main house, surrounding it in a mob composed of interchangeable black faces, "eyes gleaming, mouth half open to shout" (42). The family manages to escape, though Pierre dies in the process. Antoinette, meanwhile, is injured (physically and emotionally) when her former friend, Tia, throws a rock and hits her in the forehead (45). Annette, already seemingly unstable, descends into distraction. She develops an intense hatred for Mason, whom she blames for the recent tragedy; In response, he tucks her away out of sight, installing her in a remote farmhouse, essentially a prisoner. Antoinette, meanwhile, is sent away to a convent to continue her schooling, later receiving word there that her mother has died.

The second section of *Wide Sargasso Sea* is narrated primarily by an unnamed Englishman, obviously the Edward Rochester of *Jane Eyre*, who has come to Jamaica to marry Antoinette. Even more than Mason, who is now deceased, Rochester is an obvious opportunist. The second son of a wealthy English family, he will get essentially no inheritance, as his older brother will inherit the estate. But he is paid a dowry of 30,000 pounds to marry Antoinette and meanwhile, under British law, gains ownership of all of her assets after their marriage. He does find his new wife beautiful, though he also finds her disturbing. His feelings for her thus mirror his feelings for the West Indies, which he find seductively appealing, but vaguely frightening, seething with forces that seem beyond his control.

Rochester and Antoinette travel for their honeymoon to a Windward Island, presumably Dominica. There, they stay on a small estate formerly owned by Antoinette's mother, attended by servants who include Baptiste, the estate manager, Christophine, and Amélie, a beautiful, young "half-caste" woman. At first, the husband and wife seem to get on well, especially sexually, but their honeymoon is disturbed when Rochester begins receiving letters from Daniel Cosway, who claims to be the son of Antoinette's father and a slave woman. These letters warn Rochester of the checkered history of the Cosways and suggest that madness and miscegenation run in the family. Rochester is greatly disturbed by the letters, especially as they reinforce the sense of unease he already feels about his new wife, who seems to him vaguely associated with the mysteries of the West Indies. For him (in the classic fashion of European fantasies about the colonial world),[3] these mysteries include exotic and forbidden sexuality and mysterious supernatural forces, particularly obeah, of which he knows Christophine is rumored to be a practitioner.

Rochester feels for Antoinette a mixture of fascination and repulsion that can be seen as representative of the European attitude toward the non-European world as a whole. It is thus not surprising that his apparent love begins to turn to aggression and hatred. He begins to spurn her affections and then, in an overt attempt to hurt Antoinette, sleeps with Amélie, who has, from the beginning, attracted him—and for many of the reasons that Antoinette initially attracted him. Rochester's seduction of Amélie is an overt exercise of racial power, clearly placing him in the line of succession of the slave masters who used women slaves for sexual pleasure for hundreds of years. In so doing, he also seeks indirectly to assert his power over Antoinette. Indeed, Rochester has already observed that the two women seem to resemble one another, causing him, with his growing obsession with miscegenation, to suspect that they are related. "It's possible," he mused to himself, "it's even probable in this damned place" (127).

This suspicion that Amélie and Antoinette may be related is ostensibly furthered by the fact that Amélie is partly white. However, there is a clear way in which Rochester regards Antoinette as partly black, or at least as having somehow partaken of the foreignness of the West Indies. He thus notices that, while she may be a purely white Creole, her eyes appear dark and alien, "not English or European either" (67). After the sexual encounter with Amélie, Rochester experiences a moment of racial revulsion, suddenly concluding that "her skin was darker, her lips thicker than I had thought" (140). But he is also repelled by fear of what he sees as her mysterious power and by the sense that Amélie, unimpressed by his privileged position as a wealthy, white, European male, is pursuing an agenda of her own, one that eludes his control. In the same way, his growing revulsion toward Antoinette is partly racial, partly due to his sense that she is not European.

Rochester attempts to assert his domination of Antoinette in numerous ways, as when he insists on calling her Bertha, despite her preference for the name Antoinette. He also seeks to eliminate Christophine, whom he regards as Antoinette's most powerful ally, especially after he realizes that Christophine has been using obeah to try to reignite his passion for Antoinette. Rochester eventually drives Christophine away by threatening to use the full power of the British colonial justice system against her, thus suggesting that British guns and laws are even stronger (and more frightening) than obeah. By this time, however, Rochester's feelings toward Antoinette are composed mostly of fear and dread. Regarding her exotic sexuality as something he can never fully master and as something that may overwhelm him if he is not cautious, he pushes her away from him.

After his father and brother both die, leaving him the master of the family estate, Rochester returns to England with Antoinette, but has no further congress with her, instead locking her away in the attic (as Mason had locked away her mother) on the premise that she is mad. *Jane Eyre* presents this madness as a fact, but *Wide Sargasso Sea* suggests that Antoinette may not be nearly so mad as Rochester appears to want to think her to be.

Still, the ending of Rhys's book is to an extent determined by that of Brontë's book: Antoinette sets fire to Thornfield Hall (reenacting the burning of the house at Coulibri) and kills herself.

Wide Sargasso Sea presents the predicament of the postslavery white planters in the West Indies as a tragic one: Caught between their black former slaves and their white cousins back in England, they are despised by both and do not fully belong either to Europe or to the West Indies.[4] Rhys presents this predicament effectively. She also capably presents the Orientalist stereotypes through which Europeans view the black inhabitants of West Indies and in which the white planters are indirectly implicated. Ultimately, however, the book's most important contribution may have to do with its treatment of gender and with its subtle delineation of parallels between patriarchal attitudes and colonialist ones.[5] Rochester desires to master and dominate Antoinette, while at the same time fearing that she may be the bearer of mysterious powers. His feelings for her are thus not only representative of patriarchal attitudes toward women, but of European attitudes toward the colonial world.

At the same time, *Wide Sargasso Sea* is a book with important shortcomings; For one thing, it may be overly sympathetic to the plight of white planters in the Caribbean, paying too little attention to the centuries in which they had lived in relative ease and luxury through the brutal exploitation of African slaves. For another, the book does not really present effective alternatives to Rochester's Orientalist fantasies. Antoinette is essentially a passive victim, while the black characters in the book, even when they are drawn as strong, such as Amélie and (especially) Christophine, derive their relative strength from seemingly mysterious sources. The book never really challenges the representation of blacks as a sinister and terrifying presence in the West Indies.[6] Indeed, blacks are never presented from their own perspective, but are seen only through the eyes of Europeans, who never regard them as fully human.

Biographical Background

Jean Rhys, christened Ella Gwendolyn Rees Williams, was born in Roseau, Dominica, in 1894, the daughter of a Welsh doctor and a third-generation Dominican Creole. As a teenager, she moved to London to live with her aunt. In 1919, she married a Dutch poet and artist and spent the next decade living in Paris and traveling about Europe. After her husband was imprisoned for trafficking in stolen art objects, Rhys turned to writing, with the encouragement and patronage of the prominent author Ford Madox Ford, to help support herself.

In 1927, Rhys published her first book, *The Left Bank*, a collection of sketches based on her experience of life in the bohemian circles of European art. She published several novels during the next decade, receiving praise from aficionados, but not achieving widespread recognition. These novels included *Postures* (1928, published in the United States as *Quartet* in 1929), *After Leaving Mr. Mackenzie* (1931), *Voyage in the Dark* (1934), and *Good Morning, Midnight* (1939). These novels are set in Europe and feature essentially European protagonists, though Anna Morgan of *Voyage in the Dark* spent her childhood on a West Indian island. These novels can be viewed as an interlinked sequence. After 1939, Rhys essentially fell silent, though she reemerged after a BBC dramatization of her fourth novel. In the 1960s, she published several short stories, followed in 1966 by *Wide Sargasso Sea*, her first and only novel to be set primarily in the Caribbean. Rhys was working on an autobiography when she died in 1979.

Historical Background

The island of Dominica, with a surface area of 290 sq. mi. (750 sq. km) and a total population of about 83,000, is an independent republic in the Windward Islands between Guadeloupe to the north and Martinique to the south. The capital city is Roseau, with a population of about 16,000. English is the official language, though a French patois is widely spoken. The island's French background is also reflected in religion; more than three-fourths of the population are Catholics. The population is almost entirely of African descent, though a few Carib Indians still live on the island. Dominica produces bananas and other fruits and has a growing tourist industry, but it is one of the poorest of all Caribbean nations.

Dominica was first sighted by Columbus in 1493, but the Caribs, who had earlier taken the island from the Arawaks, resisted repeated European attempts at conquest until well into the nineteenth century, when the British, who gained official control of the island in 1815, finally defeated the Caribs, virtually exterminating them, though about 500 Caribs still live on a reservation on the eastern side of the island. Dominica, a member of the West Indies Federation from 1958 to 1962, gained independence from British rule in 1978. For the history of Jamaica, see chapter 6.

Notes

1. For fuller discussions of Rhys's subversive response to Brontë, see Nebeker 1981 (122–94) and Michael Thorpe 1977. For an especially cogent description of the ways in which Rhys's novel points out the shortcomings of the Western

feminist celebration of a colonialist text such as *Jane Eyre*, see Spivak 1985 (243).

2. At the same time, Ramchand is relatively positive in his treatment of *Wide Sargasso Sea*. Elsewhere, he argues strongly that the book is a central work of West Indian literature, if only because of the important questions it raises about the nature of that literature (Ramchand 1976). For an even more vehement argument concerning the effectiveness of Rhys's book as a West Indian novel, see Look Lai 1968.

3. See Edward Said's *Orientalism* (1979) for the classic account of these fantasies.

4. In so doing, Rhys also obliquely comments upon growing racial tensions in Britain itself. Ferguson, in fact, argues that the book partly responds to the Notting Hill race riots of 1958, in which white Britons expressed their anger and fear over growing black immigration from the colonies to England (Ferguson 1993, 114).

5. For more on this aspect of Rhys's work, see Tiffin 1978.

6. Granted, some of this atmosphere of terror derives from the Gothic mode that Rhys adapts from Brontë's text. See Luengo 1990 and Howells 1991 (114).

Chapter 18

Merle Collins:
Angel

Angel (1987) follows the (rather autobiographical) life story of its protagonist, Angel McAllister, from infancy into her mid-thirties. However, the book is really the story of modern Grenada, and Angel's experiences are used primarily as a focal point to allow Collins to trace the rise of anticolonial resistance in colonial Grenada, followed by independence and subsequent political turmoil, including the only successful revolution ever to be undertaken anywhere in the former territories of the British Empire. As such, *Angel* is really more a historical novel than a bildungsroman, though, by demonstrating the interconnectedness of the stories of the protagonist and her country, the book also suggests that these two genres need not be mutually exclusive. This is particularly the case in a postcolonial fiction like this one, which narrates the coming of age of a new, young nation, just as the bildungsroman narrates the growth and maturation of a new individual.[1]

Perhaps the most striking (and sometimes difficult) aspect of *Angel* is the language in which it is written. Though parts of the narrative are conveyed in standard English, the texture of the narrative consists primarily of Grenadian creole, a complex patois in which the English matrix is modified by French and indigenous Grenadian elements. This language reflects the linguistic consciousness of the Grenadian working class, not only announcing Collins's sense of solidarity with that class, but also, as Maria Helena Lima notes, suggesting that Collins views the Grenadian working class as the principal audience for her novel (Lima 1993, 37). In addition, this linguistic texture is supplemented by the periodic insertion (in large boldface print) of proverbial expressions that reinforce the thematic material in the narrative, while also suggesting strong connections between the novel and Grenadian oral culture.[2]

A similar appeal to oral culture resides in Collins's decision to allow the creole speech of the characters to spill over into the narration, thus refusing to establish a linguistic boundary between these two levels of discourse. Moreover, by shifting freely back and forth between creole and standard English in the narration, Collins also challenges the notion that these two languages are fundamentally different, particularly that standard English is more "literary" and more appropriate for the construction of verbal art, while rejecting the concomitant notion that creole is a debased form not suited to such lofty applications. In short, *Angel* establishes a dialogue, in the sense meant by Mikhail Bakhtin, between creole and standard English. And, precisely as indicated by Bakhtin in his work, this dialogic interaction between styles undermines any pretensions to authority on the part of one style or another, suggesting a democratic encounter between British and Grenadian cultural traditions that opposes the long history of British cultural domination of Grenada.

Collins directly thematizes this conflict of languages in her book, thus reinforcing the implications of this dialogue between styles. In particular, after the seven-year-old Angel wins a scholarship that allows her to pursue her education at a respected Catholic school, she finds that her working-class dialect is an object of mockery to the other students, who generally come from more affluent backgrounds. Angel, worried that she "caan speak proper," attempts to learn to speak in more standard English. In the meantime, not wishing to be identified as a poor, country girl among her more sophisticated classmates, she claims that she is from Aruba and speaks the way she does because of her Aruban accent (91). In this way, Collins indicates the class divisions of colonial Grenada, with the upper classes scrambling to imitate their British masters, whose cultural superiority they have uncritically accepted. The young Angel accepts this superiority as well, though in the course of the book she will learn to challenge such hierarchies.

The story of the book is, in this sense, the story of Angel's gradual education in colonial politics, an education that eventually enables her to overcome the stereotypes that have been imposed on Grenadian society by the legacy of British colonial rule. At the same time, the book relates the parallel story of the political education of Grenada itself. Lima notes that the novel "depicts the history of Grenada against and through the lives of its characters," thereby demonstrating a historical "transformation in attitudes, ideas, and language" (Lima 1993, 43). Appropriately, Angel is an infant as the book begins, in 1951, when the Grenadian independence movement is also in its infancy. Grenadians begin to experience a new sense of pride as the Leader (based on the historical figure of Eric Gairy), a black Grenadian, becomes the main impetus behind an emergent labor movement that helps Grenadian workers to stand together to resist their exploitation by their white bosses. The early sections of *Angel* occur during this strike. Angel's uncle, Regal, is a key aide to the Leader and keeps the strike going when the Leader is jailed. Angel is thus directly connected to the strike, though she, of course, does not understand what is going on at the time.

The terms of the strike are not made clear, but it appears to end successfully, as the Leader, soon after his release from jail, declares the strike won. Unfortunately, this triumph is short-lived. For one thing, there are early hints that the Leader may not be the virtuous figure many believe him to be. Regal, in fact, soon grows disillusioned at signs that the Leader is largely out for his own personal gain. Meanwhile, soon after the strike, Grenada is hit by a major hurricane that wreaks considerable damage on the island. Angel's family, who lives in a newly-constructed brick house, are relatively unaffected, though subsequent conditions on the island contribute to their increasing poverty. Eventually, Angel's father, Allan, decides to go to the United States as a migrant farm worker in an effort to make money for the family, though he finds conditions there difficult and is able to send back only a very small sum. In the meantime, Angel's mother, Doodsie, keeps the family (which at this point includes Angel and her younger brother, Simon) going.

After Allan returns, the economic status of the family slightly improves, and they eventually move to a larger house on an estate where he finds work. Angel, meanwhile, distinguishes herself as a young student and wins her way into the Catholic school. She continues to be a good student there, though, as she grows older, she becomes troubled by the Eurocentric bias of her education, noting that the literature she reads seems to feature mostly blonde, blue-eyed heroines (113). She is also troubled to learn that, in the eyes of her Catholic teachers, her parents are not truly married, because Doodsie is not a Catholic and she and the Catholic Allan were not married in the Catholic Church. Allan's philandering leads to other difficulties in the marriage, as well, and Angel to some extent retreats into her studies as a refuge from her troubled home life.

After graduation, Angel, seeking more education and a broader experience of the world, goes away to Jamaica to college. There, she struggles with constant financial difficulties, but does well in her studies. She also encounters an entirely new world among the highly-politicized black students on the campus. It is the end of the 1970s, and the black power movement is in full swing. By the time she returns to Grenada with her degree, three years later, Angel herself has been radicalized. She is by now contemptuous of the Leader, who is taking Grenada toward a full independence that will clearly have few benefits for the common people. Doodsie is deeply bothered by Angel's new militant attitude, and particularly by her daughter's new hostility to religion as a tool of oppression. Angel also comes into conflict with Allan, who remains a strong supporter of the Leader. Eventually, she and her father have a nasty confrontation, and Angel moves out of the house.

After 1974, postindependence Grenada is in virtual chaos, with the economy in ruins and the Leader's oppressive regime seeking to eliminate all opposition. The situation, in short, is a direct fulfillment of Frantz Fanon's dire warnings in *The Wretched of the Earth* (1968) that independence cannot lead to liberation in former colonies if it merely means that white oppressors are replaced by black ones, preserving the unequal class divisions of colonial society. As Angel tells Doodsie in the midst of one of their political debates, the Leader's regime is anything but the kind of black power that she has been advocating: "So because you Prime Minister skin black, you figure he interested in black people? Look how much he have for heself and watch who his friends are!" (201).

Eventually, the Leader's abusive regime encourages the growth of a powerful opposition group, the "Horizon" (obviously based on the New Jewel Movement). Eventually, in 1979, a revolution unseats the Leader's regime, leading to the establishment of a new leftist government under the leadership of the Chief (based on Maurice Bishop). Angel is a strong supporter of the new government, which is presented in largely positive terms as a genuine attempt to build a better society for the people of Grenada. The new leaders conduct public meetings in an attempt to be directly responsive to the people. Government support for education, virtually nonexistent in the Leader's regime, is dramatically increased. New programs also help to ensure that all of the people have sufficient food, while an extensive program of development (supported largely through foreign aid from Cuba and other sympathetic sources) leads to the construction of new roads and a new airport.

This new government is not without its own troubles, however, and an internal disagreement in the new ruling party eventually leads to violent conflict between opposing factions. In 1983, this conflict leads to the killing of the still-popular Chief, but the situation eventually begins to calm. People go back to work, children return to school, and things begin to return to normal (274). Then, seizing the opportunity to eliminate Grenada's leftist revolutionary government once and for all, the United States military leads an invasion of the island on the pretext of restoring order, even though order has largely been restored. Angel and her young brother, Rupert, join other Grenadians in taking arms to resist the invasion, but of course they are no match for the awesome forces that are arrayed against them. The Americans soon secure the island and depose the government, installing a provisional puppet regime.

Angel herself is seriously wounded in the conflict and has to be flown to the United States for emergency medical treatment. She survives, but loses an eye, replaced by a glass substitute. As the book ends, she returns to Grenada and her family. There, she conducts a sort of personal wake for those killed in the U.S. invasion and for the dreams that were destroyed by the unseating of the revolutionary government. Hope, however, remains, and it is clear that Angel has not given up the expectation of building a just society in Grenada. Through this ritual, she hopes to have exorcised the ghosts of the past, opening the way, as Patrick Taylor notes, for a better future (Taylor 1991, 51). Indeed, Andrew Salkey interprets the ending to suggest that "Angel expects a resumption of her revolutionary fervor, this time to be reborn of a crucial loss of fear" (Salkey 1989, 151).

Historical Background

The state of Grenada consists of the main island of Grenada and the southern half of the Windward Island group known as the Grenadines, with a total land area of about 133 sq. mi. (340 sq. km), making it the smallest independent nation in the Western Hemisphere. The mostly black total population of approximately 100,000 is heavily Catholic, which reflects the area's French heritage, as does the French-influenced creole spoken on the island in addition to English, the official language. The main island of Grenada is a mountainous volcanic island whose economy relies primarily on the production of agricultural products such as cocoa, bananas, nutmeg, and fruits. Tourism is also an important industry. The capital, St. George's, is the most important city, with a population of about 7,000. Education is compulsory until age fourteen, and different surveys place the literacy rate between 85 percent and 98 percent. The annual per capita gross domestic product is relatively low, just under $3,000, slightly less than that of Jamaica, but considerably less than the per capita GDP of $8,700 in Barbados or $8,000 in Trinidad.

The island of Grenada was sighted by Columbus in 1498, but fierce resistance from the Carib Indians who inhabited the island prevented Spanish colonization. A British attempt to colonize the island in the early seventeenth century was repelled by the Caribs, as well. The French finally managed to subdue (and essentially exterminate) the Caribs in 1651, establishing control of the island, which officially became a French colony in 1674, though the island remained sparsely settled. The first census, in 1700, showed a population of 257 whites, 525 black slaves, and 53 free blacks. Fort Royal was constructed during the period 1705-1710, and the French gradually increased their presence on the island until 1763, when it was ceded to the English in the Treaty of Paris. The French recaptured the island in 1779, but British control was reaffirmed in the Treaty of Versailles in 1783, eventually leading to the establishment of Grenada as a Crown Colony in 1877.

This colonial status continued through the first half of the twentieth century, though Eric Gairy's Grenada United Labour Party (GULP) headed an anticolonial resistance movement that announced its growing power with the declaration of a general strike in 1951. Gairy and his party remained at the forefront of Grenadian politics as the colony moved toward independence, though it was rivaled in the 1960s by the Grenada National Party of Herbert Blaize. Grenada became an associated state within the British Commonwealth in 1967 and achieved independence in 1974 in the midst of another general strike, with Gairy as the first prime minister.

Gairy's regime was corrupt and oppressive; it has been compared to the notorious Duvalier regime in Haiti. It was strongly opposed in the late 1970s by the so-called New Jewel Movement, led by Maurice Bishop and Bernard Coard. In 1979, Bishop and Coard overthrew the Gairy government via a successful Marxist-oriented revolution. Their new People's Revolutionary Government instituted major social reforms and important development programs, making Grenada a close ally of the Castro-led socialist government in Cuba, which supplied substantial foreign aid to the new government in Grenada. However, factional disputes between supporters of Bishop and Coard led to violence in 1983, culminating in the execution of Bishop. The United States and its Caribbean allies seized this opportunity to invade Grenada and to depose the People's Revolutionary Government in the name of restoring order, though all signs suggested that order had largely been restored before the invasion.

American troops occupied Grenada until the end of 1984, when elections returned Blaize, a relic from the 1960s, to power as prime minister. U.S. troops finally left the island in the summer of 1985. Blaize was displaced in the subsequent 1990 elections, but his successors have kept Grenada within the orbit of U.S. aid and influence. In the last decade, the island has focused on economic development, placing special emphasis on the promotion of tourism.

Notes

1. Noting the important use of history in the book, Lima suggests that it might be considered a "documentary bildungsroman" (Lima 1993, 44).

2. For such reasons, Andrew Salkey praises the "demotic sweep" of the novel, which he believes delivers "a consummate, artistic folk experience" that reinforces the verisimilitude of the book's "gradually unfolding historical panorama" (Salkey 1989, 151).

Chapter 19

Earl Lovelace:
Salt

Salt, (1996) the winner of the 1997 Commonwealth Writers' Prize, is a complex historical novel that details the ongoing legacy of slavery and colonialism in postcolonial Trinidad. The novel is primarily set in the postcolonial era, focusing especially on the career of Alford George, a schoolteacher turned politician. Meanwhile, the experiences of Alford and the other contemporary characters are paralleled to events surrounding the emancipation of Trinidad's African slaves in the 1830s. These parallels suggest that the past experience of slavery still haunts modern Trinidad and that, before the new nation can move forward into a genuinely new era, it must deal with this past in a productive way. In particular, Lovelace suggests that the black population should be paid reparations, in some form, for the centuries during which their ancestors were not only forced to work without pay, but subjected to continual abuse and degradation.

Salt begins with the mythical story of Guinea John, who flew back to Africa during the political unrest that surrounded the emancipation of Trinidad's slaves in the 1830s, taking with him "the mysteries of levitation," and leaving the island's remaining black population behind to deal with life there, a return to Africa not being a realistic option. This opening scene, with its resonances of African myth, seems to announce that *Salt* will be narrated in a form of magical realism, much in the mode associated with writers such as Gabriel García Márquez or Alejo Carpentier. It turns out, however, that Lovelace's novel is actually quite realistic, though the complex, nonlinear narrative, which must be pieced together by readers as they go, differs substantially from the usual conventions of realism. The story of Guinea John is being told by Bango

Durity, the uncle of one of the novel's multiple narrators, in order to make a point about Trinidadian history. Bango seeks to emphasize the importance of the African heritage of the black people of Trinidad, while at the same time reminding all of the people of Trinidad that the island's blacks are now Trinidadians, not Africans, and that their future is in Trinidad, not Africa.

For Bango, this future can only be fulfilled after the past has been put to rest; and the past can be put to rest only after the island's white population acknowledges the wrongs done during the period of slavery and makes some sort of reparations for them. Indeed, Bango has made this demand for reparations a lifelong project, organizing a number of demonstrations, including annual marches on Independence Day, to try to make his point. Unfortunately, most of his neighbors in the village of Cascadu and the nearby town of Cunaripo seem to regard him merely as a colorful eccentric. We learn, however, that he began his activism in reaction to a very specific experience of economic exploitation. Working as a sharecropper on land owned by the white Carabon family, the young Bango struggled to try to save the money to buy a forty-acre plot, which he had been told was the minimum amount that could be purchased. He then learned that the land was actually being sold off in five-acre plots and that the land on which his own rickety cabin sat had been sold to Moon Lochan, an East Indian who worked on the estate (150).

Bango recognizes this experience as a direct repetition of the experience of his great-great-grandfather, Jo-Jo, a freed slave who was promised that he could buy the land he was working, only to see it given to one of the East Indian indentured laborers brought in to replace slave labor in the wake of emancipation (185). It was, in fact, Jo-Jo who began the campaign for reparations that Bango continues. Jo-Jo's experience and the general experience of emancipation in Trinidad are narrated through a series of flashbacks, including a lengthy explanation given by Bango to Alford George after the latter becomes a government minister. When slavery was officially abolished in the British Empire in 1834, the British government agreed to pay huge reparations to the planters who thus lost their "property," but offered nothing to the black men and women who had been treated as property for so long. In addition, the slaves, instead of winning immediate freedom, were forced to serve an additional period of uncompensated "apprenticeship" under their former owners, ranging from four to six years, depending on the nature of their work. This betrayal of the promise of freedom led to widespread protests, which were brutally put down by the British colonial government, accompanied by propaganda that characterized the revolt as evidence that blacks were subhuman savages. Meanwhile, the "civilized" government beheaded several leaders of the rebellion and displayed their heads on poles to intimidate would-be rebels. By 1838, the governor of the island proclaimed a general emancipation that ended slavery on the island. Soon afterward, the planters responded by importing indentured laborers from China and India to replace the freed slaves, who were often, like Jo-Jo, displaced from land on which they had lived their entire lives and of which they had been promised the opportunity to gain ownership.

Thus, in a more general sense, Bango recognizes the sale of his land to Moon as a kind of allegory recapitulating the historical experience of Trinidad's black population, used as slaves for hundreds of years, then further abused and exploited even after emancipation. Indeed, Bango's experience is widely repeated; Alford George's father, Dixon George, is saved from losing his own land in a similar way only when young Alford, a star student in local schools, sacrifices the money that has been saved for his further education in England so that his father can buy the land. The vehemence and doggedness with which Bango carries on his program of protest are thus clearly justified, even if few in the area seem to understand that fact.

Alford, until late in the book, seems to learn little from the parallels between his own experience and that of Bango. Indeed, somewhat in the mode of Ivan Morton in Lovelace's *The Wine of Astonishment* (1982), Alford, by virtue of his education, begins to lose touch with his peasant roots altogether. In this sense, Lovelace's depiction of Alford is reminiscent of the comments of the Italian Marxist Antonio Gramsci, who argued the crucial importance of intellectuals in leading the fight for justice for Italy's peasant population, but who also argued that even intellectuals who originate in the peasantry tend, by virtue of the process that makes them intellectuals, to lose their sense of organic connection to their former class. Thus, "the mass of the peasantry, although it performs an essential function in the world of production, does not elaborate its own 'organic' intellectuals . . . although it is from the peasantry that other social groups draw many of their intellectuals" (Gramsci 1971, 6).[1]

Alford does, however, mean well. Having been forced to give up his dream of studying in England, he works as a teacher in the Cunaripo Government School, where he himself had been a student. He establishes a reputation as a successful teacher within the existing system. He eventually concludes, however, that the school, based on the old British colonial educational system, is not serving the needs of the people of the newly-independent Trinidad. In particular, the curriculum is heavily oriented toward the identification of an elite few, who are then prepared for special examinations to compete for scholarships to study in England. Not only are the majority of students virtually ignored by this system, but the elite few are themselves alienated from the general population.

Alford begins to agitate for educational reform, but is unable to get the attention of the government authorities in Port of Spain. Desperate, he decides to take his inspiration from the anticolonial activism of India's Mahatma Gandhi. He thus begins a hunger strike, sitting outside the building that houses the Ministry of Education and refusing to eat until the system of college exhibition examinations is changed. This campaign gets considerable media attention, and Alford becomes an instant celebrity. He also succeeds in getting the government to agree to a full inquiry into the current examination system. Alford returns to teaching for a time, now attempting to root his pedagogy in practical Trinidadian reality. He also publishes a book of poems, which suggests that his connection to the practical world may not be as strong as he thinks.

Alford works with some allies to found a new political party to further his campaign for reform. However, as elections near, he is offered a spot on the ticket of the ruling National Party. He accepts the offer and is elected to the Legislative Assembly as the representative of Cascadu and Cunaripo. He also joins the cabinet, becoming minister of social and environmental rehabilitation. He pursues his work as minister, believing that he is at last in a position to work real change. However, when he encounters his former lover, Vera, working as a cleaning woman in the ministry's office building, he begins to suspect that his life is growing more and more distant from that of the common people. Eventually, he concludes that he has been entirely co-opted by the system he had hoped to change:

> I have forgotten my mission. I have become part of the tapestry of
> pretence at power. I who ought to have been the one to disturb this
> numbing peace have now become the keeper of that peace. I have
> joined the gang of overseers that help to keep this place a planta-
> tion. (130)

With elections again approaching, Alford decides to change his course. Seeking a way to reconnect with the people, he reaches out to Bango, hoping to join with the old man to agitate for reform. Learning of the earlier loss of Bango's land, Alford offers to see to it that Bango and his wife, Myrtle (the stepfather and mother of Vera), are given a piece of land. Bango, however, responds that he does not want simply to be given a private reward. Instead, he demands that the land be given publicly and that the transfer be openly identified as a partial reparation for the past abuses suffered by the black population of Trinidad. He then relates the story of Jo-Jo and the other slaves involved in the emancipation movement of the 1830s, emphasizing that he is simply seeking justice and not following a course of racial hatred: "I ain't come here to make the Whiteman the devil," he tells Alford. "I not here to make him into another creature inhabiting another world outside the human order. . . . I come to call him to account, as a brother, to ask him to take responsibility for his humanness" (167).[2]

Alford, realizing that Bango's personal experience is typical of a broad phenomenon, decides to start working for a large-scale program of land redistribution in Trinidad. This new attitude horrifies the National Party and its leader, the prime minister, unnamed in the text, but obviously a figure of Eric Williams, the noted scholar, historian, and leader of the People's National Movement (PNM), the principal political party that had worked for the independence of Trinidad from British colonial rule. Williams served as the leader of Trinidad and Tobago from independence in 1962 until his death in 1981. He is treated rather harshly in Lovelace's text, reflecting the historical fact that, especially in the 1970s, he grew increasingly unpopular with black militants, who saw him as aligning himself more and more with special interests and growing aloof from the common people during the last years of his life. In response to the land redistribution plan, the prime minister removes Alford from the cabinet. Alford then resigns from the National Party and from the legislature. Returning to Cunaripo for the Independence Day celebrations, he feels a sense of shame as he observes Bango leading his annual march and realizes that he and the other members of the community have left it to Bango alone to protest the historical injustices that have been done to all of the black people of the area and the entire country. Alford completes the speech he has been giving, then joins Bango's march, resolving to stand with Bango in the future.

Alford thus becomes a Gramscian organic intellectual of Trinidad's black peasantry, in this resembling Lovelace, who has himself devoted a great deal of time and energy to the fight for the proposition that all countries that participated in and benefited from slavery and the slave trade should make reparations for their past crimes.[3] Lovelace's work, of course, is particularly focused on reparations for the descendents of former slaves in Trinidad, but it is part of an international movement that has agitated for reparations throughout the 1990s. *Salt* can be seen as a contribution to this particular project, but it is also a powerful historical novel that provides important reminders of the links between the past phenomenon of slavery and the ongoing social and economic problems that continue to plague contemporary Trinidad.

Notes

See chapter 4 for historical background.

1. For a further discussion of Gramsci's ideas on intellectuals, and in particular of the relevance of those ideas to the postcolonial world, see San Juan 1998 (86–99).

2. In the same vein, Lovelace includes in *Salt* the relatively sympathetic stories of the white Adolphe Carabon and his family and the Indian Sonan Lochan and his family, thus emphasizing that he, too, is interested in justice rather than racial vendettas.

3. See Lovelace's comments on this project in his interview with Celia Sankar (1998).

Bibliography

Allfrey, Phyllis Shand. 1953. *The Orchid House*. London: Constable.

Althusser, Louis. 1971. *Lenin and Philosophy and Other Essays*. Trans. Ben Brewster. London: Monthly Review Press, 170-83.

Anthony, Michael. 1963. *The Games Were Coming*. London: André Deutsch.

———. 1965. *The Year in San Fernando*. London: André Deutsch.

———. 1967. *Green Days by the River*. London: André Deutsch.

———. 1976. *Streets of Conflict*. London: André Deutsch.

———. 1981. *All that Glitters*. London: André Deutsch.

———. 1996. *In the Heat of the Day*. Portsmouth, NH: Heinemann.

Ashcroft, Bill, Gareth Griffiths, and Helen Tiffin. 1989. *The Empire Writes Back: Theory and Practice in Post-Colonial Literatures*. London: Routledge.

Austen, Jane. 1996. *Mansfield Park*. 1814. New York: Penguin.

Bakan, Abigail B. 1990. *Ideology and Class Conflict in Jamaica: The Politics of Rebellion*. Montreal: McGill-Queen's University Press.

Bakhtin, M. M. 1981. *The Dialogic Imagination*. Ed. Michael Holquist. Trans. Caryl Emerson and Michael Holquist. Austin: University of Texas Press.

———. 1984. *Rabelais and His World*. Trans. Helene Iswolsky. Bloomington: Indiana University Press.

Baldeosingh, Kevin. 1996. *The Autobiography of Paras P.* Portsmouth, NH: Heinemann.

———. 1997. *Virgin's Triangle*. Portsmouth, NH: Heinemann.

Balutansky, Kathleen. 1989. "We Are All Activists: An Interview with Merle Hodge." *Callaloo* 12.

Barrett, Leonard E. 1997. *The Rastafarians*. Boston: Beacon Press.

Baugh, Edward. 1988. "Friday in Crusoe's City: The Question of Language in Two West Indian Novels of Exile." *Critical Perspectives on Sam Selvon*. Ed. Susheila Nasta. Washington, DC: Three Continents Press, 240–49.

Baugh, Edward, ed. 1987. Special V. S. Reid Issue. *Journal of West Indian Literature* 2.1.

Beckles, Hilary. 1984. *Black Rebellion in Barbados: The Struggle against Slavery, 1627–1838*. Bridgetown: Carib Research and Publications.

———. 1990. *A History of Barbados: From Amerindian Settlement to Nation-State*. Cambridge: Cambridge University Press.

Behn, Aphra. 1997. *Oroonoko*. 1688. New York: Norton.

Bell, Madison Smartt. 1995. *All Souls Rising*. New York: Pantheon.

Birbalsingh, Frank. 1977. "Samuel Selvon and the West Indian Literary Renaissance." *Ariel* 8 (1977): 5–22.

Bolland, O. Nigel. 1988. *Colonialism and Resistance in Belize: Essays in Historical Sociology*. Benque Viejo del Carmen, Belize: Cubola Productions.

Bontemps, Arna. 1939. *Drums at Dusk*. New York: Macmillan.

Booker, M. Keith. 1997. *Colonial Power, Colonial Texts: India in the Modern British Novel*. Ann Arbor: University of Michigan Press.

———. 1998a. *The African Novel in English: An Introduction*. Portsmouth, NH: Heinemann.

———, M. Keith. 1998b. *The Modern British Novel of the Left: A Research Guide*. Westport, CT: Greenwood Press.

Booker, M. Keith, and Dubravka Juraga. 1997. "The Reds and the Blacks: The Historical Novel in the Soviet Union and Postcolonial Africa." *Studies in the Novel* 29.3: 274-96.

Brand, Dionne. 1996. *In Another Place Not Here*. Toronto: Knopf.

Brathwaite, Edward Kamau. 1960. "The New West Indian Novelists, Part I." *Bim* 8.31: 199–210.

———. 1967a. "Jazz and the West Indian Novel, Part I." *Bim* 11.44: 275–84.

———. 1967b. "Jazz and the West Indian Novel, Part II." *Bim* 12.45: 39–51.

———. 1968. "Jazz and the West Indian Novel, Part III." *Bim* 12.46: 115–26.

———. 1974. Introduction to *Brother Man* by Roger Mais. Portsmouth, NH: Heinemann, v–xxi.

———. 1984. *History of the Voice: The Development of National Language in Anglophone Caribbean Poetry*. London: New Beacon Books.

Brathwaite, Lloyd. 1975. *Social Stratification in Trinidad*. Jamaica: ISER.

Brennan, Timothy. 1990. "The National Longing for Form." *Nation and Narration*. Ed. Homi K. Bhabha. London: Routledge, 44–70.

Brodber, Erna. 1980. *Jane and Louisa Will Soon Come Home*. London: New Beacon Books.

———. 1988. *Myal*. London: New Beacon Books.

———. 1994. *Louisiana: A Novel*. Jackson: University of Mississippi Press.

Brontë, Charlotte. 1996. *Jane Eyre*. 1847. New York: Penguin.

Buhle, Paul. 1988. *C.L.R. James: The Artist as Revolutionary*. London: Verso.

Buhle, Paul, ed. 1986. *C.L.R. James: His Life and His Work*. London: Allison and Busby.

Cannadine, David. 1983. "The Context, Performance, and Meaning of Ritual: The British Monarchy and the 'Invention of Tradition,' c. 1820–1977." *The Invention of Tradition.* Ed. Eric Hobsbawm and Terence Ranger. Cambridge: Cambridge University Press, 101–64.

Carby, Hazel V. 1987. *Reconstructing Womanhood: The Emergence of the Afro-American Woman Novelist.* New York: Oxford University Press.

———. 1988. "Proletarian or Revolutionary Literature?: C.L.R. James and the Politics of the Trinidadian Renaissance." *South Atlantic Quarterly* 87.1: 39–52.

Carew, Jan. 1958a. *Black Midas.* London: Secker and Warburg.

———. 1958b. *The Wild Coast.* London: Secker and Warburg.

———. 1961. *The Last Barbarian.* London: Secker and Warburg.

———. 1964. *Moscow Is Not My Mecca.* London: Secker and Warburg.

———. 1976. *Save the Last Dance for Me.* London: Longman.

Cary, Norman Reed. 1988. "Salvation, Self, and Solidarity in the Work of Earl Lovelace." *World Literature Written in English* 28.1: 103–14.

Césaire, Aimé. 1972 *Discourse on Colonialism.* Trans. Joan Pinkham. New York: Monthly Review Press.

Chang, Victor. 1986. Introduction to *The Children of Sisyphus* by Orlando Patterson. London: Longman, vii–xvi.

Chevannes, Barry. 1994. *Rastafari: Roots and Ideology.* Syracuse, NY: Syracuse University Press.

Christian, Barbara. 1980. *Black Women Novelists: The Development of a Tradition, 1892–1976.* Westport, CT: Greenwood Press.

———. 1991. "Paule Marshall." *African-American Writers.* New York: Charles Scribner's Sons, 289–304.

Clarke, Austin. 1964. *Survivors of the Crossing.* London: Heinemann.

———. 1965. *Amongst Thistles and Thorns.* London: Heinemann.

———. 1967. *The Meeting Point.* London: Heinemann.

———. 1973. *Storm of Fortune.* Boston: Little, Brown.

———. 1975. *The Bigger Light.* Boston: Little, Brown.

———. 1977. *The Prime Minister.* Don Mills, Ontario: General Publishing Company.

Cliff, Michelle. 1980. *Claiming an Identity They Taught Me to Despise.* Watertown, MA: Persephone Press.

———. 1985. *The Land of Look Behind.* Ithaca, NY: Firebrand Books.

———. 1990a. *Bodies of Water.* New York: Dutton.

———. 1990b. "Clare Savage as a Crossroads Character." *Caribbean Women Writers.* Ed. Selwyn R. Cudjoe. Wellesley. MA: Calaloux Publication, 263–68.

———. 1993. *Free Enterprise.* New York: Dutton.

———. 1995. *Abeng.* 1984. New York: Plume-Penguin.

———. 1996. *No Telephone to Heaven.* 1987. New York: Plume-Penguin.

———. 1998. *The Store of a Million Items.* Boston: Houghton Mifflin.

Collins, Merle. 1985. *Because the Dawn Breaks!: Poems Dedicated to the Grenadian People*. London: Karia.

―――. 1987. *Angel*. Seattle, WA: Seal Press.

―――. 1992. *Rotten Pomerack*. London: Virago.

―――. 1995. *The Colour of Forgetting*. London: Virago.

Collins, Merle, and Rhonda Cobham, eds. 1987. *Watchers and Seekers: Creative Writing by Black Women in Britain*. London: Women's Press.

Conrad, Joseph. 1988. *Heart of Darkness*, 1902. Norton Critical Edition. 3rd Ed. Robert Kimbrough. New York: Norton.

Cooke, John. 1980. "Whose Child?: The Fiction of Paule Marshall." *CLA Journal* 24: 1–15.

Cooper, Carolyn. 1996. "Race and the Cultural Politics of Self-Representation: A View from the University of the West Indies." *Research in African Literatures* 27.4: 97–105.

Cudjoe, Selwyn R. 1980. *Resistance and Caribbean Literature*. Athens: Ohio University Press.

―――. 1988. *V. S. Naipaul: A Materialist Reading*. Amherst: University of Massachusetts Press.

Cudjoe, Selwyn R., and William E. Cain, eds. 1995. *C.L.R. James: His Intellectual Legacies*. Amherst: University of Massachusetts Press.

Dabydeen, David. 1991. *The Intended*. London: Secker and Warburg.

Dabydeen, David, ed. 1988. *A Handbook for Teaching Caribbean Literature*. London: Heinemann.

Dabydeen, David, and Nan Wilson-Tagoe. 1997. *A Reader's Guide to Westindian and Black British Literature*. Revised Edition. London: Hansib.

D'Aguiar, Fred. 1994. *The Longest Memory*. London: Chatto and Windus.

―――. 1996. *Dear Future*. London: Chatto and Windus.

―――. 1997. *Feeding the Ghosts*. Hopewell, NJ: Ecco Press.

Dangarembga, Tsitsi. 1989. *Nervous Conditions*. Seattle: Seal Press.

Danticat, Edwidge. 1994. *Breath, Eyes, Memory*. New York: Soho.

―――. 1995. *Krik? Krak!* New York: Soho.

―――. 1998. *The Farming of Bones*. New York: Soho.

Dawes, Kwame S. N. 1994. "Violence and Patriarchy: Male Domination in Roger Mais's *Brother Man*." *Ariel* 25.3: 29–49.

Dawes, Neville. 1960. *The Last Enchantment*. London: MacGibbon and Kee.

―――. 1978. *Interim*. Kingston: Institute of Jamaica.

de Boissière, Ralph. 1964. *No Saddles for Kangaroos*. Sydney: Australasian Book Society.

―――. 1981. *Crown Jewel*. London: Allison and Busby. (Revision of the original 1952 edition.)

―――. 1984. *Rum and Coca-Cola*. London: Allison and Busby. (Revision of the original 1956 edition.)

Defoe, Daniel. 1994. *Robinson Crusoe*. 1719. New York: Penguin.

de Lisser, Herbert G. 1913. *Jane: A Story of Jamaica*. Kingston: The Gleaner Company.

———. 1914. *Jane's Career: A Story of Jamaica*. London: Methuen.

———. 1929. *The White Witch of Rosehall*. London: E. Benn.

———. 1958. *The Arawak Girl*. Kingston: Pioneer Press.

Denniston, Dorothy Hamer. 1995. *The Fiction of Paule Marshall: Reconstructions of History, Culture, and Gender*. Knoxville: University of Tennessee Press.

Dickinson, Swift. 1996. "Sam Selvon's 'Harlequin Costume': *Moses Ascending*, Masquerade, and the Bacchanal of Self-Creolization." *MELUS* 21.3: 69–106.

Dos Passos, John. 1969a. *The 42nd Parallel*. 1930. New York: Signet-New American Library.

———. 1969b. *Nineteen Nineteen*. 1932. New York: Signet-New American Library.

———. 1969c. *The Big Money*. 1936. New York: Signet-New American Library.

Drake, Sandra E. 1986. *Wilson Harris and the Modern Tradition: A New Architecture of the World*. Westport, CT: Greenwood Press.

Eagleton, Terry. 1981. *Walter Benjamin: Towards a Revolutionary Criticism*. London: Verso.

Edgell, Zee. 1982. *Beka Lamb*. Portsmouth, NH: Heinemann.

———. 1991. *In Times Like These*. Portsmouth, NH: Heinemann.

———. 1997. *The Festival of San Joaquin*. Portsmouth, NH: Heinemann.

Edmondson, Belinda. 1993. "Race, Privilege, and the Politics of (Re)writing History: An Analysis of the Novels of Michelle Cliff." *Callaloo* 16.1: 180–91.

Endore, Guy. 1991. *Babouk*. 1934. New York: Monthly Review Press.

Erapu, Laban. 1974. Introduction to *Miguel Street* by V. S. Naipaul. Portsmouth, NH: Heinemann, ix–xvi.

Fabre, Michel. 1982. "Moses and the Queen's English: Dialect and Narrative Voice in Samuel Selvon's London Novels." *World Literature Written in English* 21.2: 385–92.

———. 1988. "From Trinidad to London: Tone and Language in Samuel Selvon's Novels." *Critical Perspectives on Sam Selvon*. Ed. Susheila Nasta. Washington, DC: Three Continents Press, 213–22

Fanon, Frantz. 1968. *The Wretched of the Earth*. Trans. Constance Farrington. New York: Grove Press.

Faulkner, William. 1995. *Absalom, Absalom!* 1936. New York: Vintage-Random House.

Ferguson, Moira. 1993. *Colonialism and Gender Relations from Mary Wollstonecraft to Jamaica Kincaid: East Caribbean Connections*. New York: Columbia University Press.

Fernandez, Julio A. 1989. *Belize: A Case Study for Democracy in Central America.* Aldershot, UK: Avebury

Firbank, Ronald. 1924. *Sorrow in Sunlight.* London: Brentano's.

Foucault, Michel. 1978. *Discipline and Punish: The Birth of the Prison.* Trans. Alan Sheridan. New York: Vintage-Random House.

———. 1980. *The History of Sexuality, Volume I: An Introduction.* Trans. Robert Hurley. New York: Vintage-Random House.

Gerschel, Liz. 1988. "Merle Hodge: *Crick Crack, Monkey.*" *A Handbook for Teaching Caribbean Literature.* Ed. David Dabydeen. London: Heinemann, 71–85.

Gikandi, Simon. 1992. *Writing in Limbo: Modernism and Caribbean Literature.* Ithaca, NY: Cornell University Press.

Gilkes, Michael. 1975. *Wilson Harris and the Caribbean Novel.* London: Longman.

———. 1981. *The West Indian Novel.* Boston: Twayne.

Gilroy, Beryl. 1986. *Frangipani House.* Portsmouth, NH: Heinemann.

———. 1989. *Boy-Sandwich.* Portsmouth, NH: Heinemann.

———. 1991. *Stedman and Joanna, a Love in Bondage: Dedicated Love in the Eighteenth Century.* New York: Vantage Press.

———. 1996. *Inkle and Yarico.* Leeds, UK: Peepal Tree.

Gordimer, Nadine. 1980. *Burger's Daughter. 1979. New York: Penguin.*

Gorra, Michael. 1997. *After Empire: Scott, Naipaul, Rushdie.* Chicago: University of Chicago Press.

Gramsci, Antonio. 1971. *Selections from the Prison Notebooks.* Ed. and Trans. Quintin Hoare and Geoffrey Nowell Smith. New York: International Publishers.

Greene, Graham. 1967. *The Comedians.* 1966. New York: Penguin.

Hamilton, Cynthia. 1992. "A Way of Seeing: Culture as Political Expression in the Works of C.L.R. James." *Journal of Black Studies* 22.3: 429–43.

Hamner, Robert D., ed. 1979. *Critical Perspectives on V. S. Naipaul.* London: Heinemann.

Harris, Michael. 1992. *Outsiders and Insiders: Perspectives of Third World Culture in British and Post-Colonial Fiction.* New York: Peter Lang.

Harris, Wilson. 1960. *The Palace of the Peacock.* London: Faber and Faber.

———. 1961. *The Far Journey of Oudin.* London: Faber and Faber.

———. 1962. *The Whole Armour.* London: Faber and Faber.

———. 1963. *The Secret Ladder.* London: Faber and Faber.

———. 1964. *Heartland.* London: Faber and Faber.

———. 1967. *Tradition, the Writer, and Society: Critical Essays.* London: New Beacon.

———. 1993. *The Carnival Trilogy.* London: Faber and Faber.

Hart, Richard. 1989. *Rise and Organize: The Birth of the Workers and National Movements in Jamaica, 1936–1939.* London: Karia.

Head, Bessie. 1971. *Maru*. London: Gollancz.

Hearne, John. 1955. *Voices under the Window*. London: Faber and Faber.

———. 1956. *Stranger at the Gate*. London: Faber and Faber.

———. 1961. *Land of the Living*. London: Faber and Faber.

———. 1981. *The Sure Salvation*. London: Faber and Faber.

Heath, Roy. 1974. *A Man Come Home*. London: Longman.

———. 1978. *The Murderer*. London: Allison and Busby.

———. 1979. *From the Heat of the Day*. London: Allison and Busby.

———. 1981a. *One Generation*. London: Allison and Busby.

———. 1981b. *Genetha*. London: Allison and Busby.

———. 1982. *Kwaku*. London: Allison and Busby.

———. 1997. *The Ministry of Hope*. London: Marion Boyars.

Hercules, Frank. 1961. *Where the Hummingbird Flies*. New York: Harcourt Brace.

Hodge, Merle. 1972. "Peeping Tom in Nigger Yard." *Tapia* 25 (April 2): 11–12.

———. 1981. *Crick Crack, Monkey*. 1970. Oxford: Heinemann.

———. 1990. "Challenges to Sovereignty: Changing the World Versus Writing Stories." *Caribbean Women Writers*. Ed. Selwyn Cudjoe. Amherst: University of Massachusetts Press, 202–206.

———. 1993. *For the Life of Laetitia*. New York: Farrar, Straus, Giroux.

Holt, Thomas C. 1992. *The Problem of Freedom: Race, Labor, and Politics in Jamaica and Britain, 1832–1938*. Baltimore: Johns Hopkins University Press.

Howells, Coral Ann. 1991. *Jean Rhys*. New York: St. Martin's.

Huggan, Graham. 1988. "Anxieties of Influence: Conrad in the Caribbean." *Commonwealth Essays and Studies* 11.1: 1–12.

Hutchinson, George. 1995. *The Harlem Renaissance in Black and White*. Cambridge, MA: Belknap-Harvard University Press.

James, C.L.R. 1937. *World Revolution, 1917–1936: The Rise of the Communist International*. London: Secker and Warburg.

———. 1989. *The Black Jacobins: Toussaint L'Ouverture and the San Domingo Revolution*. 1938. 2d ed. 1963. New York: Vintage-Random House.

———. 1993a. *American Civilization*. Cambridge: Blackwell.

———. 1993b. *Beyond a Boundary*. 1963. Durham, NC: Duke University Press.

———. 1997. *Minty Alley*. 1936. Jackson: University Press of Mississippi.

James, Louis. 1968. *The Islands in between: Essays on West Indian Literature*. London: Oxford University Press.

———. 1999. *Caribbean Literature in English*. London: Longman.

Jameson, Fredric. 1986. "Third-World Literature in the Era of Multinational Capitalism." *Social Text* 15: 65-88.

———. 1991. *Postmodernism, or, The Cultural Logic of Late Capitalism*. Durham, NC: Duke University Press.

Johnson, Lemuel A. 1990. *"A-beng:* (Re)calling the Body in(to) Question." *Out of the Kumbla: Caribbean Women and Literature."* Ed. Carol Boyce Davies and Elaine Savory Fido. Trenton, NJ: Africa World Press, 111–42.

Jones, Bridget. 1975. "Some French Influences in the Fiction of Orlando Patterson." *Savacou* 11–12: 27–38.

Jones, Evan. 1993. *Stone Haven.* Kingston: Institute of Jamaica.

Joyce, James. 1968. *A Portrait of the Artist as a Young Man.* 1916. New York: Viking, 1968.

———. *Ulysses: The Corrected Text.* 1922. Ed. Hans Walter Gabler with Wolfhard Steppe and Claus Melchior. New York: Random House.

Julien, Eileen. 1992. *African Novels and the Question of Orality.* Bloomington: Indiana University Press.

Juneja, Renu. 1996. *Caribbean Transactions: West Indian Culture in Literature.* London: Macmillan.

Katrak, Ketu H. 1995. "'This Englishness Will Kill You': Colonial(ist) Education and Female Socialization in Merle Hodge's *Crick Crack, Monkey* and Bessie Head's *Maru." College Literature* 22: 62–77.

Khan, Ismith. 1961. *The Jumbie Bird.* London: MacGibbon and Kee.

———. 1964. *The Obeah Man.* London: Hutchinson.

Kiberd, Declan. 1995. *Inventing Ireland.* Cambridge, MA: Harvard University Press.

Kincaid, Jamaica. 1986. *Annie John.* 1985. New York: Plume-Penguin.

———. 1990. *Lucy.* New York: Farrar, Straus, Giroux.

———. 1996. *The Autobiography of My Mother.* New York: Farrar, Straus, Giroux.

King, Bruce, ed. 1995. *West Indian Literature.* 2d ed. Carbondale: Southern Illinois University.

King, Stephen, and Richard J. Jensen, Jr. 1995. "Bob Marley's 'Redemption Song': The Rhetoric of *Reggae* and Rastafari." *Journal of Popular Culture* 29.3: 17–36.

Lamming, George. 1958. *Of Age and Innocence.* London: M. Joseph.

———. 1960. *Season of Adventure.* London: M. Joseph.

———. 1971. *Water with Berries.* New York: Holt, Rinehart and Winston.

———. 1991. *In the Castle of My Skin.* 1953. Ann Arbor: University of Michigan Press.

———. 1992a. *The Pleasures of Exile.* 1960. Ann Arbor: University of Michigan Press.

———. 1992b. *Conversations: Essays, Addresses, and Interviews, 1953–1990.* London: Karia Press.

———. 1992c. *Natives of My Person.* 1972. Ann Arbor: University of Michigan Press.

———. 1994a. "The Caribbean Intellectual and Western Education." *Crossroads of Empire: The Europe-Caribbean Connection, 1492–1992.* Ed. Alan

Cobley. Cave Hill, Barbados: University of the West Indies Department of History, 78–93.

———. 1994b. *The Emigrants*. 1954. Ann Arbor: University of Michigan Press.

Lewis, W. A. 1939. *Labour in the West Indies: The Birth of a Worker's Movement*. London: Fabian Society.

Lima, Maria Helena. 1993. "Revolutionary Developments: Michelle Cliff's *No Telephone to Heaven* and Merle Collins's *Angel*." *Ariel* 24.1: 35–56.

Lionnet, Françoise. 1995. *Postcolonial Representations: Women, Literature, Identity*. Ithaca, NY: Cornell University Press.

Looker, Mark. 1996. *Atlantic Passages: History, Community, and Language in the Fiction of Sam Selvon*. New York: Peter Lang.

Look Lai, Wally. 1968. "The Road to Thornfield Hall: An Analysis of Jean Rhys's *Wide Sargasso Sea*." *New Beacon Reviews: Collection One*. Ed. John La Rose. London: New Beacon Books, 38–52.

Lovelace, Earl. 1965. *While Gods Are Falling*. London: Collins.

———. 1968. *The Schoolmaster*. London: Collins.

———. 1979. *The Dragon Can't Dance*. London: A. Deutsch.

———. 1983. *The Wine of Astonishment*. 1982. Portsmouth, NH: Heinemann.

———. 1997. *Salt*. 1996. New York: Persea Books.

Luengo, Anthony. 1990. "*Wide Sargasso Sea* and the Gothic Mode." *Critical Perspectives on Jean Rhys*. Ed. Pierrette M. Frickey. Washington, DC: Three Continents Press, 166–77.

Lukács, Georg. 1983. *The Historical Novel*. Trans. Hannah Mitchell and Stanley Mitchell. Lincoln: University of Nebraska Press.

Lynch, Kevin. 1960. *The Image of a City*. Cambridge, MA: MIT Press.

MacDonald, Bruce F. 1979. "Language and Consciousness in Samuel Selvon's *A Brighter Sun*." *English Studies in Canada* 2 (Summer): 202–15.

Maes-Jelinek, Hena. 1976. *The Naked Design: A Reading of* Palace of the Peacock. Aarhus, Denmark: Dangaroo Press.

Mair, Christian. 1989. "Naipaul's *Miguel Street* and Selvon's *Lonely Londoners*: Two Approaches to the Use of Caribbean Creole in Fiction." *Journal of Commonwealth Literature* 24.1: 138–54.

Mais, Roger. 1974. *Brother Man*. 1954. Portsmouth, NH: Heinemann.

———. 1981. *The Hills Were Joyful Together*. 1953. Portsmouth, NH: Heinemann.

———. 1983. *Black Lightning*. 1955. Portsmouth, NH: Heinemann.

Marshall, Paule. 1959. *Brown Girl, Brownstones*. New York: Random House.

———. 1961. *Soul Clap Hands and Sing*. New York: Atheneum.

———. 1973. "Shaping the World of My Art." *New Letters* (Autumn): 97–112.

———. 1983a. *Praisesong for the Widow*. New York: Putnam.

———. 1983b. *"Reena" and Other Stories*. Old Westbury, NY: Feminist Press.

———. 1991. *Daughters*. New York: Atheneum.

———. 1992. *The Chosen Place, the Timeless People.* 1969. New York: Vintage-
Random House.

Marx, Karl, and Frederick Engels. 1978. *The Marx-Engels Reader.* 2d ed. Ed.
Robert C.Tucker. New York: Norton.

McDonald, Avis G. 1989. "Writing Down Babylon: Movement and Stasis in
Orlando Patterson's *The Children of Sisyphus.*" *SPAN* 29 (October): 62–
76.

McHugh, Roland. 1976. *The Sigla of* Finnegans Wake. Austin: University of
Texas Press.

McKay, Claude. 1928. *Home to Harlem.* New York: Harper.

———. 1929. *Banjo.* 1929. New York: Harper.

———. 1933. *Banana Bottom.* New York: Harper.

Mendes, Alfred H. 1934. *Pitch Lake: A Story from Trinidad.* London: Duckworth.

———. 1935. *Black Fauns.* London: Duckworth.

Middleton, Darren J. N. 1995. "Christ Recrucified: The Portrayal of the
Rastaman in Roger Mais's *Brother Man.*" *Notes on Contemporary Literature* 25.2: 10–12.

Mittelholzer, Edgar. 1941. *Corentyne Thunder.* London: Eyre and Spottiswoode.

———. 1950. *A Morning at the Office.* London: Hogarth Press.

———. 1952. *Children of Kaywana.* London: Peter Neville.

———. 1954. *The Harrowing of Hubertus.* London: Secker and Warburg.

———. 1958. *Kaywana Blood.* London: Secker and Warburg.

Moretti, Franco. 1987. *The Way of the World: The Bildungsroman in European
Culture.* London: Verso.

Morris, Mervyn. 1984. Introduction to *Moses Ascending* by Sam Selvon.
Porstmouth, NH: Heinemann, vii–xviii.

Morrison, Toni. 1981. *Tar Baby.* New York: New American Library.

———. 1987. *Beloved.* New York: Knopf.

Munro, Ian, and Reinhard Sander. 1972. *Kas-Kas: Interviews with Three Caribbean Writers in Texas, George Lamming, C.L.R. James, and Wilson Harris.*
Austin: University of Texas African and Afro-American Research Institute.

Murdoch, H. Adlai. 1995. "James's Literary Dialectic: Colonialism and Cultural Space in *Minty Alley.*" *C.L.R. James: His Intellectual Legacies.* Ed.
Selwyn R. Cudjoe and William E. Cain. Amherst: University of Massachusetts Press. 61–71.

Naipaul, V. S. 1957. *The Mystic Masseur.* Harmondsworth: Penguin.

———. 1958. *The Suffrage of Elvira.* London: André Deutsch.

———. 1961. *A House for Mr. Biswas.* London: André Deutsch.

———. 1962. *The Middle Passage: Impressions of Five Societies, British, French
and Dutch, in the West Indies and South America.* London: André Deutsch.

———. 1964. *An Area of Darkness.* London: André Deutsch.

———. 1967. *The Mimic Men.* London: André Deutsch.

———. 1968. *An Area of Darkness.* London: Penguin.

———. 1971. *In a Free State*. London: André Deutsch.

———. 1974. *Miguel Street*. 1959. Portsmouth, NH: Heinemann.

———. 1975. *Guerrillas*. New York: Knopf.

———. 1979. *A Bend in the River*. New York: Knopf.

———. 1984. *The Loss of El Dorado*. 1970. New York: Vintage-Random House.

———. 1987. *The Enigma of Arrival*. New York: Knopf.

———. 1994. *A Way in the World*. New York: Knopf.

Nair, Supriya. 1996. *Caliban's Curse: George Lamming and the Revisioning of History*. Ann Arbor: University of Michigan Press.

Narinesingh, Roy. 1981. Introduction to *Crick Crack, Monkey* by Merle Hodge. Oxford: Heinemann, vii–xiv.

Nasta, Susheila, ed. 1988. *Critical Perspectives on Sam Selvon*. Washington, DC: Three Continents Press.

Nebeker, Helen. 1981. *Jean Rhys: Woman in Passage*. Montréal: Eden Press Women's Publications.

Ngugi wa Thiong'o. 1992. *Decolonising the Mind: The Politics of Language in African Literature*. London: James Currey.

———. 1993. *Moving the Centre: The Struggle for Cultural Freedoms*. Portsmouth, NH: Heinemann.

Nichols, Grace. 1986. *Whole of a Morning Sky*. London: Virago.

Nielsen, Aldon Lynn. 1997. *C.L.R. James: A Critical Introduction*. Jackson: University Press of Mississippi.

Nixon, Rob. 1992. *London Calling: V. S. Naipaul, Postcolonial Mandarin*. New York: Oxford University Press.

Omolade, Barbara. 1983. *Desire: The Politics of Sexuality*. Ed. A. Snitow, C. Stansell, and S. Thompson. New York: Monthly Review Press, 350–67.

Paquet, Sandra Pouchet. 1982. *The Novels of George Lamming*. London: Heinemann.

———. 1991. Foreword to *In the Castle of My Skin* by George Lamming. Ann Arbor: University of Michigan Press.

Patterson, Orlando. 1967a. *An Absence of Ruins*. London: Hutchinson.

———. 1967b. *The Sociology of Slavery: An Analysis of the Origins, Development, and Structure of Negro Slave Society in Jamaica*. London: MacGibbon and Kee.

———. 1972. *Die the Long Day*. New York: Morrow.

———. 1982. *Slavery and Social Death: A Comparative Study*. Cambridge, MA: Harvard University Press.

———. 1986. *The Children of Sisyphus*. 1964. London: Longman.

Paul-Emile, Barbara. 1995. "Gender Dynamics in James's *Minty Alley*." *C.L.R. James: His Intellectual Legacies*. Ed. Selwyn R. Cudjoe and William E. Cain. Amherst: University of Massachusetts Press, 72–78.

Payne, Anthony J. 1995. *Politics in Jamaica*. New York: St. Martin's.

Peedle, Ian. 1999. *Belize: A Guide to the People, Politics, and Culture*. London: Interlink Books.

Philip, Marlene Nourbese. 1988. *Harriet's Daughter.* Portsmouth, NH: Heinemann. Phillips, Caryl. 1985. *The Final Passage.* London: Faber and Faber.

Phillips, Caryl. 1986. *A State of Independence.* London: Faber and Faber.

———. 1989. *Higher Ground.* New York: Viking.

———. 1991. *Cambridge.* London: Bloomsbury.

———. 1993. *Crossing the River.* London: Bloomsbury.

———. 1997. *The Nature of Blood.* New York: Knopf.

Potash, Chris. 1997. *Reggae, Rasta, Revolution: Jamaican Music from Ska to Dub.* New York: Schirmer Books.

Pynchon, Thomas. 1987. *Gravity's Rainbow.* 1973. New York: Penguin.

Ramchand, Kenneth. 1970. "Concern for Criticism." *Caribbean Quarterly* 16.2: 51–60.

———. 1976. *An Introduction to the Study of West Indian Literature.* Sunbury-on-Thames: Thomas Nelson and Sons.

———. 1983. *The West Indian Novel and Its Background.* 2d Ed. London: Heinemann.

———. 1997. Introduction to *Minty Alley* by C.L.R. James. 1971. Jackson: University Press of Mississippi, 5–15.

Ramraj, Victor. 1983. "Selvon's Londoner's: From the Center to the Periphery." *Language and Literature in Multicultural Contexts.* Ed. Satendra Nandan. Suva, Fiji: University of the South Pacific, 297–306.

Redcam, Tom. 1909a. *Becka's Buckra Baby.* 1903. Kingston: Jamaica Times Printery.

———. 1909b. *One Brown Girl and* —. Kingston: Jamaica Times Printery.

Reid, V. S. 1949. *New Day.* New York: Knopf.

———. 1958. *The Leopard.* London: Heinemann.

———. 1978. *The Jamaicans.* 2d ed. Kingston: Institute of Jamaica.

———. 1983. *Nanny-Town.* Kingston: Jamaica Publishing House.

———. 1985. *The Horses of Morning: About the Rt. Excellent N. W. Manley, Q. C., M. M., National Hero of Jamaica: An Understanding.* Kingston: Caribbean Authors Publishing Company.

Rennie, Bukka. 1973. *The History of the Working Class in the 20th Century (1919–1956): The Trinidad and Tobago Experience.* Toronto: New Beginning Movement.

Rhys, Jean. 1927. *The Left Bank and Other Stories.* New York: Harper.

———. 1928. *Postures.* London: Chatto and Windus.

———. 1931. *After Leaving Mr. Mackenzie.* New York: Harper and Row.

———. 1934. *Voyage in the Dark.* London: Constable and Company.

———. 1939. *Good Morning, Midnight.* New York: Harper.

———. 1982. *Wide Sargasso Sea.* 1966. New York: Norton.

Riley, Joan. 1985. *The Unbelonging.* London: Women's Press.

———. 1987. *Waiting in the Twilight.* London: Women's Press.

———. 1988. *Romance.* London: Women's Press.

————. 1992. *A Kindness to the Children*. London: Women's Press.

Rodney, Walter. 1982. *A History of the Guyanese Working People, 1881–1905*. Baltimore: Johns Hopkins University Press.

Rogozinski, Jan. 1994. *A Brief History of the Caribbean: From the Arawak and the Carib to the Present*. New York: Meridian-Penguin.

Ross, Jack. 1992. "Wilson Harris, Joseph Conrad, and the South American 'Quest' Novel." *Landfall* 46.4: 455–68.

Roy, Namba. 1961. *Black Albino*. London: New Literature.

Rushdie, Salman. 1991. *Midnight's Children*. 1980. New York: Viking-Penguin.

Ryan, Selwyn D. 1972. *Race and Nationalism in Trinidad and Tobago: A Study of Decolonization in a Multiracial Society*. Toronto: University of Toronto Press.

Said, Edward. 1979. *Orientalism*. New York: Vintage-Random House.

Salik, Roydon. 1992. "Compromising Life: Autobiography in Selvon's *A Brighter Sun*." *Environment and Labor in the Caribbean*. Ed. Joseph Lisowski. New Brunswick, NJ: Transaction Publishers, 69–76.

Salkey, Andrew. 1958. *A Quality of Violence*. London: Hutchinson.

————. 1960. *Escape to an Autumn Pavement*. London: Hutchinson.

————. 1968. *The Late Emancipation of Jerry Stover*. London: Hutchinson.

————. 1969. *The Adventures of Catullus Kelly*. London: Hutchinson.

————. 1976. *Come Home, Malcolm Heartland*. London: Hutchinson.

————. 1989. Review of *Angel*. *World Literature Today* 63.1: 151.

Sander, Reinhard W. 1988. *The Trinidad Awakening: West Indian Literature of the Nineteen-Thirties*. Westport, CT: Greenwood Press.

San Juan, E., Jr. 1998. *Beyond Postcolonial Theory*. New York: St. Martin's.

Sankar, Celia. 1998. "Earl Lovelace: Unsettled Accounts." *Americas* 50 (January-February): 38–43.

Scott, Paul. 1966. *The Jewel in the Crown*. New York: William Morrow.

Sealy, Clifford. 1973. "*Crown Jewel:* A Note on Ralph De Boissière." *Voices* 2, 3 (March): 1–3.

Selvon, Samuel. 1963. *I Hear Thunder*. New York: St. Martin's.

————. 1979. *Turn Again Tiger*. 1958. Portsmouth, NH: Heinemann.

————. 1983. *An Island Is a World*. 1955. London: Longman.

————. 1984. *Moses Ascending*. 1975. Portsmouth, NH: Heinemann.

————. 1985a. *A Brighter Sun*. 1952. London: Longman.

————. 1985b. *The Lonely Londoners*. 1956. London: Longman.

————. 1986. *The Plains of Caroni*. 1970. Toronto: Williams-Wallace.

————. 1987. *Moses Migrating*. 1983. London: Longman.

————. 1990a. *The Housing Lark*. 1965. Washington, DC: Three Continents Press.

————. 1990b. *Those Who Eat the Cascadura*. 1972. Toronto: TSAR.

Sembène, Ousmane. 1962. *Gods Bits of Wood*. Trans. Francis Price. New York: Doubleday.

Shinebourne, Janice. 1986. *Timepiece*. Leeds, UK: Peepal Tree Press.

Spillers, Hortense J. 1985. "*Chosen Place, Timeless People:* Some Figurations on the New World." *Conjuring: Black Women, Fiction and Literary Tradition.* Ed. Marjorie Pryse and Hortense J. Spillers. Bloomington: Indiana University Press, 155–75.

Spivak, Gayatri Chakravorty. 1985. "Three Women's Texts and a Critique of Imperialism." *Critical Inquiry* 12 (Autumn): 243–61.

Stephens, Evelyne Huber. 1986. *Democratic Socialism in Jamaica: The Political Movement and Social Transformation in Dependent Capitalism.* Basingstoke, United Kingdom: Macmillan.

Stevenson, Robert Louis. 1994. *Treasure Island.* 1883. New York: Penguin.

St. Omer, Garth. 1964. *Syrop. Introduction 2: Stories by New Writers.* London: Faber and Faber, 139–87.

———. 1968a. *A Room on the Hill.* London: Faber and Faber.

———. 1968b. *Shades of Grey.* London: Faber and Faber.

———. 1969. *Nor Any Country.* London: Faber and Faber.

———. 1972. *J–, Black Bam and the Masqueraders.* London: Faber and Faber.

Taylor, Patrick. 1991. "Deconstruction and Revolution: Merle Collins's *Angel.*" *The C.L.R. James Journal* (January): 12–17.

———. 1995. "Rereading Fanon, Rewriting Caribbean History." *Postcolonial Discourse and Changing Cultural Contexts.* Ed. Gita Rajan and Radhika Mohanram. Westport, CT: Greenwood Press, 17–31.

Thelwell, Michael. 1980. *The Harder They Come.* New York: Grove.

———. 1987. *Duties, Pleasures, and Conflicts: Essays in Struggle.* Amherst: University of Massachusetts Press.

———. 1991. "*The Harder They Come:* From Film to Novel." *Grand Street* 37: 135–65.

Thieme, John. 1981. "Calypso Allusions in Naipaul's *Miguel Street.*" *Kunapipi* 3.2: 18–32.

Thomas, H. Nigel. 1991a. "From 'Freedom' to 'Liberation': An Interview with Earl Lovelace." *World Literature Written in English* 31.1: 8–20.

———. 1991b. "'Progress' and Community in the Novels of Earl Lovelace." *World Literature Written in English* 31.1: 1–7.

Thorpe, Marjorie. 1977. "The Problem of Cultural Identification in *Crick Crack, Monkey.*" *Savacou* 13: 31–38.

———. 1982. Introduction to *The Wine of Astonishment* by Earl Lovelace. Oxford: Penguin, vii–xiv.

———. 1984. "In Search of the West Indian Hero: A Study of Earl Lovelace's Fiction." *Critical Issues in West Indian Literature: Selected Papers from West Indian Literature Conferences, 1981–1983.* Parkersburg, IA: Caribbean Books, 90–100.

———. 1990. "The Other Side: *Wide Sargasso Sea* and *Jane Eyre.*" *Critical Perspectives on Jean Rhys.* Ed. Pierrette M. Frickey. Washington, DC: Three Continents Press, 178–85.

Tiffin, Helen, 1978. "Mirror and Mask: Colonial Motifs in the Novels of Jean Rhys." *World Literature Written in English* 17: 328–41.

———. 1986. "The Novels of George Lamming: Finding a Language for Post-Colonial Fiction." *Essays on Contemporary Post-Colonial Fiction.* Ed. Hedwig Brock and Albert Wertheim. Munich: Max Hueber Verlag, 253–74.

Torres-Saillant, Silvio. 1997. *Caribbean Poetics: Towards an Aesthetic of West Indian Literature.* Cambridge, Cambridge University Press.

Turner, Terisa E., and Bryan J. Ferguson, eds. 1994. *"Arise Ye Mighty People!" Gender, Class, and Race in Popular Struggles.* Trenton, NJ: African World Press.

Warner-Lewis, Maureen. 1987. "Rebels, Tyrants, and Saviours: Leadership and Power Relations in Lovelace's Fiction." *Journal of West Indian Literature* 2.1: 76–89.

Waters, Anita M. 1989. Race, Class, and Political Symbols: Rastafari and Reggae in Jamaican Politics. New Brunswick, NJ: Transaction Books.

Watt, Ian. 1957. *The Rise of the Novel: Studies in Defoe, Richardson, and Fielding.* Berkeley: University of California Press.

Waugh, Alec. 1955. *An Island in the Sun.* New York: Farrar, Straus, and Cudahy.

Webb, Barbara J. 1992. *Myth and History in Caribbean Fiction: Alejo Carpentier, Wilson Harris, and Edouard Glissant.* Amherst: University of Massachusetts Press.

Williams, Denis. 1963. *Other Leopards.* London: Hutchinson.

Williams, Eric. 1944. *Capitalism and Slavery.* New York: Putnam.

———. 1984. *From Columbus to Castro: The History of the Caribbean, 1492–1969.* 1970. New York: Vintage.

Williams, Haydn Moore. 1986. "Reactions to Entrapment in 'Backward Places': V. S. Naipaul's *Miguel Street* and Ruth Jhabvala's *A Backward Place.*" *A Sense of Place in the New Literatures in English.* Ed. Peggy Nightingale. St. Lucia: University of Queensland Press, 68–74.

Williamson, Karina, and David Dabydeen. 1988. "Roger Mais: *The Hills Were Joyful Together.*" *A Handbook for Teaching Caribbean Literature.* Ed. David Dabydeen. London: Heinemann, 63-70.

Worcester, Kent. 1996. *C.L.R. James: A Political Biography.* Albany: State University of New York Press.

Wyke, Clement. 1991. *Sam Selvon's Dialectical Style and Fictional Strategy.* Vancouver: University of British Columbia Press.

Zola, Émile. 1994. *Germinal.* 1885. Trans. Havelock Ellis. New York: Vintage-Random House.

Index

About the Authors

M. KEITH BOOKER is Professor of English at the University of Arkansas, Fayetteville. He is the author of *The African Novel in English: An Introduction* (Heinemann, 1998).

DUBRAVKA JURAGA has published essays on postcolonial, Russian, and East European literature. She is coauthor of *Bakhtin, Stalin, and Modern Russian Fiction: Carnival, Dialogism, and History.*